Praise for *On* **Language, Democracy,** *and* **Social Justice**

"*On Language, Democracy, and Social Justice* provides a forum for Noam Chomsky to articulate crucial insights, while offering an uplifting narrative describing a concerned individual's personal correspondence, and then interaction, with Chomsky himself. As such, it's a useful book that addresses contemporary issues, most notably regarding Haiti, but it's also a behind-the-scenes description, one of a multitude, of how Chomsky relates to people concerned with making a difference in the world, and what they (and in turn we) can learn from such intellectual, and personal, encounters."

—*Robert Barsky, Professor, Vanderbilt University*

"*On Language, Democracy, and Social Justice* is a thoughtful and transformative book that raises crucial questions about the death of democracy and the rise of a unique form of authoritarianism in the United States. Reclaiming the connection between education and social change, it offers its readers an accessible, provocative, and insightful analysis of a number of issues that extend to social justice and the promise of a democracy to come to the savage ideologies, practices, and policies of neoliberalism. Moving lucidly between a language of critique and a discourse of possibility, the book offers a stinging critique of American-style casino capitalism and its attack on those vital public values, ideologies, and institutions that give meaning to any viable democratic society while also providing a number of suggestions about the promise of collective struggle, organized resistance, and the possibilities for a more just future."

—*Henry Giroux, Global Television Network Chair in English and Cultural Studies, McMaster University*

"Critical educators such as Pierre W. Orelus have consistently challenged the colonial matrix of power in an attempt to redress the crisis within the geoculture of the modern/colonial world, and in doing so have challenged epistemologies of power and the social relations of production in which these epistemologies are forged. Professor Orelus is from Haiti, and his interest in learning more about the colonization of his homeland is what first led him to become interested in Noam Chomsky's work."

—*from the foreword by Peter McLaren*

"…what is facilitative rather than debilitating about this new book is that it doesn't only offer a language of critique, it simultaneously creates and encourages a collective praxis to make change in the world."

—*from the afterword by Pepi Leistyna*

On LANGUAGE, DEMOCRACY, *and* SOCIAL JUSTICE

Studies in the Postmodern Theory of Education

Shirley R. Steinberg
General Editor

Vol. 458

―――――――――

The Counterpoints series is part of the Peter Lang Education list.
Every volume is peer reviewed and meets
the highest quality standards for content and production.

―――――――――

PETER LANG
New York • Washington, D.C./Baltimore • Bern
Frankfurt • Berlin • Brussels • Vienna • Oxford

Pierre W. Orelus *with* **Noam Chomsky**

On LANGUAGE, DEMOCRACY, *and* SOCIAL JUSTICE

Noam Chomsky's Critical Intervention

PETER LANG
New York • Washington, D.C./Baltimore • Bern
Frankfurt • Berlin • Brussels • Vienna • Oxford

Library of Congress Cataloging-in-Publication Data
Orelus, Pierre W.
On language, democracy, and social justice: Noam Chomsky's critical intervention /
Pierre W. Orelus, Noam Chomsky.
pages cm. — (Counterpoints: studies in the postmodern theory of education; vol. 458)
Includes bibliographical references and index.
1. Chomsky, Noam. 2. Sociolinguistics. 3. Democracy. 4. Social justice.
I. Orelus, Pierre W. II. Title.
P85.C47A5 410.92—dc23 2013023709
ISBN 978-1-4331-2448-8 (hardcover)
ISBN 978-1-4331-2447-1 (paperback)
ISBN 978-1-4539-1190-7 (e-book)
ISSN 1058-1634

Bibliographic information published by **Die Deutsche Nationalbibliothek**.
Die Deutsche Nationalbibliothek lists this publication in the "Deutsche
Nationalbibliografie"; detailed bibliographic data is available
on the Internet at http://dnb.d-nb.de/.

© 2014 Pierre W. Orelus & Noam Chomsky
Peter Lang Publishing, Inc., New York
29 Broadway, 18th floor, New York, NY 10006
www.peterlang.com

All rights reserved.
Reprint or reproduction, even partially, in all forms such as microfilm,
xerography, microfiche, microcard, and offset strictly prohibited.

DEDICATION

*This book is dedicated to teachers,
community activists, and concerned citizens
who have been at the forefront of struggles
aimed at fighting colonized schooling,
the devastating effects of western neoliberalism and
neocolonialism on the poor, and
the assault on democracy.
May their collective spirit remain strong so they continue this noble fight!*

CONTENTS

Acknowledgments ix

Foreword xi
 by Peter McLaren

Introduction 1

1 Professional and Personal Encounters With Noam Chomsky:
  A Critical Self-Reflection 7

2 Noam Chomsky and the Linguistic, Political, and Activist World:
  A Critical Analysis 23

3 Democracy, Schooling, and U.S. Foreign Policy 43
  Noam Chomsky and Pierre Orelus in Dialogue

4 Democracy and Language Rights of Minority Groups. 53

5 Neoliberalism: The Rich Over the Poor. 65
  Noam Chomsky and Pierre Orelus in Dialogue

6 Market Democracy in a Neoliberal Order: Doctrines and Reality 77

7 Third World Countries Under Western Siege 97
  Noam Chomsky and Pierre Orelus in Dialogue

8 Re-Envisioning Social Justice 107
  Noam Chomsky and Pierre Orelus in Dialogue

9 What Should Be the Role of Intellectuals in the Twenty-First Century?. 113

Afterword: Passing the Torch. 125
 by Pepi Leistyna

Index. 171

ACKNOWLEDGMENTS

This book would not have been a reality without the support of many people. I wish to begin by thanking Professor Noam Chomsky for all of his support; I feel deeply indebted to him. I also want to thank Peter McLaren for gracefully agreeing to write the foreword. Likewise, I am deeply grateful to Professor Pepi Leistyna for writing the afterword. Moreover, I want to sincerely thank Professors Henry Giroux and David Barsky for endorsing the book. A sincere thanks goes to Anthony Arnove for his genuine help with the book contract and beyond. Also, I wish to thank Shirley Steinberg and Chris Myers for their support and the trust they placed in this book project. Finally, I want to thank my partner, Romina Pacheco, for her support.

FOREWORD

by Peter McLaren

Noam Chomsky is widely held to be one of the twentieth century's greatest luminaries. His genius, perhaps more than that of any other contemporary figure, epitomizes the ideal of social justice. He is considered to be among history's most influential and impassioned critics of U.S. foreign policy and an outspoken opponent of the abuses of authority. Few scholar-activists have exposed with such nuanced singularity the contradictions and limitations of liberal democracy and its culture of diminishing expectations of what it means to be human. A diversely talented polymath, Chomsky is a seminal figure in linguistics but is held in equally high regard for his scathing attacks on war, imperialism, and the illegitimate use of political authority. Aside from Bertrand Russell, no contemporary scholar has stepped as far outside of political convention and displayed such contempt for society's most powerful factions and institutions and the political orthodoxies that sustain them—and achieved international renown within his own lifetime for his forays into polemics—as Noam Chomsky. His knowledge of political history and geopolitics is without precedent, and his book with Edward Herman, *Manufacturing Consent* is considered a paradigm of political criticism. Deploying a staggering knowledge of history that he can recall effortlessly, even at the age of 84, Chomsky has vigorously debunked the strategies and tactics of the world's greatest terrorist states, including the United States. Of course, one of the primary means by which the U.S. security state can manufacture consent is through the use of the media. Citing the work of Barry Sanders, P. Ramesh (2003) notes that television "does not stimulate the brain; 'it feeds both stimulus and response into the infant-child brain as a single-paired effect.' Even the video game does not have 'active' let alone 'interactive' participants, for the simple reason that 'the rules of the game dominate as thoroughly as any totalitarian regime.'" Ramesh continues: "TV creates the most vicious of cycles: it makes a person more susceptible to manufactured images by diminishing that person's ability to generate his own, a condition akin to the suppression of the immune system, a kind of electronic AIDS." During the twentieth century, human beings were slaughtered in wars at rates exceeding anything known in modern history. And our historical segue into the twenty-first century has shown little to convince us that the bloody history of humanity will be abated. Human beings have been reduced in the scientific worldview to inert statistics, and in religious worldviews to "terrorists" or enemies of Christ. Sanders (2010) writes:

> How did we arrive at a state of affairs so catastrophic that fathers, sons, husbands, wives, daughters, lovers and friends—the rag and bone of human existence—could have collapsed so conclusively into images, pixels, ciphers, ghosts, gross numbers, into the palatable euphemisms of death? Why does virtually every loss of human life now resemble that frightening model of anonymity from the inner city, the drive-by random assassination, where, once again, victims do not die but get "dusted," or "wasted," "popped" or "blown away," and nobody is responsible? Under every hoodie, we have begun to believe, lurks a hoodlum: a case of our own fear turning us into racial profilers at the level of the street. We walk our neighborhoods unarmed, most of us, but still feeling trigger-happy. We drive the streets feeling somewhat safe, most of us, but still shaking in our shoes. Ghosts haunt us in the airport and at the supermarket; they stalk us on the sidewalks and in the shadows. Just past the edge of our well-tended lawns, a clash of civilizations, a war of terror, rages endlessly. We live in fear, and come alive in anger. How did we lose our substance and our identities so immaculately? Where have all the human beings gone? In short, when did we stop caring?

Chomsky is one who has never stopped caring. As a renowned scholar whose political activism challenges all forms of media disinformation and falsehoods, including those spawned by society's most powerful factions and their institutions, his aggressive disclosures have been discredited and his character impugned by reigning institutional powers, and his ideas are rarely voiced within the establishment media. And when they are voiced, the criticisms are mainly directed at the hallmarks of his presentation style, which in the hands of the corporate media pundits can become crude caricature: a lack of expressiveness in his delivery, a biting sarcasm, a sweeping knowledge of facts, incessant finger-pointing at those whom he considers responsible for injustice, a withering repetition of the horrors of war and cruelty resulting in a desensitizing effect, and a tendency toward argumentative simplicity. These criticisms are to be expected of an iconoclastic activist who has arguably done more to educate readers worldwide about the perils of abuses of authority and the contradictions of liberal democracies than any other single person, bringing to mind such slogans as: "Whoever you vote for, the Government gets in," "If voting could change anything, it would be made illegal," and "Guy Fawkes was the only person to enter Parliament with honest intentions."

Critical educators such as Pierre Orelus have consistently challenged the colonial matrix of power in an attempt to redress the crisis within the geoculture of the modern/colonial world, and in doing so have challenged epistemologies of power and the social relations of production in which these epistemologies are forged. Professor Orelus is from Haiti, and his interest in learning more about the colonization of his homeland is what first led him to become interested in Noam Chomsky's work. Very little is known among the U.S. public at large about the political history of Haiti. Haiti is often caricatured in U.S. popular culture as a land where zombies reign. In keeping with the popular emphasis on Haiti as one of the birthplaces of the zombie, specifically within Haitian vodou (the other being the continent of Africa), I would like to use the figure of the zombie to emphasize the horror of capitalism and its casualties.

Capitalism was not given birth to by a mad scientist in a Gothic cape whose laboratory is filled with the crackling electric currents of a Jacob's Ladder, bubbling beakers, flasks, cathode ray oscilloscopes, and electrodes designed to reanimate dead tissue. Unlike a horror film, where there is always an imperfection in the makeup or the plot or the acting, the horror of capitalism is perfect. Even its imperfection is perfect. This horror is cleansed of any supplementarity, it rationalizes away all criticism, it is completely hygienic. It is beyond ideology. Capitalism delivers a measure of objectivity. It knows what it wants—surplus value at all costs and as such it devours all living labor—whether proletarian or cognitarian. The horror of capitalism severs all nouns from their corresponding verb forms: Alienation is never alienating, democracy is never democratizing, emancipation is never emancipatory. Every action or activity within the orbit of capitalism is turned into pure commodity. All of our heroes give capitalism endless chances to redeem itself, and we simultaneously look to capitalism to redeem ourselves.

The zombie represents the abject victim of all colonial encounters, the expelled worker from the capitalist plutocracy, whose agency is vomited up like a magmatic eruption; the naturalization of the unreal, the ghostly other of capitalism and colonial violence that returns to haunt the very process that created it. The vast indefiniteness that is the zombie thus must be put back into the service of capital as a perfect colonial "everyman" whose cauterized brain removes the zombie from any form of protagonistic agency. In early zombie accounts (i.e., *The Magic Island*, the 1929 novel written by William Seabrook, the journalist who is often credited with importing zombies to the United States), we are compelled to treat the zombie as an enemy of colonial progress and to restore the zombie to the status of willing, rather than unwilling, slave of capital.

Examining zombie stories and films in relationship to the geopolitics of neoliberal capitalism has been a recent project of David McNally in his important work *Monsters of the Market: Zombies, Vampires and Global Capitalism*. Marx describes capital as a "mechanical monster whose body fills whole factories," where workers become "conscious organs of the automaton." He brilliantly illustrates how workers have become mere appendages of the "animated monster" of the market and how they have become, in David McNally's words, zombified, that is, reduced to "dismembered body-parts activated by the motions of the grotesque corpus of capital," to "become nothing but bearers of undifferentiated life-energies, dispensed in units of abstract time" (2011, p. 142). In the jaws of this capitalist beast, "abstract time, time measured and calibrated according to mathematical efficiencies, becomes the basis of concrete activity" (p. 142). McNally identifies a powerful connection between Marx's description of what capital does to workers to what witches are said to do when they create a zombie. Broadly speaking, McNally sees the process of zombification as the reduction of behavior to basic motor functions and social utility to raw labor. According to McNally's provocative thesis, zombie myths most often associated with Africa and the Caribbean, but also those reflected in recent Hollywood films, have embedded within them "poetic knowledge" of some of the most axiomatic features of capitalist modernity.

The occult ability of capitalists to purchase labor-power as a commodity and "squeeze more from it than the value of the wages paid"—that is, the ability of capital to add value to itself—happens, as McNally puts it, "in the darkness of the hidden abode of production" and constitutes the "invisible powers of capitalist exploitation and accumulation" (p. 145). McNally's intention is to provide a type of "dialectical optics" or "night vision" that can shed light on this nocturnal abode of capitalist production.

In order to appreciate McNally's thesis, we need to look briefly at Marx's value theory of labor. According to Marx's provocative thesis, the production of value is not the same as the production of wealth. The production of value is historically specific and emerges whenever labor assumes its dual character. This is most clearly explicated in Marx's discussion of the contradictory nature of the commodity form and the expansive capacity of the commodity known as labor power. In this sense, labor power becomes the supreme commodity, the source of all value. For Marx, the commodity is highly unstable, and non-identical. Its concrete particularity (use value) is subsumed by its existence as value-in-motion or by what we have come to know as "capital" (value is always in motion because of the increase in capital's productivity that is required to maintain expansion).

McNally stresses how, for Marx, it is imperative not to confuse the value of something with its material being. Value is supra-sensible—it is spectral—since every conceivable good can possess a marker of it universal exchangeability because all value-bearing goods in a world of commodity exchange do not reside in any of their material properties. Value is invisible and intangible and operates by means of what Marx called a "phantom-like objectivity" (McNally, 2011, p. 206); value, in other words, is something all commodities share "irrespective of their sensible differences" (p. 206). The gods of capital and value are clearly elevated above sensuous human agents as a strange and esoteric process of sorcery. The process of fetishization is not what is commonly viewed as commodity fetishism: the worshipping of the material object of human labor instead of worshipping—as Luther would have us do—God's creation of nature. Rather it is but the opposite—it is attributing supernatural powers to an immaterial, spectral-like substance: value. It is conducting daily life as if the transactions of capital possessed extraordinary phantom-like powers. Capitalism could therefore be considered a religion of the non-sensuous that contrasts sharply with African religion and its worship of the irreducibility of the material and the corporeal. According to McNally, Marx located fetishism in the process of de-valuations and dislocations of human activity and in the denigration of the human that occurs within capitalism "when people become subordinated to things and powers of their own making" (p. 207). Protestantism fetishizes the immaterial and invisible process of value production and sees the products of human labor as artificial and impure. The African tales of the zombies "carry a defetishising charge in their insistence that something strange and mysterious, something that threatens the bodily and moral foundations of social life, is at work in the global circuits of capital-accumulation." According to McNally,

> Africa continues to be plundered for the products of nature: ivory, rubber, diamonds, cocoa, cotton, gold, oil. Digging, cutting and pumping, slashing through forest and jungle, blasting great holes into the earth, capitalism in Africa seems intent on nothing less than a veritable war against nature. And, with each manic effort to seize their continent's natural wealth, Africans have been captured, whipped, beaten, worked to death, structurally adjusted—all so that nature might be despoiled, people might be downtrodden, and capital might accumulate. The fury directed against nature and laborers has swelled into a monstrous system of violence and mayhem: private militias, state and colonial armies have marauded across the continent, insuring that the natural resources ripped from the earth stay in the hands of the richest and most powerful. (p. 208)

Those Africans who were not enslaved during Africa's insertion into the European world-economy were the victims of colonial taxation, dispossessed of their land and forced to work in the textile or palm oil industries, or other industries. The most potent of the zombie tales coming from Sub-Saharan Africa and elsewhere render zombies as forced laborers, as "unseen laborers of a global imperial economic order" (p. 211) who, lacking in identity, self-consciousness, memory, and agency, nevertheless perform drudging labor for others. Here we recognize how wage labor "obliges workers to treat their creative, corporeal energies as divisible bits to be auctioned off" (p. 147).

Analee Newitz (2006) wonders why "monster stories are one of the dominant allegorical narratives used to explore economic life in the United States." For Newitz, the capitalist monster that has been haunting America since the late nineteenth century has been "mutated by backbreaking labor, driven insane by corporate conformity, or gorged on too may products of a money-hungry media industry" (2006, p. 2). These fiends "cannot tell the difference between commodities and people…they confuse living beings with inanimate objects" (p. 2). Furthermore, "because they spend so much time working, they often feel dead themselves" (p. 2). These "capitalist monsters embody the contradictions of a culture where making a living often feels like dying" (p. 2). Newitz elaborates that the narratives of the capitalist monster genre are often too violent to fit within "the usual aesthetic system," but "such violence offers an intensely raw expression of what it means to live through financial boom and bust, class warfare, postcolonial economic turmoil, and even everyday work routines" (p. 5). Drawing from Marx's concept of capital as dead labor, Newitz describes the process of moving from life time into working time as "a symbolic death." She writes that "capitalism, as its monsters tell us more or less explicitly, makes us pretend we're dead in order to live" (p. 6). Newitz warns that this "pretense of death, this willing sacrifice of our own lives simply for money, is the dark side of our economic system" (p. 6).

Filmic representations of zombies could be found in Depression-era America, such as the classic *I Walked with a Zombie*, by Jacques Tourneur (1943), which depicted the decline of colonial capitalism. Around this time, as McNally points out, a new and innovative "zombie music" was emerging along with new practices and cultures of resistance among African Americans. McNally describes the jazz of Thelonious Monk as quintessential zombie music in its "angular phrasing, highlighted by unusual intervals, dissonance and displaced notes" (2011, p. 262). Here Monk's music expresses "the rhythms of a world out of joint, a space of reification in which people are reduced to things—and in which they violently awaken from their frozen state." McNally writes that

> in Monk's compositions, we hear not only the jarring sounds of things coming to life; more than this, we heed the rhythms of zombie-movement, the ferocious sounds of the dance of the living dead. It is now widely recognized that the entire African American experience is bathed in living death, in the "double consciousness" of being both person and thing. And Monk's music captures this in the monstrously beautiful cadences of the banging, smashing, crashing chords of an emerging African-American protest music, one that gave a new urban cadence to 'the rhythmis cry of the slave,' to use Du Bois' apt expression (p. 263)

McNally further writes that the music of the enslaved is a language of doubling, "both song of sorrow and cry of freedom," and that the "poly-rhythms, shifting tempos, and displaced notes" captured the "ugly beauty" of this experience, the clash of freedom and bondage: "In giving voice to bodies in pain, it howls these wounds, names them, explores them, accents them" (p. 263).

Gore-soaked zombies dragging the entrails of their victims have been shuffling across movie screens for decades, and they are still being produced at breakneck speed. *Zombie Island* is in production, *World War Z* is to appear on the giant screen with Brad Pitt in 2013, and a fifth *Resident Evil* film is expected soon.

Director George A. Romero gave the genre new life with his 1968 classic *Night of the Living Dead*. Romero is still making zombie movies, but they lack the bite of his best shockers like *Dawn of the Dead*. According to McNally, Romero's re-figuration of the zombie as a flesh-eating ghoul repositions zombies as hyperconsumers rather than as displaced laborers of the 1943 film *I Walked with a Zombie*, or the zombie myths of Sub-Saharan Africa, and de-radicalizes the image of zombie revolt. This appears to be what Henry Giroux is arguing in his book *Zombie Politics and Culture in the Age of Casino Capitalism*, in which he sees zombie culture as synonymous with predatory capitalism and the politics in which it was spawned.

> Zombie values find expression in an aesthetic that is aired daily in the mainstream media, a visual landscape filled with the spectacle of destruction and decay wrought by human parasites in the form of abandoned houses, cars, gutted cities and trashed businesses.... Zombie culture hates big government, a euphemism for the social state, but loves big corporations and is infatuated with the ideology that, in zombieland, unregulated banks, insurance companies, and other megacorporations should make major decisions not only about governing society but also about who is privileged and who is disposable, who should live and who should die. (Giroux, 2011a, pp. 32–33)

Giroux explains his use of the zombie metaphor thusly:

> The zombie metaphor does more than suggest the symbolic face of power, it points dramatically to a kind of "mad agency that is power in a new form, death-in-life" agency without conscience and bereft of social democratic imagination or hope. This is what Achille Mbembe calls necropolitics in which "death is the mediator of the present—the only form of agency left." What is new about this type of politics is that it is not hidden, lurking in the shadows but appears daily and unremarkably in memos, reports, and policies justifying illegal legalities such as the use of state secrets, indefinite detention without charge, the massive incarceration of people of color, hidden prisons, a world of night raids, the bailout of corrupt corporations that led to the direct destitution of millions, and the full-fledged attack on a weakened oppositional culture of thoughtfulness and critique, itself all but left for dead. The figure of the zombie utilizes the iconography of the living dead to signal a society that appears to have stopped questioning itself, that revels in its collusion with human suffering, and is awash in a culture of unbridled materialism and narcissism. (Giroux, 2011b, June 2)

If the zombie metaphor has this much heuristic value, then it is indeed fitting that McNally turns precisely to those zombie myths that have emanated from

Sub-Saharan Africa where such fables reflect most tellingly capitalist modernity's "tendency to mortify living labor, to zombify workers in order to appropriate their life-energies in the interests of capital" (2011, p. 143). McNally is worth quoting at length:

> It was West Africans who, after all, captured as commodities in order to fuel the capitalist plantation-economy, most fully experienced the mortifying tendencies of capitalism…. By reducing people—sentient, creative, passionate, loving, hating, desiring humans—to property, capitalist slavery imposed a death-in-life. Even after the abolition of slavery, anti-black racism continues to reproduce central aspects of this life-denying reification. (p. 143)

What is very significant in McNally's discussion of the zombie films is his insight that Hollywood's contemporary zombies are creatures of consumption, "brazenly mobbing stores and malls and consuming human flesh, not living-dead producers of wealth for others" (p. 210). This neoliberal view of the zombie has displaced the image of the living-dead laborer of the 1930s and 1940s for that of the "ghoulish consumer." The object of critique is consumerism, not capitalism. According to McNally, "it moved the image away from those features that are particularly resonant in the African context in the neoliberal era" (p. 213). This pattern persists in today's so-called postcolonial contexts, as "even those that sought an 'African socialism' found themselves, sooner or later and to differing degrees, re-colonized by the world-market" (p. 217). The revival of the zombie movies within a neoliberal milieu "tend to offer biting criticism of the hyper-consumptionist ethos of an American capitalism characterized by excess. But this deployment comes at the cost of invisibilizing the hidden world of labor and the disparities of class that make all this consumption possible" (p. 260). McNally writes that the "occlusion of the zombie-laborer also de-radicalizes images of zombie-revolt" (p. 261). In other words, it hides the carnage implied in the advances of globalized capitalism. Zombies, after all, were symbols of rebellion, as the horror of the zombie film was in the awakening of the zombie, not the passive, walking-dead zombie. Here we need "to read the post-Hegelian treatment of the master-slave relation through Fanon as much as Marx" (p. 265) as society's rulers become zombified and the oppressed become awakened. Today, critical pedagogy is a means to help awaken zombies through "the liberation of monstrous corporeality and sensuous existence from the abstracting circuits of capital" through a dialectical reversal which brings about the political victory of the oppressed and the defeat of zombieism, and what McNally refers to as "de-reification, the reanimation of the relations amongst things and persons via the liberation of things, as well as persons, from circuits of abstraction" (p. 267).

It seems, then, that there are two types of sociological zombies: Marxist zombies and Weberian zombies (after Max Weber), those that draw attention to the circulation of commodities and that are a threat to bourgeois social relations and middle-class lifestyles, and those that point to the objective class relations and exploitation at the origin of capitalist production.

Torie Bosch (2011) recently noted that the second season of *The Walking Dead* television series premiered to astonishingly high ratings, and she reminds us that the studios and publishers keep the zombie pop culture coming: "Colson Whitehead's 'literary zombie novel' *Zone* has just hit bookshelves, a movie version of Max Brooks' 2006 book, *World War Z* will star Brad Pitt, and who could forget the tour de force that is *Pride and Prejudice and Zombies*?"

Bosch claims that what is new about the current zombie craze is its "white-collar shine." She writes:

> No longer are zombies the beloved genre of the lonely, virgin teenage male, the macabre flipside of girls' obsession with unicorns. The undead have gone from lowbrow guilty pleasure to the favored monster of the erudite. (Sorry, Grendel.) At the risk of reading too deeply into a guilty pleasure, I can't help but believe that this current Era of the Dead draws its power from our economic malaise. If you work in the many white-collar fields that have suffered in this recession, zombies are the perfect representation of the fiscal horror show. The zombie apocalypse is a white-collar nightmare: a world with no need for the skills we have developed. Lawyers, journalists, investment bankers—they are liabilities, not leaders, in the zombie-infested world. (The exception to this rule, of course, is doctors.) In *The Walking Dead*, the strongest survivors come from blue-collar backgrounds—cops, hunters, mechanics. Perhaps the weakest of the band is Andrea, a former civil rights attorney who can't be trusted with a gun and who is overly indulgent in grieving her sister, a college student, who wasn't alert enough while peeing in the woods and got bit for her neglectfulness. In the zombie apocalypse, your J.D. is worthless—which is actually not so different from the real world of recent years. As we watch humans battle zombies, we see a social order upended.

In effect, Bosch is saying that the zombie apocalypse is not a world where the bourgeoisie are becoming obsolete because "robots take over industries like the law, medicine, even scientific discovery" but rather "the zombie apocalypse is the opposite scenario, in which our white-collar skills become worthless not through technical advance but through total system collapse." She writes that zombie stories are tales of comeuppance for the working class; they are tales of triumph where auto mechanics, farmers, plumbers, and electricians land blue-collar folks at the top of the new social order. But the zombie apocalypse is now an era in which the bourgeoisie with college degrees are having to get down and dirty by fixing generators. She explains:

> These highbrow zombie stories are not just about watching the newly humbled struggle to make sense of the topsy-turvy world. The suburbanite/urbanite viewer who can't hunt, can't slaughter animals, can't grow her own food, is meant to shudder at her ill-preparedness while watching. It's the existential fear of the economy writ large: I sometimes wonder what I would do if I lost everything. Move in with my mother? Crash on a generous

friend's couch? Somehow put my supercharged typing skills to use? The zombie apocalypse scenario takes these fears and explodes them.

In a way, these highbrow zombie scenarios are terrifying the bourgeoisie who feel the working class will fare better in the coming economic apocalypse. Bosch comments:

> While watching *The Walking Dead*, I am reminded that I would be nothing but a drag in a survivalist scenario. There will be a greater supply than demand for storytellers. I've never gone fishing. I can't even make a fire without a lighter. I can't lie to myself and think that I would survive the initial chaos of a zombie invasion (or any other apocalyptic event). Realistically, I'd be one of the brain-devouring hordes, not a scrappy, fighting human. Indulging in these zombie films gives an outlet to more realistic fears of personal economic collapse.

Bosch concludes with this sentiment:

> Should the economy recover, I suspect that we will abandon zombies as entertainment. The zombie boom will be a reminder of the frightening uncertainties of this decade. After all, we white-collar workers enjoy the illusion that our skills are meaningful. Once we no longer have to exorcise our fears of a society in which contract negotiation and SEO-optimization are nonsense, how will we terrify ourselves about the future? Perhaps we'll see a robot-apocalypse entertainment bubble.

For Bosch, highbrow zombie entertainment evokes the fear of the learned and refined classes having to compete with the working class on their own terms.

In his book *Magical Marxism* (2011), Andy Merrifield takes a different approach to zombies, noting that it is precisely the notion of the primitive that can be called upon to muster resistance, since the term primitive can be viewed productively as a "structure of feeling" that calls us out of our zombiehood. Here Merrifield links zombiehood to the history of colonialism and slavery, to the culture created by the master. For Merrifield,

> Zombies feed on the blandest of diets and the fog of forgetfulness and insensitivity has made them unaware of their condition, the generalized condition we call our life today, circa 2010, after a history that other zombies tell us has ended, has expended all its creative capacities to invent something else, to organize its political, economic, and cultural life differently. (Merrifield, 2011, p. 184)

In the quote above, Merrifield describes a scenario of zombiehood similar to Marx's notion of false consciousness. He calls on present-day zombies to find their primitive within and to defend themselves from the charge that they are reifying the exoticness of the Caribbean or Latin America by claiming that "'primitive thought' is not the exclusive domain of specific faraway peoples, with traditional life-forms, but is a structure of feeling that is appropriate to all of us, that defines our poetic impulses, our primal desires, our radical spirit" (p. 184).

For Merrifield, "To make the leap from zombie-hood, the leap out of our insomnia plague, into a world of magical desire and dream-images, into a living, troubling world of magical politics and potions is, in a nutshell…a call to sneak about subversively, to summon up the magician, to enter into another realm of reality, a raw, vivid, marvelous reality…" (p. 184). Merrifield calls for a magical Marxism that works toward a materialist fantasy and a "de-materialized flexibility" that is liberated from those old shopworn debates about class and the role of the state.

It is true, of course, as McNally notes, that for Marx, "the overcoming of the rule of the market thus also means a restoration of the world of concrete objectivity, so that objects might become things 'that are touched and loved and worn'" and also entails "their reconnection with things in their concrete, sensuous, textured particularities" (p. 267). But for Marx, this means significantly more than seeking the primitive within but achieving, as McNally notes, the kind of dialectical reversal that not only names the horrors of capitalism through a counter-magic to the sorcery of capitalism, through a tearing off of the "magic-cap of modernity" in our efforts to demystify the capitalist mode of production, but through the hard work of class struggle that is necessary to bring about the political victory of the oppressed.

Not only has Noam Chomsky managed to tear off the "magic-cap of modernity" with a clear and fearless analysis of the contemporary political landscape and the powerful elites that dominate it, he has also revealed it to be nothing more than a fool's coxcomb. The horrors of crimes committed in the name of democracy thus stand exposed. After an encounter with Noam Chomsky, modernity's pretense of having perfected democracy, and the United States' claim to the mantle of the world's greatest living democracy, can only be seen as bald-faced lies.

The illuminating dialogues between Chomsky and Orelus underscore the reality that we can act within history. We have a choice of which historical destinies—and there are many—we can choose from as a basis of our politics. Especially at this current historical moment, when our own experiences are overshadowed by despair and tethered to oblivion, we need a political analysis than can help us to understand more critically our experiences of daily life and to forge a political imagination that will help us in making important choices that could change the future for generations that follow. It is for this purpose that *On Language, Democracy, and Social Justice: Noam Chomsky's Critical Intervention* was written.

References

Anderson, P. (Director). *Resident Evil: Retribution* {Motion picture]. United States: Screen Gems.

Bosch, T. (2011, October 25). First, eat all the lawyers: Why the zombie boom is really about the economic fears of white-collar workers. *Slate*. Retrieved June 14, 2013, from http://www.stage.slate.com/articles/arts/culturebox/2011/10/zombies_the_the_zombie_boom_is_inspired_by_the_economy_.single.html

Forster, M. (Director). (2013). *World War Z* [Motion picture]. United States: Paramount Pictures.

Giroux, H. (2011a). *Zombie Politics and Culture in an Age of Casino Capitalism*. New York: Peter Lang.

Giroux, H. (2011b, June 2). Zombie politics: Dangerous authoritarianism or shrinking democracy—Part II. *Truthout*. Retrieved June 14, 2013, from http://truth-out.org/news/item/1356:zombie-politics-dangerous-authoritarianism-or-shrinking-democracy-part-ii

Herman, E., & Chomsky, N. (1988). *Manufacturing Consent*. New York: Pantheon Books.

McNally, D. (2011). *Monsters of the market: Zombies, vampires and global capitalism*. Leiden, The Netherlands, and Boston: Brill.

Merrifield, A. (2011). *Magical Marxism: Subversive politics and the imagination*. London and New York: Pluto Press.

Newitz, A. (2006). *Pretend we're dead: Capitalist monsters in American pop culture*. Durham, NC: Duke University Press.

Ramesh, P. (2003, July). Review of *A is for ox: the collapse of literacy and the rise of violence in an electronic age*, Barry Sanders. *Journal of the Krishnamurti Schools*. Retrieved June 15, 2013, from http://journal.kfionline.org/issue-7/review-of-a-is-for-ox-the-collapse-of-literacy-and-the-rise-of-violence-in-an-electronic-age-barry-sanders

Romero, G. A. (Director). (1968). *Night of the Living Dead* [Motion picture]. United States: The Walter Reade Organization.

Romero, G. A. (Director). (1978). *Dawn of the Dead* [Motion picture]. United States: United Film Distribution Company.

Sanders, B. (2010). Excerpt from *Unsuspecting souls*. Retrieved June 14, 2013, from http://www.thenervousbreakdown.com/bsanders/2010/12/unsuspecting-souls-an-excerpt/

Seabrook, W. (1929). *The Magic Island*. New York: Harcourt, Brace and Company.

Tourneur, J. (Director). (1943). *I Walked with a Zombie* [Motion picture]. United States: RKO Radio Pictures.

INTRODUCTION

Before talking about the overarching goals of this book, it is important to situate it contextually. Parts of the book demonstrate the ways and the extent to which Noam Chomsky's work has profoundly influenced the academic, political, and activist world. Particularly, the second chapter focuses on the way Chomsky's work has inspired many activists, activist-scholars, and public intellectuals, including myself. In my own case, it was my early exposure to Chomsky's work that stirred my intellectual curiosity to reach out to him, engaging him in several dialogues over the course of 8 years.

Many scholars and activist intellectuals have inspired me and influenced my scholarly work. Noam Chomsky is one of the few I have had the honor of meeting and developing a professional relationship with. This factor alone, I feel, makes a great difference in terms of how I see Noam Chomsky and his scholarly and activist work. Meeting and interacting with him on numerous occasions has heightened my respect for him both as a person and a dissident intellectual.

Chomsky's scholarly, activist, and political work has had a tremendous impact on the world. However, not many books have specifically analyzed the extent to which his work—along with his humility, kindness, and compassion for the weak and the poor—has profoundly influenced and inspired individuals who have had the privilege of knowing him. Hence, in the first chapter I use narratives stemming from professional and personal encounters with him to draw attention to his humility and genuine concern for the poor. In the remainder of the book,

Chomsky and I examine a wide range of important social justice issues, such as language rights of marginalized groups, democratic schooling, neoliberalism, and the effect of U.S. foreign policy on developing countries, particularly those that were colonized, are neocolonized, or are occupied. Through dialogues and essays, we provide the reader with a comprehensive view of these issues.

As a master's candidate in applied linguistics at the University of Massachusetts–Boston learning about Noam Chomsky's scholarly and activist work, never in my wildest dreams did I think that someday I would have the honor of meeting the most celebrated contemporary linguist and political dissident intellectual and develop a professional relationship with him, let alone collaborate on a book project with him. I had my first face-to-face dialogue with Professor Chomsky in 2005 while I was a doctoral student at the University of Massachusetts–Amherst. Additional in-person interactions, phone interviews, and email correspondence have taken place between Noam Chomsky and me ever since.

However, the idea of embarking on this book project did not cross my mind until my last dialogue with him in November 2010 at his office at the Massachusetts Institute of Technology. Of all the dialogues that I had with Professor Chomsky, the last one was the most profound in that it enabled me to bear witness to his humility, kindness, and compassion for the weak while talking about language, political, educational, and socioeconomic issues. This dialogue finally made me realize that writing this book would be valuable not merely as a way to explore the aforementioned issues, but also to highlight the impact that Chomsky has had on the academic, activist, and political world.

Before I decided to embark on this project, many questions crossed my mind. Even though I was convinced of its worth, I could not help but ask myself: How would the public receive it? How much weight or impact would it have on the academic and political worlds? Aren't there already many books about Noam Chomsky that highlight his scholarly and activist work in the world? Finally, does Noam Chomsky need an emerging scholar like myself to author a book on/with him that talks about the effect of his work on academics, activists, and ordinary people?

Further, before I took on this book project, close friends, colleagues, and some family members asked me if I thought about the possible association people might make between Noam Chomsky and me. Specifically, they were concerned that both the U.S. academy and some political pundits might draw the conclusion that I am a Chomskyan, and therefore, like Chomsky, I must be, for example, against Western imperial violence targeted at people and countries around the world. Some of them indirectly suggested to me that I should wait until I got tenure before I wrote this book, for fear that my current institution might assume that I am a "radical" and deny me tenure. The concern of my friends, colleagues, and family members is understandable, given that—in my view—the U.S. academy is by and large a conservative place in which minimal space is allotted to progressive intellectuals and activist-scholars to engage in critical work aimed at challenging the status quo.

I am also aware that the American public in general adheres to this conservative bent. However, I remain convinced that, like me, there must be deans, provosts, and university presidents who believe in academic freedom, upon which no institution should infringe. No one should allow an institution or dominant conservative group to silence one's voice, for one's freedom is in one's voice. I argue that if an institution denies a professor tenure because of what he or she stands for—that is, because of his or her uncompromising democratic principles, ideology, and firm stance against social injustice and inequality—rather than because of poor academic performance, this professor cannot have any respect for the institution. Having made that statement, let me also point out that I am fully aware that there are indeed many examples of excellent scholars, researchers, and teachers being denied tenure because of their ideological and political positions, not because of poor performance. Ideology matters (Freire & Macedo, 2002), and I am well aware of that. I am articulating these views so that the reader knows where I stand politically and ideologically.

Unlike what some readers might assume, this book is not intended to glorify Noam Chomsky by placing him on a pedestal. (And the humble Noam Chomsky, I am sure, would not want to be glorified, for this would contradict the democratic principles for which he has stood for over half a century.) Rather, this book is part of a larger educational and political project aimed at talking about the social justice issues mentioned earlier, while at the same time making concrete proposals for possible co-construction of a more humane world.

My narrative about my personal and professional interactions with Noam Chomsky is offered in the first chapter of the book. These interactions have shaped my view of Chomsky professionally and personally. As noted earlier, he is among the very few world-renowned intellectuals whom I have had the honor to meet. His humility, warmth, and genuine concern for the weak and the poor have prompted me to become a more caring and thoughtful thinker. Academically, he has inspired me to breach the academic imperial code to speak truth to power.

Overarching Goals of the Book

This book examines social justice issues such as unbalanced relationships between dominant and subjugated languages, democratic schooling, neoliberalism, colonization, and the harmful effect of Western globalization on developing countries, particularly on the poor living in those countries. These are issues that should concern us all as human beings regardless of our social, political, and ideological position in society. Unfortunately, because of corporate greed, selfishness, and self-interest, many of us fail to show genuine concern about these matters.

While those in power strive to maintain their hegemonic positions by exploiting and oppressing others, billions of people around the world, including children, are starving and deprived of basic needs such as shelter, clean water, and food. Powerful countries and individuals have used wars as political and economic tools to enrich themselves at the expense of invaded, occupied, and neocolonized people whose lives are often destroyed by cluster bombs and other military weapons. Stoking divisions among a country's ethnic groups or different segments of the population in order to invade and conquer them is the technique that many Western colonial, neocolonial, and imperial powers have used to maintain their economic and political hegemony in the world. Meanwhile, our education system has become more standardized than ever, and, as a consequence, teachers spend more time preparing students for standardized tests than actually teaching them (Apple, 2001, 2009; Au, 2008; Sleeter, 2005, 2007).

Further, while billions are spent on wars every year, our public schools do not have the resources teachers require to effectively educate students. For example, the Obama administration has allocated billions of dollars to the military while public school teachers and employees are losing their jobs. Moreover, while many teachers are being laid off, more money has been allocated to recruit high school and college students for the army. Finally, while the U.S. government continues to violate the basic human rights of people in Guantanamo and raid the houses of peace activists and freedom fighters, the false idea has been widely disseminated in the mainstream media by politicians—including President Barack Obama—that this government does not torture and that it is a beacon of freedom and a champion of democracy.

In the meantime, the United States has been trying to impose its manufactured form of democracy on people of other countries, even though participatory democracy is not yet a reality here (Apple & Beane, 2007; Carr, 2011; Chomsky, 1994, 2002; Denzin, 2009; Giroux, 2007; Macedo, 2009). If democracy exists in this country, it only works for the super rich, because they are the ones who get tax breaks from the government and get away with corruption and exploitation of the most vulnerable groups—poor, working-class people who are selling their labor in factories and sweatshops (Giroux, 2003; Smiley & West, 2012; West, 2004). Democracy works only for the powerful, who control the means of production and thereby control the wealth of the country (Apple, 2009). It is a buzzword for those the system has been oppressing. As Chomsky often pointed out during my dialogues with him, participatory democracy has succeeded in poor countries such as Bolivia, with the election of President Evo Morales in 2005 and then again in 2010, and in Haiti, with the election of President in 1990. But Western imperial powers such as the United States will not acknowledge that.

How can we have a school system that is democratic if the country in which it is located is not itself democratic? Moreover, how can we convince students of the presence of democracy when the basic human rights of these students, their parents, other family members, and their friends have been violated? Likewise, how can we have democracy when people are forbidden to speak their native languages in school and are afraid of revealing their religion and nationality to xenophobic and racist people who they fear might attack them? Democracy remains, unfortunately, a fancy word that many people in society can only dream about. Like participatory democracy, equal access to quality education and resources has yet to become a reality for many people, especially the poor. In short, social justice for all remains, unfortunately, a noble objective that many people have yet to see their country or government achieve. These are some of the issues that this book aims to address.

Overview of Chapters

The first two chapters illuminate the extent to which the scholarly and activist work of the borderless intellectual Noam Chomsky has profoundly impacted the intellectual and activist community. Chapters 3 and 4 explore language-based discrimination, schooling, and democracy. Chapters 5, 6, and 7 examine the negative effect of the Western neoliberal agenda on the poor, particularly those living in developing countries. Likewise, Chapter 8 examines the concept of social justice, while the last chapter discusses what role the public and activist intellectuals should play in the fight against social injustice. All of the chapters explore the matrix of linguistic, educational, class, and socioeconomic inequalities in a larger context. It is worth emphasizing that each chapter critically examines a set of entangled issues, except the first chapter, in which I detail how I got to know Professor Chomsky professionally and the extent to which he has deeply inspired me professionally, academically, and personally.

While in some dialogues I engage Chomsky in a deep conversation that examines the way corporate-driven school policies affect students' learning, particularly poor students, in others we talk about the myth of U.S. democracy that has been circulated throughout the mainstream media and the world. In subsequent dialogues, we focus on the way in which people in Third World countries have resisted the effects of U.S. foreign policy on their lives. While each chapter attempts to address a particular issue, the inevitable occurs—that is, interwoven issues run through all of them. A summary precedes all dialogues and provides the reader with a brief overview of their content and the context in which they occurred.

Intended Audience and Final Thoughts

This book will appeal to social justice scholars and activists, as well as undergraduate and graduate students majoring in education, language studies, political science, and history. It echoes the thoughts and authentic voices of a world-renowned intellectual, Noam Chomsky, who has profoundly influenced many disciplines and communities around the globe, and myself, Pierre Orelus, an emerging scholar committed to speaking truth to power. It is hoped that people will find this book helpful in their quest for social justice.

References

Apple, M. (2001). *Educating the "right" way: Markets, standards, God, and inequality.* New York: Routledge.

Apple, M. (2009). *Global crises, social justice, and education.* New York: Routledge.

Apple, M., & Beane, J. (2007). *Democratic schools: Lessons in powerful education* (2nd ed.). Portsmouth, NH: Heinemann.

Au, W. (2008). *Unequal by design: High-stakes testing and the standardization of inequality.* New York: Routledge.

Carr, P. (2011). The quest for a critical pedagogy of democracy. In C. Malott & B. Porfilio (Eds.), *Critical pedagogy in the twenty-first century: A new generation of scholars* (pp. 187–210). Charlotte, NC: Information Age.

Chomsky, N. (1994). *Secrets, lies and democracy.* Berkeley, CA: Odonian Press.

Chomsky, N. (2002). *Media control: The spectacular achievements of propaganda.* New York: Seven Stories.

Denzin, N.K. (2009). Critical pedagogy and democratic life or a radical democratic pedagogy. *Cultural Studies—Critical Methodologies, 9*(3), 379–397.

Freire, P., & Macedo, D. (2002). *Ideology matters.* Lanham, MD: Rowman & Littlefield.

Giroux, H. (2003). *The abandoned generation: Democracy beyond the culture of fear.* New York: Palgrave Macmillan.

Giroux, H. (2007). Democracy, education, and the politics of critical pedagogy. In P. McLaren & J. Kincheloe (Eds.), *Critical pedagogy: Where are you now?* (pp. 1–5). New York: Peter Lang.

Macedo, D. (2009). Unmasking prepackaged democracy. In S. Macrine (Ed.), *Critical pedagogy in uncertain times: Hopes and possibilities* (pp. 79–96). New York: Palgrave Macmillan.

Sleeter, C.E. (2005). *Un-standardizing curriculum: Multicultural teaching in the standardized-based classroom.* Routledge: New York.

Sleeter, C.E. (2007). *Facing accountability in education: Democracy & equity at risk.* New York: Teachers College Press.

Smiley, T., & West, C. (2012). *The rich and the rest of us: A poverty manifesto.* Carlsbad, CA: Smileybooks.

West, C. (2004). *Democracy matters: Winning the fight against imperialism.* New York: Penguin.

ONE

Professional and Personal Encounters With Noam Chomsky

A Critical Self-Reflection

I was first exposed to Noam Chomsky's nativist theory in 1994 in an introductory psychology course that I took at Massachusetts Bay Community College. As the professor was talking about language development, she briefly mentioned nativist theory. Although her explanation about this theory was rather brief (she was trying to contrast it with behaviorism), it caught my attention. I attempted to ask her a question about nativist theory, but I was not fully able to do so, since my limited English at the time prevented me from making myself completely clear. Therefore, the professor seemed unsure about what I wanted to ask her. I felt somewhat embarrassed and said to her hastily, "I am sorry. I didn't mean to interrupt you," realizing I could not adequately articulate the question. She replied, saying, "That's okay Pierre. You're not interrupting me. What question did you want to ask?" I remained silent for a while and then said, "Actually I don't have any question. I am sorry."

The truth was that I did not want to embarrass myself in front of my classmates for fear that I would not be able to make myself clear while asking questions about nativist theory. Nonetheless, because I was able to read English fairly well, I went home that day and carefully read the short section in my psychology textbook that addressed this theory and gained a basic understanding of nativist theory. In that section there was no mention of Noam Chomsky's activist and political work (which was perfectly understandable, given that it was a psychology textbook).

Despite the temporary language barrier I faced in my introductory psychology class, I completed it successfully. It was not until 6 years later, while I was working on a master's degree in applied linguistics at the University of Massachusetts–Boston, that I was introduced to Noam Chomsky's scholarly and activist/political work. Specifically, while working on my degree, I was fortunate to have as a professor Pepi Leistyna, who skillfully and painstakingly helped me understand Noam Chomsky's work in the most profound and critical way.

Professor Leistyna provided me with the foundational knowledge of behaviorist, nativist, and social interactionist theories through inspiring mini-lectures and small group discussions, where my classmates and I discussed the key tenets of these theories. In addition, he used documentaries in class, which enabled me to deepen my understanding about these important theories. Equally important was the information that Professor Leistyna shared with me beyond the classroom about Professor Noam Chomsky's activism, including his firm political stance against U.S. imperialist policy and human rights violations. I was fascinated by what I learned from Professor Leistyna regarding Chomsky's political and scholarly work.

I remember saying to Professor Leistyna that in the next 15 years or so he would become the next Noam Chomsky, given his broad knowledge of world affairs, language, literacy, culture, identity, and sociopolitical issues, as well as the depth of his critical analysis of these topics. Being the humble professor he is, he acknowledged my compliment, saying, "Thank you. That's nice of you." I looked up and have continued to look up to Professor Pepi Leistyna, who is now a dear colleague of mine. He and another distinguished professor, Donaldo Macedo, with whom I took a sociolinguistics class at the Applied Linguistics program at the University of Massachusetts–Boston, have helped me to understand the politics of language by exposing me to the scholarly work of Robert Phillipson (1992, 2010), Tove Skutnabb-Kangas (2000), James Gee (2011), and Pierre Bourdieu (1999), among others.

Acquiring knowledge about nativist theory in Professor Leistyna's psycholinguistics class helped me to better understand the limitations of behaviorism as conceptualized and promoted by B.F. Skinner (1938, 1953, 1957, 1968). Behaviorist theory heavily emphasizes memorization, repetition, and drill practices, which have proven to be very limited and mechanistic in many ways. Behaviorism grossly fails to explain the complexity of language acquisition and learning. To paraphrase Chomsky (1959, 1965), language is too complex to be acquired through drill and mechanistic practices and methods that proponents of behaviorism suggest.

Before Chomsky came up with his breakthrough theory, behaviorism was dominant. In fact, until late 1950s and early 1960s, many researchers and educators believed that behaviorism was the most effective approach to teaching languages. It was used in many traditional and non-traditional settings, such as the U.S. Army and schools, to teach languages. Many language teaching methods, such as the audiolingual method and the grammar-translation method, stem from behaviorism. Gaining a sound understanding of the limitations of behaviorism as a master's degree candidate challenged me to critically reflect on the trajectory of my learning experience.

I vividly remember the way in which my elementary, middle school, and high school teachers—and even some of my college professors—used the behaviorist approach to teaching. My teachers would have me repeat after them prepackaged sentences in English and Spanish under the assumption that this was the right way to teach me these languages. For example, in my high school English class, my classmates and I were expected to memorize verbs, nouns, and sentences in the hope that this mechanistic learning strategy would help us to speak English.

However, like many of my classmates, I spent about 5 years memorizing tons of English verbs, adjectives, nouns, idiomatic expressions, and whole sentences, but was never able to speak English until I came to the United States, where I learned it through social interaction with friends and co-workers. In addition to my English course, I often memorized sections of my biology and physiology textbooks when I was preparing for midterm and final exams. However, I did not retain for long what I was able to memorize for these exams. In fact, 3 or 4 days after the exams, I forgot virtually everything that I had memorized about these subjects.

Having the opportunity to be exposed to the scholarly work of the authors mentioned earlier, as well as others, I developed a consciousness that has enabled me to think critically about important social justice and political issues such as the oppressive nature of the school system and the unequal power relationship between the oppressors and the oppressed. For example, while Chomsky's work has challenged me to critically reflect on and question the way I was taught English and Spanish as third and fourth languages, respectively, Phillipson's and Skutnabb-Kangas's work on linguicism has helped me become aware of the language divide between speakers of dominant and subjugated languages. As an educator who has been teaching language and culture courses for the last decade, I have been encouraged by their work to constantly question and reflect on the politics of language. Specifically, the work of Phillipson and Skutnabb-Kangas has helped me tremendously in understanding the lopsided power relations between languages spoken by minority groups and those considered languages of opportunity, such as English, and the negative impact these unequal relations have had on the subjectivity and material conditions of speakers of languages considered inferior. More important, their work has made me realize that conscientious and critically aware intellectuals have a historic and moral obligation to counteract the negative effects of linguicism (Skutnabb-Kangas, 2000) and linguistic imperialism (Phillipson, 1992, 2010) on linguistically and culturally diverse groups, particularly those who have been marginalized because of their linguistic, cultural, and socioeconomic backgrounds.

Although I appreciate the knowledge that I acquired in Pepi Leistyna's course about Noam Chomsky's nativist theory, which has proven to be helpful to me throughout my career as a professor teaching language acquisition courses, I was most appreciative (and still am) of the vital information that he provided me in class about Noam Chomsky's political, activist, and human rights work. Professor Leistyna's engaging mini-lecture on and enthusiasm about Chomsky's political work inspired me to further explore Chomsky's scholarly and activist work.

While completing my master's degree, I read Chomsky's books insatiably and listened to interviews he gave and debates in which he was involved concerning the U.S. war in Vietnam, the U.S. invasion and occupation of other countries, its foreign policy, and its violations of human rights, among many other things. While I was a high school teacher, I learned through a friend that Professor Chomsky was going to give a talk about U.S. foreign policy at the University of Massachusetts–Boston and that my former professor, Pepi Leistyna, was one of the organizers of the event. I attended the talk and brought with me one of my favorite books, Chomsky's *The Culture of Terrorism*, to have him sign it.

Because it was the first time I was to have the honor of listening to Noam Chomsky, I was extremely excited and felt intellectually energized. I sat in the large room filled with hundreds of people where he was scheduled to talk, waiting impatiently for him to arrive and looking in the meantime at other Chomsky books that a gentleman was selling. As soon as I finished browsing through these books, I saw my former professor, Pepi Leistyna, walking in the hallway behind Chomsky. A professor whom I did not know introduced Chomsky, who spoke for about an hour. Somewhere in his talk, Chomsky mentioned Haiti as he spoke about unfair U.S. trade and foreign policy.

During the question-and-answer period, I asked Chomsky the following question: To what extent do you think U.S. foreign policy has damaged the economic and political system of Haiti? Professor Chomsky gave a much lengthier response to my question than I expected. He started by talking about the major impact the Haitian revolution had had on the entire Western hemisphere, as well as other parts of the world. He went on to explain how Haiti has been paying a heavy political and economic price for being the first black republic to gain its independence from France.

Professor Chomsky went further by talking about how the United States at the time refused to recognize the independence of Haiti and sided with France, which was demanding that this newly independent nation pay the French government a sum of 90 million gold francs, supposedly as indemnity. Moreover, he explained in detail how the U.S. government, through unfair trade and foreign policy, has exploited and destabilized Haiti and other Third World countries for decades. He concluded his detailed answer by citing the example of President Jean Bertrand Aristide, who was democratically elected in 1990 but was deposed by the U.S. government with the complicity of some segments of the Haitian bourgeoisie and the Haitian army. The United States had created and left behind this army after its occupation of Haiti from 1915 to 1934.

I was intellectually moved by Professor Chomsky's response and went back home that day to read more of his work on U.S. foreign policy. Later, as a first-year doctoral student, I continued to read about U.S. foreign policy with regard to Third World countries, and I developed a keen interest in further exploring this issue. In doing my research, I gained a deeper understanding of the history of Western colonialism and its effect on these countries. The knowledge that I acquired inspired me to write some essays on the historical, socioeconomic, and political conditions of formerly colonized Third World countries, particularly Haiti.

While working on these essays, especially the ones on Haiti, I could not help but quote Noam Chomsky throughout. Suddenly, the idea crossed my mind of writing Chomsky a letter requesting an interview to further discuss the negative effect of U.S. trade and foreign policy on Haiti and other impoverished countries. However, I did not act on this idea right away but instead waited about 6 months before writing my request, since I assumed that Chomsky, as a highly respected intellectual, might not have the time to reply to someone he did not know. But I was mistaken, as the email that I received from him illustrates.

Dear Mr. Orelus,

Most interested to hear from you. I'm sorry you hesitated to write. Everything reaches me, unless, by accident, it gets lost in the deluge, which is enormous. I hope that you will be able to visit. Hate to be bureaucratic, but the only way to arrange it is to contact Bev Stohl (same address). She knows the details (I don't), and arranges everything. Would have to pass anything by her anyway.

I was ecstatic at the opportunity to engage in a face-to face dialogue with this premier linguist and world-renowned, borderless intellectual. I followed Professor Chomsky's suggestion and contacted his personal assistant to set a time to meet with him. Bev Stohl offered me a choice of several days and times. I went back and forth by email with her before she confirmed that I was scheduled to meet with Chomsky on March 18, 2005.

Before the meeting, I asked Professor Chomsky if it would be okay to send him a draft of two of the essays that I was working on, since our dialogue would mostly concern the content of those essays. I made that request because I wanted him to have a better idea of what my mini-project was about, and he agreed to receive and review the essays before the meeting. I immediately had a positive impression of the man whose scholarly work I had deeply explored in graduate school.

My First Encounter With Noam Chomsky

In addition to the essays that I sent to Noam Chomsky, I developed a set of questions aimed at guiding me throughout the interview. In addition, I bought a digital voice recorder with me to record the dialogue, as I planned to transcribe it. The night before our meeting, I was extremely nervous at the thought of meeting Noam Chomsky. Even though I was quite familiar with his work, I was concerned as to how I would articulate my arguments and formulate my questions. This stemmed mainly from the fact that Chomsky was a renowned world intellectual and that I was not sure how, as a graduate student, I would impress him with the knowledge that I had acquired about his scholarly and activist work.

On the appointed day, I drove about 2 hours from western Massachusetts to meet with Professor Chomsky in his office at the Massachusetts Institute of Technology in Cambridge, practicing the questions with my wife during the drive. We arrived early and found parking not too far from the building where Chomsky's office is located. When we arrived at his office, I told his personal assistant that I had an appointment with him. She recognized my name and asked me to sit outside and wait for her to call me in.

As I was waiting, my anxiety level increased. I was so nervous that I felt like leaving, but knowing the importance of the dialogue that I was about to have with Chomsky, I decided to make an extra effort to control my nervousness. My wife, who noticed my anxiety, assured me that everything would be okay. About 45 minutes later, Bev came out and told me that Professor Chomsky was ready for the dialogue and that I could come in. On the way into the office, Chomsky told me that it was okay for my wife to come in with me, a considerate gesture that was much appreciated.

My wife sat in for the whole dialogue but did not take part in it. However, before Professor Chomsky and I started talking, he acknowledged her presence and briefly spoke with her. Before we started engaging in the dialogue, he pulled out the essays that I had sent him and on which he had made comments in the margins. In addition, he mentioned that I had raised some important points in the essays.

I was very nervous at the beginning of the interview. However, I soon felt comfortable, thanks to Professor Chomsky's humility, calm temperament, and friendliness. The dialogue lasted about 30 minutes but seemed longer. It went smoothly and calmly. Afterwards, I could not stop telling my wife that Professor Noam Chomsky was the humblest and nicest intellectual that I had ever met. I felt so comfortable interacting with him. I did not feel any sense of intellectual arrogance and self-praise in his voice and in his responses to my questions.

He treated me respectfully and showed interest in what I had to say. He sat in his chair, listening carefully to my questions and answering them as candidly as possible. Because I wanted to get the most detailed responses to my questions, I decided not to interject while he was talking, as I normally would have. He provided extended and profound responses to my questions throughout the dialogue.

As seemed to be the protocol, his personal assistant came back and knocked on his office door to signal that the time allotted for our dialogue was up. However, Professor Chomsky continued to talk, expanding on his responses to my questions. Bev came in a second time and informed him that another person was waiting for him outside, and a few minutes later our conversation ended. Before I left his office, I quickly asked him if it would be possible to continue the dialogue with him at a later time. He nodded and said, "*Sure. Please make the request through Bev.*"

On my way home from MIT, I listened to the tape of the interview over and over, all the while reflecting on the positive experience that I had had dialoguing with Chomsky. I asked myself: Has he been humble and kind like this all his life? Or has he cultivated these qualities as he has gotten older? I felt tempted to ask him these questions while dialoguing with him, but I thought it would be inappropriate to do so.

After I had the interview transcribed, I sent Chomsky a copy of the transcript, a copy of a picture that I took with him, and a thank-you note saying that my wife and I enjoyed the discussion we had with him. I asked him to review the transcript to make sure that everything that we talked about during our discussion was accurate. He confirmed receipt of these materials and informed me that he would be giving a talk at Hampshire College and at the University of Massachusetts–Amherst. He stated:

> *Just picked up the transcript, disk, photo. Glad you both enjoyed the discussion. Me too. I will be in Amherst in the fall, for an Eqbal Ahmad memorial lecture at Hampshire, and a talk at UMass organized by the linguistics department. Bev Stohl, at my office, would have the details. About the transcript, do you happen to have an electronic version? Easier to make corrections that way. If not, will do it by pen and mail.*

As requested, I sent him an electronic version of the transcript. Two weeks later Chomsky sent me back his edits of the interview via email with the following note: "*I picked it up and went through the transcript. Attached. Phrases to be deleted are in boldface within square brackets. Phrases to be inserted are in boldface, separated from the text. Hope it is comprehensible.*"

About 3 months after meeting Professor Chomsky at MIT, I attended his talks at the University of Massachusetts–Amherst and at Hampshire College. At UMass–Amherst the ballroom where he was speaking was full of people, including some students I had known through activist work on that campus. Before

Chomsky began his speech, I had the privilege of greeting him and briefly interacting with him. I also attended the talk at Hampshire College, but I did not have the opportunity to speak to him because of my late arrival. However, since I sat next to the podium where he was standing, we were able to acknowledge each other's presence through eye contact. Six months or so later, I went back to MIT to meet with him for a second time.

My Second Encounter With Professor Chomsky

I felt so inspired by my first meeting with Professor Chomsky that I wanted to continue the dialogue with him, so I met with him the second time to further discuss the issues that we had examined in our first dialogue. By the time we met again, I had already written about seven essays that I wanted to expand into a book. He agreed to meet with me to discuss this book project, which he encouraged me to pursue. Chomsky replied to my email saying, "*Glad to learn that you're contemplating a book project. I'd be glad to have a chance to talk to you about it. Usual procedure: contact Bev Stohl (same e-mail address), and see what you can work out with her.*"

Professor Chomsky tried to help me find a publisher for the book by referring me to Anthony Arnove, who, in turn, referred me to an editor at South End Press. Even though the book, *Education Under Occupation*, was not published by South End, Chomsky's genuine initial interest in this book project inspired me to strive to finish the manuscript and find another publisher for it. Chomsky graciously endorsed the book, as the email below with the blurb for the book shows:

> Pierre—
>
> *Finally was able to carve out a little time to read your ms, with great pleasure. Hope it's not too late for a few words, below.*
>
> Noam
>
> Interweaving the perspectives of subject and critical observer, Pierre Orelus reveals multiple dimensions of the material and psychological devastation left in the wake of Western imperial conquest. His ruminations focus on his native Haiti, once the world's richest colony, severely punished for daring to become the first free country of free men in the hemisphere, now its most deeply impoverished and brutalized society. But his thoughts and their implications reach well beyond, yielding valuable insight into the pain and suffering of the traditional victims, and their resilience and hope.

Our second meeting was very informal. Chomsky invited my wife, who was going to sit outside and wait for me, to take part in the dialogue. We talked about the social movement that was taking place in Latin America with leftist and progressive leaders, such as the late Venezuelan president Hugo Chávez, Bolivian

President Evo Morales, and former Brazilian President Luiz Inácio Lula da Silva. Professor Chomsky seemed fascinated by the elections that had taken place in these countries leading to the presidency of these leaders. He was particularly impressed with the Bolivian election, where indigenous people organized themselves and elected their leader, Evo Morales. He said that the election experience in Bolivia was a good example of a participatory form of democracy that the West, including the United States, should follow.

We talked briefly about our professional and personal backgrounds. I shared with Chomsky that I am from a working-class family and that my father was a carpenter and my mother a street vendor. He told me that his father was a professor of linguistics and that his mother stayed home to take care of him and his younger brother. He also shared with me that he had been to Haiti and had had the opportunity to interact with many Haitians involved in grassroots movements. He was impressed with the way the poor and the masses in Haiti had organized to elect former priest Jean Bertrand Aristide as president in 1990. Overall, he seemed fascinated by the grassroots movement taking place on the island and the resilience of the Haitian people, particularly the poor.

Toward the end of our conversation, we commented on a painting hanging in his office, agreeing that it truly reflected the human condition, wars, and poverty. In fact, I remember Professor Chomsky deconstructing for us the message the artist intended to convey. In his office was also a portrait of Bertrand Russell, who I later discovered greatly influenced him. Like Chomsky, Russell was a dissident intellectual who, throughout his career, spoke against the abuse of human rights and Western imperialism.

While talking with Chomsky, my wife asked him if he had plans to go to Venezuela any time soon; he responded that he had almost made it there but had to cut his trip short for family reasons. Before we ended the conversation, Professor Chomsky asked me to let him know when I finished the book manuscript that I was still working on. Approximately 6 months later, I emailed him to let him know that I was done with the manuscript and asked him if he was still willing to endorse it. He agreed to do so and kept his promise, as noted earlier.

When I tell friends, classmates, and professors that I met with Noam Chomsky several times and that I have been in touch with him via email, they are curious to know how this happened. At first they have a hard time believing my version of how my encounters with Professor Chomsky took place, as they assume that Chomsky is unreachable and that only a few well-connected people could have access to him, but not a doctoral student such as I was. (As mentioned earlier, I had made similar assumptions myself.) The truth is that I just took a chance by contacting him.

In short, my first two meetings with Professor Chomsky and my contacts with him by email for the last 8 years have been inspiring and transformative, both personally and professionally. After I met with him for the second time in 2006, I did not see him face-to-face until November 2010. This was partly because, upon completion of my doctorate in 2008, I moved from Massachusetts to Las Cruces, New Mexico, in 2008 to take a tenure-track faculty position at New Mexico State University.

My Third Encounter With Noam Chomsky

Before I met with Chomsky in person for the third time, we had a phone conversation that lasted about 45 minutes. I was working on a book project that addressed such issues as neoliberalism, schooling, and democracy, among others. I emailed Noam and asked him if I could interview him to gain further insights about these issues for a book. He agreed and asked me once again to make an appointment through Bev Stohl, who set up the date and time for a phone interview. Like the previous dialogues that I had with him, the phone interview was pleasant and went smoothly. Even though the interview was scheduled for 25–30 minutes, we ended up talking for about 45 minutes. In fact, I felt that we could have talked longer, because Professor Chomsky seemed very interested in the issues we were discussing. It was once again a great pleasure talking with him.

As for our third face-to-face dialogue, it was prompted as follows. After the damaging earthquake that took place in Haiti on January 12, 2010, I wanted (1) to write some essays that critically examined the so-called reconstruction project of Haiti proposed by the UN and the Obama administration, and headed up by former U.S. President Bill Clinton, and (2) to make a short documentary movie on Haiti in which I would interview scholar activists like Chomsky to talk about neoliberalism and democracy in the context of Haiti. To this end, I decided that I would ask Professor Chomsky for another face-to-face interview. Though he was going to be extremely busy during the time in which I wanted to have the interview with him, he suggested that I contact Bev to arrange a time to meet with him. He replied to my request saying, "*Not sure where I'll be those days. Best idea, as always, is to check with Bev Stohl, at my e-mail address. Hope there'll be a way to get together.*"

I wanted Chomsky to be one of the interviewees in this documentary, since he is politically aware and very knowledgeable about what has been happening in Haiti since its independence. However, before the in-person interview between us took place, we went back and forth by email discussing issues regarding Haiti, the 2010 earthquake, and its aftermath. What follows is an excerpt of the online discussion we had about these issues.

* * *

Pierre (March 3, 2010): Dear Noam, I hope you're well. I want to inform you that a second edition of my first book "Education Under Occupation" will be released soon—

hopefully in a month. With the approval of the publisher, I decided that I would change the title and possibly the subtitle, as I feel the previous title did not fully capture the gist/focus of the book. I would also include a new chapter regarding what has been happening in Haiti, especially after the earthquake. The content of the book will be the same except that a new chapter will be included in it. I am letting you know about this since you were one of the distinguished scholars who graciously endorsed this book.

Noam (March 3, 2010): Good news, though I'm sorry that it was such a horrendous catastrophe that led to the new chapter. Hope that things are going well.

Pierre (March 5, 2010): Hi Noam, you're right. Here is what prompted my decision to write a new chapter about Haiti in the second edition of the book. I feel it is my responsibility as a public intellectual and as a person who was born and grew up in Haiti to provide the reader a different view about what has been happening in Haiti, especially during and after the earthquake. I am curious to know your view on what has been happening in Haiti during and after the earthquake, particularly about Obama's decision to select former Presidents George W. Bush and Bill Clinton to facilitate the relief effort supposedly designed to "save" Haiti. As you know, these two presidents have politically destabilized and economically paralyzed Haiti with their neoliberal policy. In my view, the Canadian, French, and US hidden/overt agenda is to use this tragedy as a political move to take over Haiti. Would you share that view?

Noam (March 5, 2010): The decision to use Bush and Clinton was either colossal ignorance or indescribable cynicism. But the fact is that awful as it is to say, these gangsters can at least bring in some badly needed aid. Sometimes choices are not appealing. I don't think there's any hidden agenda. The US and France have so totally destroyed Haiti that there's not much left to take over. Canada by now is hardly a country just taking orders from the Master.

Pierre (March 8, 2010): Hi Noam, you may be right "these gangsters can at least bring in some badly needed aid." However, I question what kind of aid this would be. It is unquestionable that the poorest of the poor in Haiti particularly are so desperate that they would accept anything from whomever. I would call envoys such as Clinton and Bush and others neocolonial missionaries. In my view, the long-term consequences of Clinton's and Bush's agenda aiming to widely open Haiti's doors to Western corporations might be even more disastrous than the present horrible socioeconomic conditions in which many Haitians find themselves. I do not intend to be pessimistic but I am very skeptical of Clinton and other so-called Western liberal humanists who sound like they care about Haitians more than anybody else. Would you share my pessimism/skepticism?

Noam (March 10, 2010): The skepticism is appropriate, and there are alternatives, such as directing aid to popular organizations and communities—as in fact suggested in an op-ed in the Boston Globe a day or two ago. But they are unlikely to be implemented, unfortunately, unless there is a great deal of popular pressure, so far missing.

Pierre (March 11, 2010): Indeed, there are alternatives. As you suggested, the best option will be to send the aid to popular organizations and communities directly involved in working with the poor. For example, sending aid to Partners in Health will be the right thing to do because this organization has been taking care of and curing the sick, training many Haitian health technicians, and creating employment for many. Would you go to Haiti sometime? I know you have been there in the past.

Noam (March 11, 2010): No chance in the near future, I'm afraid. Nothing much I could contribute even if I went. Last time it was to try to publicize the terror that the US was supporting and to provide some support and publicity for dissidents, some underground.

Pierre (March 15, 2010): I know you are one of the few scholars/activists who are genuinely concerned about Haiti and other oppressed nations. Would you be able to do anything from here that may be an inspiration to some grassroots organizations in Haiti that are fighting for social justice and equality on the ground? If you plan on doing something of that sort, please let me know how you would like me to be involved. I might be able to provide some "insider" insights since I grew up there.

Noam (March 15, 2010): I haven't been able to do anything beyond speaking and writing about it, sometimes for Haitian support groups. Don't know what more I can do.

Pierre (March 27, 2010): Hi Noam, I just finished revisiting your book with Paul Farmer and Amy Goodman "Getting Haiti Right This Time." It makes me seriously think about what is happening now in Haiti. In this book you, Paul, and Amy talk about the resilience of Haitian people in such a profound way. How far do you think such a resilience can get Haitian people? Are you hopeful that Haiti will stand on its feet someday, given the corporate interests involved in the so-called reconstruction project taking place there?

Noam (March 27, 2010): Friends who have just been there, including a Haitian colleague, are impressed with the resilience, which is really incredible after what they have been through. I wouldn't dare to guess.

Pierre (March 27, 2010): I agree with you. I guess my sense of optimism has been partly affected by my recent trip to this island. What I saw happening there was heartbreaking. Based on what you have read and been told about Haiti since the earthquake occurred there, what is your overall assessment of the socioeconomic and political situations of the country? Would you make any prediction of what would happen, say, 5–10 years from now? Would it be appropriate to compare Haiti to other occupied countries such as Palestine and/or Iraq? I would appreciate your analysis/response.

Noam (March 27, 2010): I wouldn't predict. I don't think comparisons to Iraq or Palestine are very helpful. Too many differences.

Pierre (April 2, 2010): Hi Noam, as I was watching DemocracyNow!, I learned that you will have a conversation with Amy Goodman and Arundhati Roy. I look forward to it. Bill Clinton just apologized for destroying the Haitian rice, through his foreign policy, that hard-working and resilient Haitian farmers have grown and depended on to survive. I was wondering what you think of his apology.

Noam (April 2, 2010): I was glad to hear his apology, but it's far too late, far too limited, and far too quiet.

* * *

As this personal communication between Chomsky and me demonstrates, Professor Chomsky is not only keenly aware of the socioeconomic and political situation in Haiti, but he also shows a genuine concern about the country. During the week in which I wanted to have the face-to-face dialogue with him, he already had several interviews set. However, he was kind enough to have his personal assistant squeeze me in for a 20–25 minute interview. She asked me via email if it was worth having this dialogue for such a short period of time and suggested that I have the dialogue at a different time so that I would have more time to interact with Professor Chomsky. As she stated, *"Dear Dr. Orelus, Yes, I have squeezed you in on Friday, November 12, at 3:30 pm, for a 20-minute meeting. It will be very quick, so please be sure it is worth your efforts to come on that day for such a short time."* Because I was no longer living in Massachusetts and could only be there during the week in which I requested the interview, I kept the appointment for the date and time she had set.

On the day I was scheduled to meet with Chomsky in his office at MIT, I had to drive from Northampton, Massachusetts, to Brown University in Providence, Rhode Island, where I attended and presented at the Haitian American Studies Association Conference. It was a hectic day. As soon as I finished presenting at that conference I rushed back to Cambridge with my wife and my 19-month-old daughter for my appointment with Professor Chomsky. As before, we managed to find a parking spot that was not too far from the building where the Department of Linguistics at MIT is housed. We took the elevator up to Professor Chomsky's office, arriving on time.

However, Professor Chomsky's personal assistant informed me that he was behind schedule and asked me to wait patiently for him until he was done with someone who was interviewing him. About 30 minutes later, Professor Chomsky came out, greeted me with a warm and genuine smile, and apologized for the delay. Meanwhile, my wife and daughter were sitting in another room waiting for me. When I realized that it would take a while before I talked to Professor Chomsky, I decided to join my wife and my daughter and stayed with them for about 20 minutes. I then returned to the little entrance corridor that served as a small waiting room.

In a while, Professor Chomsky came back outside and asked me to come in. However, he had apparently forgotten that he had a conference call at 4:00 pm. His personal assistant informed him about it. He once more apologized and asked me if I would mind coming back around 5:00 pm to have the dialogue with him. I agreed. My wife and I decided to go down to the first floor of the building, where we had tea and coffee at a small coffee shop. It seemed that it had been a hectic day for Chomsky, as it had been for me as well. However, he was calm and friendly as always. When I got back to his office, his personal assistant was about to leave. Professor Chomsky invited me into the office, and we spoke for about an hour without interruption.

On this occasion we did not have much time to chart before we had the formal dialogue, as we had before. We focused our conversation on Western neo-liberalism, U.S. foreign policy, and the earthquake in Haiti and its aftermath. Toward the end of the dialogue, I asked Professor Chomsky: Which one of your scholarly works are you most proud of, given that you have written over one hundred books? He did not directly answer the question and proceeded to say, *"I am proud that people like you are picking up the mantle and going on. I can't do it forever. So it's good to see you doing it. I don't know if I feel proud about it. I feel happy about it."*

I ended our dialogue by asking him: What would you like to be remembered for when your final day on this earth comes? He answered the question by sharing with me a moving story about his deceased wife. As he was telling me the story, he became very emotional. It was an emotional moment for me as well; I almost burst into tears as I listened to him. Professor Chomsky narrated the story this way:

> *There are things that impress me personally and that I feel emotionally moved by. This summer, I went to southern Colombia to visit some remote and endangered agricultural villages, which are trying to protect themselves and their resources, both from military attack, which is constant, but also from the predatory attack of multinational mining corporations and the Colombian government, which is trying to privatize their water and so on and so forth. It was pretty inspiring to watch. I mean it happened to be a personal connection. They were dedicating a forest to the memory of my late wife. Which is the immediate reason I went down there. That was really a moving experience. These are the kind of things that stick with me. There are a lot of things like that around the world.* (Excerpt from interview, 2010)

I was deeply touched by his response. Given the way I phrased the question, Professor Chomsky could have responded by referring specifically to what he has personally accomplished throughout his long career. Instead, he replied using an example that honored the death of his wife.

What I learned from his response is the following: What would be most satisfying to take to the grave when one's final day on earth comes is not the finest scholarly work that one has produced and the world recognition that one may have received. Rather, it is the memory of the people to whom one feels connected emotionally and intimately and loves, and the legacy of the positive impact one has on others. In short, what I inferred from Chomsky's response is that what is truly important at the end of one's life is people, especially those one loves and feels loved by, not material things and glory. The tender memory of loved ones and the positive influence one has on others last beyond death.

Having the opportunity to meet and interact with Noam Chomsky several times has challenged me to reconsider what is or should be important in my personal, academic, and professional life. As a young and an emerging scholar, I have been striving to "make it." By making it I mean trying to contribute to my field and beyond by producing high-quality scholarly work that exceeds people's expectations.

I may never be like Noam Chomsky and other incredible writers and borderless intellectuals like Edward Said, Frantz Fanon, Jean Price Mars, C.L.R. James, Stuart Hall, Eric Williams, Robert Phillipson, Tove Skutnabb-Kangas, Ngugi Wa Thiong'o, Aimé Césaire, Paulo Freire, Arundhati Roy, Howard Zinn, Andre Lord, Angela Davis, Gayatri Chakravorty Spivak, Vandana Shiva, Maryse Condé, Jacques Stephen Alexis, Jacques Roumain, bell hooks, Peter McLaren, Henri Giroux, Antenor Firmin, and Leslie Manigat, among others. The reason is that each one of us on this earth is not motivated by the same level of inner drive, desire, and passion, or may not have access to the same resources and opportunities, or possess the same level of intellect and cognitive capacity to excel and to be acknowledged worldwide. However, I will continue to fully use inspiration gained from these intellectuals and combine it with my own intellectual capacity to impact the world my way, with my scholarly and political work.

At the same time, inspired by the humble and unforgettable life and professional lessons that I have learned from Noam Chomsky in interacting with him numerous times, I will always make the effort to remind myself that what makes one great is not necessarily one's professional and academic success or fame; rather, it is one's humility, kindness, love, and compassion for others; the willingness to help and support those who are in need; and the ability to connect with oneself and others, especially loved ones.

Lastly, drawing on Noam Chomsky's embodiment of these virtues, his incredible intellectual depth, and his commitment to social justice and human rights, I argue that he is a model for humanity. He has profoundly inspired me personally, professionally, and intellectually, as he has inspired millions of people around the globe—academics and non-academics—to engage in causes aimed at fighting against human oppression. Very few intellectuals have impacted people globally in such a profound way as Noam Chomsky. I am therefore grateful that I had the honor of meeting him, getting to know him, and collaborating with him on this book project.

References

Bourdieu, P. (1999). Language and symbolic power. In A. Jaworski & N. Coupland (Eds.), *The discourse reader* (pp. 502–514). London: Routledge.

Chomsky, N. (1959). [Review of B.F. Skinner's *Verbal behavior*]. *Language, 35*(1), 26–58.

Chomsky, N. (1965). *Aspects of the theory of syntax*. Cambridge, MA: Massachusetts Institute of Technology Press.

Gee, J.P. (2011). *Social linguistics and literacies: Ideology in discourses*. New York: Routledge.

Phillipson, R. (1992). *Linguistic imperialism*. New York: Oxford University Press.

Phillipson, R. (2010). *Linguistic imperialism continued*. New York: Routledge.

Skinner, B.F. (1938). *Behavior of organisms: An experimental analysis*. New York: Appleton Century-Crofts.

Skinner, B.F. (1953). *Science and human behavior*. New York: Macmillan.

Skinner, B.F. (1957). *Verbal behavior*. New York: Appleton Century-Crofts.

Skinner, B.F. (1968). *The technology of teaching*. New York: Appleton Century-Crofts.

Skutnabb-Kangas, T. (2000). *Linguistic genocide in education—Or worldwide diversity and human rights*. Mahwah, NJ: Lawrence Erlbaum.

TWO

Noam Chomsky and the Linguistic, Political, and Activist World

A Critical Analysis

Every century has witnessed the birth and emergence of a few world-transcending intellectuals, and Noam Chomsky in the twentieth century was no exception. Chomsky is a uniquely talented intellectual who has profoundly transformed the global political landscape and the academic fields of linguistics and philosophy. He is one of the world's most respected dissident intellectuals and linguists. Noam Chomsky has influenced and transformed many minds and hearts with his scholarly and activist work. He has been interviewed and appeared in countless documentaries, where he has offered, among other things, a distinctive, dissenting voice regarding U.S. foreign policy toward the rest of the world, particularly the Middle East, Latin America, Asia, and the Caribbean.

Worldwide, Noam Chomsky is one of the leading intellectuals in the fields of linguistics, philosophy, and U.S. foreign policy, among others (Barsky, 1997, 2007; Peck, 1987; Smith, 2004). *Science Citation Index* includes 1,619 citations to Chomsky from 1974 to 1992, and one can only imagine how many more times he has been cited since then. One may disagree with Chomsky's views on many controversial issues, such as the Palestinian and Israeli conflict and U.S. foreign policy. However, he is one of the few dissident intellectuals who has consistently taken an unshakable position about this conflict, who has critically unveiled corporate propaganda and lies about his own country, and who has spoken up against many forms of oppression, such as massive exploitation and mass murder of innocent people caused by the U.S. invasions and occupation of Vietnam, Cambodia, East Timor, Afghanistan, and Iraq, among others. As Smith (2004) stated:

> Chomsky is most widely known for his excoriation of the foreign policy of his native America. For four decades he has produced a series of devastating attacks on the lies, deception, inhumanity, and murderousness of the policies of the state. Central to this sustained attack is a constant emphasis on the disparity between the actions of the government and the portrayal of those actions by the official propaganda system. Corporate propaganda always emphasizes the superior moral values and benevolence of the home country. When one looks at other countries, it is easy to be dispassionate and see self-serving deception for what it is. It is somewhat harder to accept the same evaluation of one's country. Indeed, many people are offended by the suggestion that their own country indulges in propaganda at all. "We" disseminate information; it is only "they" who peddle propaganda. (p. 189)

Along the same lines, Alexander Cockburn (1992) stated: "What Chomsky offers is a coherent 'big picture,' buttressed by the data of a thousand smaller pictures and discrete theaters of conflict, struggle, and oppression" (cited in Chomsky & Barsamian, 2008, p. xi). Noam Chomsky's dissident voice illuminates his firm conviction and determination to challenge the status quo, particularly in terms of U.S. imperialism. He has dedicated most of his career to speaking out against the brutal abuse of power and violations of human rights. Very few intellectuals have accomplished what Chomsky has in terms of revolutionizing many disciplines, such as linguistics and philosophy, and he has influenced many social and political movements around the globe.

Numerous books, articles, and documentaries have reported the positions Noam Chomsky has taken against U.S. imperialism and foreign policy and the worldwide influence of his academic and activist work (Barsky, 2007; Smith, 2004). Therefore, this chapter is designed not merely to repeat what has already been said about Chomsky. Rather, it highlights a different perspective on Chomsky's work and his influence on the world, placing it in the current sociopolitical and historical context. I begin by briefly reviewing Chomsky's biographical background, including his transformation of the linguistics field with nativist theory. I then go on to examine the effect his activist work has had on the larger activist and academic world.

Noam Chomsky: A Short Biographical Note

Noam Chomsky was born on December 7, 1928, in Philadelphia, Pennsylvania, to a middle-class Jewish family. His parents, William Chomsky and Elsie Simonofsky, had two children, Noam, and his younger brother David, who studied medicine and became a physician (Barsky, 1997). According to Barsky (1997), who wrote two books on Noam Chomsky, Chomsky's parents deeply influenced him.

Chomsky's father fled Russia and emigrated to the United States to avoid being drafted into the Czarist army (Barsky, 1997, p. 9). Before he became a high school principal and started teaching Hebrew at the college level, he "worked in a sweatshop in Baltimore, Maryland. He then managed to support his studies at Johns Hopkins University by teaching in Baltimore Hebrew elementary schools" (Barsky, 1997, p. 9). He wrote many books, including *Hebrew: The Eternal Language* (1957) and *Hebrew, the Story of a Living Language* (1947), which Noam Chomsky read when he was only 12 years old (Barsky, 1997, p. 10). Noam Chomsky's early exposure to his father's scholarly work on linguistics shaped and influenced him academic and politically. Smith (2004) states: "His father, William Chomsky, not only influenced him politically, but also exposed him early in life to classical Semitic philology: his book *Hebrew: The Eternal Language* (dedicated to Noam and his brother) appeared in the same year, 1957, as his son's *Syntactic Structures*, the accepted beginning of the Chomskyan revolution" (p. 5).

In 1949, Chomsky married Carol Schatz, a prominent intellectual in her own right. They have three children. Chomsky earned a PhD in linguistics in 1955 from the University of Pennsylvania. While studying there, he met Professor Zellig Harris, a leading linguist and political theorist who had a profound intellectual and political influence on Chomsky (Barsky, 1997; Smith, 2004). Chomsky joined Harvard University as a Junior Fellow in the early 1950s. In 1957, he joined the staff of the Massachusetts Institute of Technology and soon after became associate professor at the age of 29 and then full professor at just 32 (Barsky, 1997). Fifteen years later, he was promoted to institute professor in the Department of Linguistics and Philosophy at age 47, "an honor reserved for the most distinguished faculty" (Barsky, 1997, p. 3). He is currently institute and emeritus professor at the same institution.

Noam Chomsky has written more than 100 books. The most recent ones include *Hopes and Prospects* (2010a); *New World of Indigenous Resistance* (2010); *Making the Future: Occupations, Interventions, Empire and Resistance* (2010b); *The Science of Language: Interviews With James McGilvray* (2012); and *Power Systems: Conversations on Global Democratic Uprisings and the New Challenges to U.S. Empire* (2013). Not many intellectuals are fortunate to live long enough to witness the profound impact of their work on the academic world and beyond, and Noam Chomsky is one of the few. His intellectual work has influenced many prominent linguists and public intellectuals, including Steven Pinker, Edward Said, Christopher Hitchens, Norman Finkelstein, Peter Ludlow, Robert Fisk, Vijah Prashad, Arundhati Roy, Amy Goodman, and Tanya Reinhart, among many others.

Chomsky has received numerous honorary degrees and awards, among them the 1988 Kyoto Prize, "the Japanese equivalent of the Nobel Prize, for his contribution to basic sciences" (Barsky, 1997, p. 3). Chomsky's "theoretical viewpoints of his doctoral dissertation appeared in the monograph *Syntactic Structure*, 1957.

This formed part of a more extensive work, *The Logical Structure of Linguistic Theory*, circulated in mimeograph in 1955 and published in 1975" (Barsky, 1997).

In the field of linguistics, Noam Chomsky is mostly known for his nativist theory, encompassing generative grammar, which he started developing in the 1950s. Generally defined, generative grammar is the study of a particular way of examining different components of syntax. With the knowledge of the rules of generative grammar, one can predict which types of combinations of words will form grammatical sentences. The rules essentially determine the morphology of a sentence.

As noted earlier, until the 1950s, the most influential language theory was behaviorism, for which B.F. Skinner is mostly known, particularly through his work *Verbal Behavior*, in which he argued that "any notion of 'idea' or 'meaning' is explanatory fiction, and that the speaker is merely the locus of verbal behavior, not the cause" (Brown, 2007, p. 10). Skinner and other behaviorist theorists such as Leonardo Bloomfield have dominated the field of linguistics for decades. Prior to Noam Chomsky's nativist theory, behaviorism was the theory that linguists and others interested in language acquisition and learning generally drew on to study the syntax and morphology of language, among other things.

Behaviorists like Skinner and Bloomfield argue that language is manipulative. It can therefore be acquired and learned through manipulation. Behaviorists do not acknowledge the influence that one's innate capacity and interaction with the outside world may have on one's learning and acquisition of a language. Instead, they stress the mechanical strategy and method that can be used to study language acquisition and learning among children and adults. After Chomsky's critical review of B.F. Skinner's book *Verbal Behavior* (1959), linguists, scientists, and educators and the like started examining language acquisition and learning from a different perspective, that is, taking into account one's innate predisposition to acquire and learn languages. Specifically, with this review and other publications, Chomsky has achieved recognition in the scientific field as a linguist who has greatly influenced and contributed to the philosophy of language and mind as well as the cognitive revolution in psychology. As Collins (2008) put it:

> Today, serious philosophy of mind is largely informed by cognitive science and much of it takes innateness for granted. Similarly, contemporary philosophy of language, with its preoccupations with "knowledge of language," compositionality, logical form etc., is simply unimaginable without Chomsky. It would not be hyperbolic to say that Chomsky's work has shaped the philosophical landscape as much as that of any other of the late twentieth century. (p. 3)

In short, in modern linguistics, Chomsky has been a pioneer. His nativist approach has revealed the limitations of behaviorist theory, pointing out that languages are too complex to be acquired through drill practices and mechanical ways. The term nativist, according to Brown (2007), is "derived from the fundamental assertion that language acquisition is innately determined, that we are born with a genetic capacity that predisposes us to a systematic perception of language around us, resulting in the construction of an internalized system of language" (p. 28). However, the innateness hypotheses have been challenged, for example by the "emergentism" theory espoused by O'Grady (2003, 2005), Ellis (2005), and MacWhinney (1999), among many others.

Ellis (2005) maintains that "the complexity of language emerges from relatively simple developmental processes being exposed to a massive and complex environment. The interactions that constitute language are associations, billions of connections, which co-exist within a neutral system as organisms co-exist within an eco-system. And systematicities emerge as a result of theory interactions and mutual constraints" (p. 81). Along the same lines, Brown (2007) contends: "This perspective disagrees sharply with earlier nativist views by suggesting that there is no inborn Universal Grammar (i.e., no innate grammatical system)." Whether or not Chomsky's nativist theory has been contested, such a theory has unquestionably transformed the field of linguistics. Chomsky has also impacted the political academic and activist world, which I analyze in depth in the following sections.

Noam Chomsky and the World

Chomsky has not only revolutionized the fields of linguistics, psychology, and mathematics but has also had a tremendous impact on other fields, such as political science, international relations, and sociology, to name just a few. Transcending the restricted confines of the academy, he has influenced the thoughts and the actions of activists, grassroots movement leaders, and ordinary citizens around the globe concerned with social justice issues such as human rights and the protection of the environment. Noam Chomsky does not sit in his comfortable MIT office theorizing about the world. He has joined intellectual activists such as Howard Zinn and Daniel Ellsberg in the streets to protest against the abuse of U.S. imperial power, domestically and internationally. For daring to speak and act against this imperial power, he has been thrown in jail numerous times and has received many death threats. Further, he has been tagged by the FBI as a dangerous public intellectual (Barsky, 1997).

Historically, many world leaders have resorted to arms to counter Western imperial and colonial powers. Anti-colonial and imperialist leaders such as Toussaint L'Ouverture, Simon Bolivar, and Amical Cabral, among many others, used weapons to fight against former Western imperial powers including Spain, Portugal, and France. Chomsky, on the other hand, has successfully used his dissident voice, activism, and scholarly writings to challenge U.S. imperialism. He is an intellectual leader par excellence whose voice and words have resonated with the forgotten and impoverished masses, including exploited factory workers and farmers in developing countries who have been victims of imperialist and genocidal wars.

Noam Chomsky is both an extraordinary and an ordinary person. He is extraordinary in the sense that he has accomplished professionally and intellectually many things that many world intellectuals have not accomplished. People have compared him to Sigmund Freud, Albert Einstein, Pablo Picasso, Bertrand Russell, and Karl Marx, among others. As Neil Smith (2004) states:

> In this century his peers in influence are such disparate figures as Einstein, Picasso, and Freud, with each of whom he has something in common. Like Freud—but with added intellectual rigor—he has changed our conception of the mind; like Einstein, he blends intense scientific creativity with radical political activism; like Picasso, he has overturned and replaced his own established systems with startling frequency. Perhaps his greatest similarity is to Bertrand Russell, whose early work, *Principia Mathematica*, redefined the foundations of mathematics, and who devoted much of his life to political writing and activism. (p. 1)

I argue that Noam Chomsky is unique in the sense that, unlike many world-famous intellectuals, he has not invented any dogmatic ideology or tried to convince people to apply it to their lives—as if such an ideology could save the world. In fact, he has urged people to reject any type of dogmatic ideology and think for themselves. As noted earlier, scholars such as Bertrand Russell have influenced and inspired Chomsky to take a stance against injustice and the abuse of human rights. However, he has shown neither in his writing nor in his public speeches that he has followed and tried to implement blindly the ideas of those who have influenced him. Noam Chomsky has consistently proven throughout his career that he is an independent thinker who analyzes and sees things with a critical mind, irrespective of what his detractors have said about him. He has not dogmatically followed in the footsteps of any particular individual: Chomsky is his own intellectual and activist person. As Peck (1987) stated:

> The United States has a long history of critical intellectuals, but Chomsky does not quite fit into any American tradition of protest. He is not part of that long line of critics—from Emerson and Thoreau to J. William Fulbright and Martin Luther King, Jr.—who bemoaned America's betrayal of its promise. He does not share the belief that America is a "city on a hill," a nation that operates according to principles radically different from others, or that this is a country in which ideas flow relatively freely and without discrimination, where the truth generally wins out over falsehood. Nor does he accept a vision of America as a well-intentioned, morally inclined power whose ideals embody the best aspirations of mankind. No American dream is part of his beliefs. (p. xi)

Despite the fact that Noam Chomsky has been isolated from the mainstream media, and his fierce detractors have used this media to misrepresent his work, Chomsky's words and actions have had a much greater impact on the world than many conservative intellectuals who have been invited as experts to distort and misrepresent the reality on the ground. One might wonder how this has been possible. I used to wonder the same thing myself until I came to the realization that the truth will never be surrendered, silenced, or buried in the big ocean of lies in which professional liars have been sinking.

In making this statement I am aware of the fact that the CEOs of corporate media have spent millions to lie to, miseducate, and pollute the minds of countless citizens, and that in many cases they have been successful at doing so. However, this does not erase the fact that the truth will always emerge and prevail. Chomsky understands very well this historical fact: A people can't be lied to and misled forever. Acting on this belief, he has persisted in reaching out to students on university campuses around the world, community activists, and leaders of grassroots movements who have spread his message to others through alternative channels of communication. People who seek the truth about Western imperial abuse of power have attended Chomsky's talks not within the ivory tower but in churches and local meetings organized by grassroots activists.

What distinguishes Noam Chomsky from many public intellectuals and makes him an ordinary person with extraordinary intellectual talents is that he has shared his knowledge not only through his scholarly works but also through informal interaction with ordinary citizens. Chomsky might be the world's most accessible intellectual. As mentioned earlier, until I had the honor to meet and interact with Chomsky, I used to believe—probably like millions of people—that because of his fame it must be extremely difficult to gain access to him. However, after I met with him several times, I realized that this was a myth I had naively bought into.

Whether in giving talks at universities, or being interviewed or interacting with people after his talks, Noam Chomsky behaves like an ordinary person with genial, complex, and sophisticated ideas. He does not comport himself like a pretentious intellectual giant. Though he will fiercely defend his position using the most grounded and substantive arguments, never has he tried to look down on the intellectual capacity or violated the humanity of those who have debated him. I have seen several Noam Chomsky debates, and I have never seen him defeated intellectually by detractors such as David Horowitz, a law professor at Harvard University, or John Silber, the former president of Boston University. He has made the strongest arguments possible based on incontestible facts, although his adversaries may still accuse him of being a liar who fabricates facts (Barsky, 1997, 2007). Chomsky's late wife stated that he never lost an argument (Smith, 2004). To be able to carry the strongest possible argument grounded in irrefutable evidence requires one to not only be a good debater but also to be well-read and a good listener. Noam Chomsky is a prime example of both.

Through his writing and his talks, Noam Chomsky has proven to be a most well-read intellectual. Not only is he vastly knowledgeable about his own areas of interest; he is also incredibly conversant in other fields. In this sense, it is appropriate to compare him to Karl Marx, who never earned a degree in sociology but has been considered one of the world's greatest sociologists. Likewise, Chomsky did not earn a degree in political science or history. However, his critical analysis of historical and political events is almost incomparable. Ironically, his detractors have refused to take this into account, arguing that his analysis of the historical and political events that have shaped many parts of the world, including Latin America, is faulty and inaccurate. For example, in a debate Chomsky had with John Silber, the latter accused him of promulgating a series of falsehoods regarding brutal U.S. actions against the Contras in Nicaragua. Below is an excerpt from that debate, hosted by Chris Lydon.

Lydon: Noam Chomsky, in a short speech to the U.S. Senate, why would you be agin [sic] the Contra money?

Noam Chomsky: Well, as even the most ardent supporters of the Contras now concede, this is what they call a proxy army which is attacking Nicaragua from foreign bases, is entirely dependent on its masters for directions and support, has never put forth a political program, has created no base of political support within the country, and almost its entire top military command is Somozist officers. Its military achievements so far consist of a long and horrifying series of very well-documented torture, mutilation and atrocities, and essentially nothing else. Administration officials are now openly conceding in public that the main function of the Contras is to retard or reverse the rate of social reform in Nicaragua and to try to terminate the openness of that society. The state of siege, for example, which was imposed last fall, and which is very mild, I should say—there is much political opening in Nicaragua, as everyone there up to the American ambassador will tell you—that corresponds roughly to the state of siege which has been in place in El Salvador since early 1980, except in El Salvador it has been associated with a huge massacre of tens of thousands of people. Destruction of the press, so on and so forth. Whereas in Nicaragua it is a reaction to a war that we are carrying out against them with precisely the purpose of trying to retard social reform and to restrict the possibilities of an open and developing society. That is a cruel and savage policy, which we should terminate.

Silber: Are you going to continue that series of plain falsehoods? That's a series of falsehoods the likes of which I've never seen compacted in such a small period of time. The massacres that have occurred in Nicaragua have been the massacres by the Sandinistas of the Miskito Indians. The repression there is massive. It is more serious than anything we have seen in Central America or in any Latin American country to date. It is a genuine dictatorship imposed there. And to describe the leaders of the Contras as being supporters of Somoza is simply fabrication. Robelo, Cruz, Calero, Chamorro are not Somozistas and never have been. And when you take the leadership of the army of the Contras—some of them were members of the National Guard—but then if you are going to object to that, which would be highly unreasonable because that was an army that was not simply followers, or Somozistas, it is important to remember that Modesta Rojas, the vice chairman of the air force of the Sandinistas, was also a member of the National Guard and a very large number of members of the National Guard are the ones who are coordinators of the block committees that imposed the dictatorship by the Sandinistas. This is a series of distortions and fabrications and the effort of the Sandinistas to discredit the Contras by the manufacture of atrocities is now a point that has been very well-documented.

Silber's vicious attack on Chomsky for unveiling the long U.S. record of brutal and murderous actions against progressive groups in Latin America, particularly in Nicaragua and El Salvador, reveals the degree to which the U.S. academy is populated by intellectually indoctrinated defenders of U.S. imperialism. As Macedo argued, "By carefully reading the debate between Noam Chomsky and John Silber, we begin to see the greater the rewards, the more dogmatic the defense of the doctrinal system becomes. Silber's dogmatic defense of the indefensible doctrinal system in his debate with Chomsky needs no further comment" (cited in Chomsky, 2000, p. 175).

Ultraconservative groups in the U.S. academy and beyond often attempt to exclude voices of scholars like Chomsky who have bridged many disciplines and impacted people from all walks of life. The disrespect and complete disregard for the arguments Chomsky was making about U.S. involvement in the murder of Contra members and supporters is quite revelatory of the vicious tactics of narrow-minded intellectuals, conservative or otherwise, who feel threatened by those who speak truth to power. It is easy to dismiss another's genius by making the specious argument that one needs to write strictly in one's so-called area, not in any another. In my view, such a weak and unsubstantiated argument only perpetuates the status quo and aims at making one believe that only those in a certain field of study can have access to knowledge pertaining to that specific field. Further, such a retrograde and silly argument fundamentally aims at killing one's passion, desire, and love for encyclopedic knowledge.

Personally, I have found such a view to be ridiculously sectarian and anti-intellectual. Where is it written that a professionally-trained linguist, for example, can't be as knowledgeable about political science and sociology as political scientists and sociologists? As a doctoral student, I heard professors make this unsubstantiated claim, and as a professor, I have continued to hear colleagues, especially those who have been in the field for decades, make the same argument in order to pigeonhole emerging and younger scholars who have traversed many disciplines in their scholarship.

Some of these professors have claimed that they have looked at the intersectionality of many forms of oppression in their work. However, when scholars transcend various disciplines to cover multiple issues in their writing, they are often told that they need to restrict their writing to their area of specialty. The conclusion that I draw from such a sectarian, limited view of scholarship is that some fear that their field of expertise is being invaded by those who look at sociopolitical, racial, language, and gender issues, for example, in a holistic way.

Obviously, transcendent intellectuals like Noam Chomsky have challenged this narrow viewpoint by not allowing any group of scholars or institutions to limit their intellectual horizon. Chomsky, in particular, has not allowed anyone to dictate what he can write about in order to be considered an expert. Strictly speaking, Chomsky should be considered an expert in political science and world history, though he probably wouldn't care about such a label. How many people are there who are vastly knowledgeable about history and world politics to whom Noam Chomsky can't be compared? To my knowledge, there are none. However, because of the territorial nature of the U.S. academy and the sectarian and retrograde attitude and actions of many scholars, a prominent thinker like Noam Chomsky would not be recognized as a political scientist. He has been only fully acknowledged as a linguist, especially by those who may have felt threatened that he could embarrass them for being much more knowledgeable in their field than themselves. In this way and in many others, Chomsky is a role model for me as an intellectual.

The Conspiracy Against Chomsky's Progressive Ideas

Despite the fact that Chomsky is a world-class intellectual, there are many people who have been denied access to his ideas as a result of the pushback against his political work by the mainstream media and the U.S. academy. Chomsky's thought is treated as a dangerous doctrine, one that must be sealed in the conservative secret box of universities and colleges to keep it from influencing and inspiring students to think for themselves and to seek the truth about government corruption and abuse of human rights. These institutions, for the most part, do not want students or people in general to become well-informed, critical citizens who might ask dangerous questions that could threaten the power structure.

To test this hypothesis, I designed the following questionnaire.

Today's date:

Please answer the following questions.

1. Do you know who Noam Chomsky is?
2. If yes, say one or two things you know about him. How do you know what you know about him?
3. Is he an American?
4. Is he still alive?

I had six undergraduate students and my graduate assistant distribute this questionnaire to both graduate and undergraduate students and people at coffee shops, in church, and other settings. I was amazed to find that students in various fields did not know who Noam Chomsky is. Some who did know of him did not know that he is an American. The majority of the non-student responders did not know who Noam Chomsky is either. A few claimed that the name sounded familiar but could not say anything specific about him.

This is not a coincidence. In fact, it is an indication of the extent to which many of our students have been miseducated and therefore deprived of vital information about prominent intellectuals and leaders who have shaped the world. In 2010, a colleague of mine and I invited the now-deceased Manning Marable to deliver the keynote speech at New Mexico State University during Black History Month. I urged my undergraduate students to attend the talk. Dr. Marable's speech centered on the biography of Malcom X. Many confessed to me a week later that until they heard Dr. Marable's keynote speech, they did not know who Malcom X was. Two out of 22 students said they had heard the name before but did not know that he was an American leader. I then asked them about Martin Luther King, Jr. Several students said that they learned in high school about Martin Luther King's famous "I Have a Dream" speech. I asked them what else they knew about Dr. King besides this speech, and they admitted that they knew nothing else except that he was an African American leader who fought for the rights of African American people in this country.

Even more disappointing, I asked them if they knew anything about W.E.B. Du Bois or Marcus Garvey. All of my students responded that they did not know anything about these leaders. Because they are all Mexicans and Chicano/as, I decided to ask them to name one Mexican or Chicano/a leaders they knew or learned about in school. Only a few were able to name Cesar Chavez, while one mentioned Doroles Huerta, who fought tirelessly beside Chavez for farmers' rights.

However, all of them knew Jennifer Lopez, Michael Jordan, Kobe Bryant, Lebron James, and Tiger Woods, to name just a few. It is no coincidence that they would know these celebrities but not prominent intellectuals and leaders like Noam Chomsky and Malcolm X. They have to be kept entertained so that they will not question the actions of their government that may affect their daily lives, their future, and the generations to come. The U.S. government, in direct collaboration with corporate media, has put in place a propaganda machine to brainwash and render citizens docile, so that they will not challenge the political system that is oppressing them.

Throughout his work, Noam Chomsky has painstakingly demonstrated how the U.S. media defend the interests of corporations and corporate groups by misinforming and misleading citizens about what is happening both domestically and internationally. Chomsky (1999) maintains:

> Whether they're called "liberal" or "conservative," the major media are large corporations, owned by and interlinked with even larger conglomerates. Like other corporations, they sell a product to a market. The market is advertisers, that is, other businesses. The product is audiences. For the elite media that set the basic agenda to which others adapt, the product is, furthermore, relatively privileged audiences. So we have major corporations selling fairly wealthy and privileged audiences to other businesses. Not surprisingly, the

picture of the world presented reflects the narrow and biased interests and values of the sellers, the buyers, and the products. (p. 93)

The U.S. school system is not much different in terms of failing to provide students with the necessary information and critical tools they need to make sense of their environment and what is happening in the larger world. Instead, schools by and large have taught students to become passive spectators of the reality that shapes their daily lives. Being critical is often perceived as being a deviant and non-conformist, for what is rewarded in schools is being docile and conformist. As Chomsky went on to say,

> The media are only one part of a larger doctrinal system; other parts are journals of opinion, the schools and the universities, academic scholarship and so on. We're much more aware of the media, particularly the prestige media, because those who critically analyze ideology have focused on them. The larger system hasn't been studied as much because it's harder to investigate systematically. But there's good reason to believe that it represents the same interests as the media, just as one would anticipate. (p. 94)

It is not surprising, then, that teachers who dare to engage students in the critical work of dissident intellectuals such as Noam Chomsky, Paulo Freire, and Frantz Fanon are sometimes spied on by their conformist and retrograde colleagues and reported to deans, provosts, and presidents at their institutions. In other words, these teachers are often put under surveillance. Likewise, students who ask too many questions that threaten the status quo are often isolated and subject to oversight.

The critical writing of Noam Chomsky on political issues has not been used in schools, whereas the work of E.D. Hirsh and Allan Bloom has permeated the U.S. school system and the media. Again, this is not a coincidence, because the work of these conservative intellectuals serves to maintain the status quo, including perpetuating the canonical legacy of Western history, culture, and values. If Chomsky's political writings were used in high schools, colleges, and universities, it would help students understand the fallacy of many aspects of Western history and challenge them to question such history.

Further, if Noam Chomsky's political writings were incorporated into the school curriculum and students had the opportunity to critically discuss such work with their teachers, the students would be theoretically well-equipped to challenge U.S. imperialism and refuse to swallow corporate lies circulated in the mainstream media about so-called U.S. democracy and freedom. Moreover, had students been given the opportunity to listen to Noam Chomsky's speeches and talks in schools, they would have been inspired to do their job as citizens—that is, to demand from their government an explanation as to why their tax dollars have been used to expand the U.S. empire through wars, invasions, conquests of other lands, and subjugation of their people. Finally, I argue that if U.S. soldiers had access to Noam Chomsky's political writings, they would most likely change their view about U.S. imperialism and be critical of their mission as soldiers. Many would join other soldiers who deserted the army, refusing to take and execute bloody orders from their superiors.

For all of the reasons mentioned earlier, Noam Chomsky's political writings have to be censored in schools and the media. As Peck (1987) put it:

> Chomsky's political writings are just as central to an understanding of our time as are his linguistics writings to our understanding of language. Yet they are often studiously ignored or angrily dismissed. His rational intensity, so applauded in linguistics, is derided when he turns it upon the United States. (p. ix)

Peck goes on to state:

> Chomsky does not provide answers for the world we live in. His demystification draws on no alternative ideology. Yet his writings constitute a way of coming to understand the world without illusion. They offer a stark but not despairing view of the world—a vision without an ideology, a radicalness without blueprints or prescribed structural alternatives. There is indeed something that resonates throughout these writings that in the end is uplifting. Chomsky is not a cynical man. Nor is he disillusioned. To become disillusioned is to have been illusioned—and this Chomsky is not. There is a deep affirmation in these writings which cut through the bleakness, a certain mobility of humanity reaffirmed. This comes not just from the pressures in our time, but from the way Chomsky's willingness to stand so outside prevailing beliefs makes him so central to a reaffirmation of a concern with human freedom and dignity, with creativity, and with the commitment to seek their multiple manifestations. (p. xix)

Along the same lines, Smith (2004) maintains: "What is clear is that after half of a century of research he still has the power to surprise, pushing explanations even deeper. Chomsky is no ordinary genius" (p. 215).

Despite the conspiracy against Chomsky's political writings, these writings have somehow fallen into the hands of many people here and abroad. About 8 years ago, the late Venezuelan president, Hugo Chávez, brought with him to the United Nations one of Noam Chomsky's books, *Hegemony or Survival* (1973). While holding this book in his left hand, Chávez praised Chomsky and urged people to read the book. Such an action had an immediate global effect. The book instantly became a best seller, and millions of copies were sold worldwide. Obviously, Noam Chomsky did not necessarily need Hugo Chávez to promote his work. However, what was symbolic about Mr. Chávez's action was that he acknowledged and appreciated the unpopular stance Noam Chomsky has taken against U.S. imperial violence toward the rest of the world.

Besides Hugo Chávez, who was a controversial political figure, many ordinary citizens who have had access to Noam Chomsky's political writings have expressed the extent to which such writings have influenced and inspired them.

For example, in an interview, Sandy Carter asked Amy Ray, "Can you talk some about experiences and influences that gave birth to your views and social vision?" Ray stated:

> From an early age, I had a sense of community involvement. But my family background was very conservative. My father was a product of the 1950s, very conservative, very smart, and hard to argue with, but also very charitable and giving. By college, I was gay and had broken away from a lot of that background, become an environmentalist, and was into social welfare and down on the military. But some of my biggest changes came when I met Winona LaDuke in 1990. Through her I was able to bring environmental and indigenous activism together and that opened doors to other connections. Reading Noam Chomsky helped me see the interconnections between a broad range of issues and how the whole paradigm of society needs to change. Later, meeting the Zapatistas in Mexico and seeing change happen at the grassroots level, bottom-up, that was certainly an inspiration. (Ray, as cited in Barsky, 2007, p. 19)

Even one of Chomsky's fierce opponents, David Horowitz, has acknowledged the incredible influence of Chomsky's activist work on people. Horowitz contends: "His venomous message is spread on tapes and CDs, and the campus lecture circuit; he is promoted at rock concerts by superstar bands such as Pearl Jam, Rage Against the Machine, and U2 (whose lead singer, Bono, called Chomsky a 'rebel without a pause')" (cited in Barsky, 2007, p. 19).

These are a few examples that may not be known for the reasons mentioned earlier. Measuring the number of people who have been influenced by Noam Chomsky's political writings and activism is impossible. David Barsky eloquently captured the global influence of Chomsky in his second book on him, *The Chomsky Effect* (Barsky, 2007), meticulously documenting the extent to which Chomsky's scholarly and activist work, human compassion, and warm personality have had the deepest effect on people around the globe. To substantiate his arguments, Barsky has used prime examples of academics and non-academics who have used Chomsky's work as a political framework to effect socioeconomic and political change in their communities and beyond. Barsky's book has brilliantly captured the personal, human, professional, intellectual, and political dimensions of Noam Chomsky. In expressing his admiration for Chomsky, Barsky (2007) stated:

> What I myself find inspiring about Chomsky is the positive effect he has upon so many people who are dissatisfied with the world as they themselves experience it. We are encouraged in schools, religious institutions, the workplace, and in the society at large to respect the views of those empowered to dictate how we should react to events (teachers, journalists, "experts"), so when someone of Chomsky's intellectual and academic stature comes and says what seems to us unfair, unjust, or prejudiced in the workplace, the household, the neighborhood, or the world is indeed aberrant by standards of decency or justice—that is, when he confirms in plain and simple English that bombing innocent civilians and then starving them over a prolonged period in Iraq is perverse, that invading Grenada, bombing Tripoli, or supporting murderous Contras is obscene, and that not

assisting those in need for obviously corporate-inspired reasons while preaching freedom and equality is hypocritical, we become empowered.... This approach is one of the reasons Chomsky is admired and one of the ways he serves to popularize ideas beyond the scholarly community. (pp. 10–12)

In my view, Chomsky is an intellectual legend, though he might resist that label. By using the word legend, I am not alluding to the loose and propagandist meaning of the word that the mainstream has used to showcase individuals like Bob Marley, for instance, who has been appropriated by neoconservatives for their selfish socioeconomic and political pursuits. Rather, by stating that Noam Chomsky is an intellectual legend, I am referring to the distinctive, genuine ways in which he has engaged and profoundly impacted both the academic and non-academic world.

I have been nourishing the dream that someday the poorest of the poor in impoverished countries like Haiti, Bangladesh, Pakistan, and Afghanistan would have access to Noam Chomsky's political writings. This dream might sound overly utopian and impossible on a practical level, because the poorest in these countries might lack basic reading and writing skills. Furthermore, even if they had these skills, those in power most likely would not allow them to have access to Chomsky's political writings, for these writings might be too dangerous in the hands of the masses.

The Influence of Chomsky's Work on My Political Awareness

As someone who was born and grew up in Haiti, a country formerly colonized by France and later occupied by the United States, Noam Chomsky's scholarly and political work has helped me understand the intricacies of the aftermath of both the U.S. occupation and France's colonization on my native land. Specifically, Chomsky has provided me with the language to name the devastating educational, cultural, psychological, socioeconomic, and political effects of the U.S. occupation and the French colonial legacy that I could not name before, yet of which I have been a victim.

As I stated earlier, Chomsky, with his innovative nativist theory, helped me understand the limitations of behaviorism while working on my master's degree in applied linguistics. Prior to becoming familiar with this theory, I could not articulate the mechanical nature of behaviorist theory. Though as a high school student I did not like the behaviorist approach that my teachers employed to teach me foreign languages and other subject-content areas, I did not have the language skills to name their oppressive teaching practices. Becoming familiar with nativist and social interactionist theories has made a difference in my linguistic and intellectual repertoire in terms of being able to understand the weaknesses of behaviorist theory.

However, despite my deep appreciation for Chomsky's linguistic theory, which has opened my eyes and helped me to deeply understand the limitations of behaviorism, I must admit that I have been most inspired by Chomsky's political and activist work, which challenges Western imperialism and denounces the abuse of human rights committed by dictators supported by Western powers, including the United States and the U.K. Chomsky's courage, tenacity, and firm determination to speak truth to power is admirable and inspirational. Given his privileged socioeconomic background, he could have chosen to promote the status quo. Instead, he decided to speak against it, taking uncompromising positions to denounce the brutal exploitation of the weak and the poor by the powerful.

Chomsky's political writings and speeches have helped me gain a deeper understanding of the damaging effects of U.S domestic and foreign policy on the poor in the West and in the Third World. That is, through his analysis, Chomsky has painstakingly unraveled for me the short- and long-term consequences such policies have had on the livelihood of people living in the United States and other parts of the world. Chomsky has also critically unveiled for me the imperial agenda of the United States to conquer the world by using its military power and manipulating and controlling world institutions such as the United Nations.

When I resided in Haiti I was aware of the role the United States played and continues to play in the political and economic destabilization and impoverishment of this country. But it was not until I started reading Noam Chomsky's political work and listening to his talks that I fully understood the extent to which the United States has played a significant role in the abject poverty of my native land and other countries that have been under its imperial siege. By reading Noam Chomsky's political work, I have come to better understand why the United States has historically supported dictators around the world. As Chomsky has consistently pointed out in my dialogues with him, the main reason is that these dictators have protected U.S. hegemonic interests. In contrast, leaders who have opposed U.S. imperialist foreign policy, such as Jean Bertrand Aristide, the former Haitian president, and Patrice Lumumba, the late Congolese prime minister, have either been assassinated or overthrown.

Conclusion

In concluding this chapter, it is worth pointing out that if Robert Phillipson (1992, 2010) and Tove Skutnabb-Kangas (2000) have helped me understand linguistic imperialism and the notion of linguistic genocide; if Frantz Fanon (1963, 1965) and Ngugi Wa Thiong'o (1986) have helped me better understand the unequal power relations between colonizer and colonized; and if Paulo Freire has ideologically equipped me with the language to name different forms of oppression taking place in school and beyond; then Noam Chomsky has unveiled for me the asymmetrical relation of power between the United States and Third World countries and the impoverishment of the latter by the former through its imperialist foreign policy.

Noam Chomsky's political analysis of U.S. domestic and foreign policies has helped me to better situate myself politically and ideologically as someone who was born and grew up in a formerly occupied and neocolonized land, Haiti, and who is now a naturalized U.S. citizen. Specifically, his analysis of the U.S. empire has enabled me to better negotiate this complicated political and ideological positionality. This is not often easy for a transnational subject like myself, who is grateful for the many opportunities the United States has offered me yet critical of its policies toward my native land, Haiti, and other countries that it has invaded and occupied.

As a poor boy growing up in a marginalized and impoverished country, it would have been valuable for me to be exposed to Chomsky's political writings early on. Having access to these writings when I was in middle school or high school, for example, would have enabled me to have a much more critical understanding of the unequal power relations between Western imperialist powers and poor countries like Haiti. Such writings would also have provided me with a critical language to unmask internal corruption of the Haitian government at the time I was growing up there. Finally, and more importantly, Chomsky's political writings would have enabled me to gain a keen understanding of the power structure of Western imperial powers like the United States and Great Britain in terms of the ways the governments of these countries have destabilized the economic and political structure and infrastructure of other countries through manipulation, intimidation, invasion, and occupation.

Young people today who have access to Noam Chomsky's political writings might be better equipped politically and critically to engage the world and strive to transform it in ways that previous generations could not. Chomsky's political writings are seeds that need to be planted in places where all forms of social injustices occur. His political writings, if appropriately and contextually taught, would encourage people to transform the world into a much more humane place. Smith (2004) has painstakingly synthesized Noam Chomsky's influence in the following way:

> He has revolutionized linguistics, and in so doing has set a cat among the philosophical pigeons. He has resurrected the theory of innate ideas, demonstrating that a substantial part of our knowledge is genetically determined; he has reinstated rationalist ideas that go back centuries, but which had fallen into disrepute; and he has provided evidence that "unconscious knowledge" is what underlies our ability to speak and understand. He has overturned the dominant school of behaviorism in psychology. Chomsky has changed the way we think of ourselves, gaining a position in the history of ideas on a par with that of Darwin or Descartes. And he has done this while devoting the majority of his time to

dissident politics and activism: documenting the lies of government, exposing the hidden influences of big business, developing a model of the social order, and acting as the conscience of the West. (p. 1)

To sum it all up, Noam Chomsky is a borderless intellectual par excellence. With his nativist theory, political writings, activism, and his uncanny ability to make the most convincing arguments possible and powerfully carry them out to the end has made him the Noam Chomsky the world has known. Chomsky is among the few living intellectuals who have deeply impacted the entire world in ways that perhaps no intellectual before them had. Chomsky is not an intellectual who is afraid of making the most unpopular arguments in various contexts to unveil corporate lies and brutal uses of power of his own country. Nor has he ever been one who speaks to please a certain group of people. Chomsky speaks his mind, independent of people's opposing arguments, especially those of his detractors. He has always remained the Chomsky of principle, of high confidence, of consistency, of an unyielding sense of loyalty and commitment to humanity, of self-respect and respect for others, of deep compassion for the weak and the poor, and, finally, a man equipped with the encyclopedic knowledge and the incredible ability to critically challenge and convince people, even sometimes his opponents.

References

Barsky, R. (1997). *Chomsky: A life of dissent*. Cambridge, MA: MIT Press.
Barsky, R. (2007). *The Chomsky effect: A radical works beyond the ivory tower*. Cambridge, MA: MIT Press.
Brown, H.D. (2007). *Principles of language learning and teaching* (5th ed.). White Plains, NY: Pearson Longman.
Chomsky, N. (1959). [Review of B.F. Skinner's *Verbal behavior*]. *Language*, 35(1), 26–58.
Chomsky, N. (1992). *What Uncle Sam Really Wants*. Berkeley, CA: Odonian Press
Chomsky, N. (2000). *Chomsky on mis-education* (introduced and edited by D. Macedo). Lanham, MD: Rowman & Littlefield.
Chomsky, N. (2003). *Hegemony or survival: America's quest for global dominance*. New York: Metropolitan Books.
Chomsky, N. (2010c). *New world of indigenous resistance*. New York: City Lights.
Chomsky, N. (2010b). *Making the future: Occupations, interventions, empire and resistance*. New York: City Lights.
Chomsky, N. (2010a). *Hopes and prospects*. New York: Haymarket Books.
Chomsky, N. (2011). *9-11: Was there an alternative?* New York: Seven Stories Press.
Chomsky, N. (2012). *The science of language: Interviews with James McGilvray*. Cambridge: Cambridge University Press.
Chomsky, N. (2013). *Power systems: Conversations on global democratic uprisings and the new challenges to U.S. empire*. New York: Metropolitan Books.
Chomsky, N., & Barsamian, D. (2008). *Chronicles of dissent: Interviews with David Barsamian*. Monroe, ME: Common Courage Press.
Chomsky, W. (1947). *Hebrew, the story of a living language*. New York: Education Department, Zionist Organization of America.

Chomsky, W. (1957). *Hebrew: The eternal language.* Philadelphia: Jewish Publication Society of America.
Collins, J. (2008). *Chomsky: A guide for the perplexed.* London: Continuum.
Ellis, N. (2005). At the interface: Dynamic interactions of explicit and implicit language knowledge. *Studies in Second Language Acquisition, 27*(2), 305–352.
Fanon, F. (1963). *The wretched of the earth.* New York: Grove Press.
Fanon, F. (1965). *A dying colonialism.* New York: Grove Press.
MacWhinney, B. (Ed.). (1999). *The emergence of language.* Mahwah, NJ: Lawrence Erlbaum.
O'Grady, W. (2003). The radical middle: Nativism without universal grammar. In C. Doughty & M. Long (Eds.), *The handbook of second language acquisition* (pp. 43–103). Malden, MA: Blackwell Publishing.
O'Grady, W. (2005). *How children learn language.* New York: Cambridge University Press.
Peck, J. (1987, July). Noam Chomsky: An American dissident. *Progressive, 51*(7), pp. 22–25.
Phillipson, R. (1992). *Linguistic imperialism.* New York: Oxford University Press.
Phillipson, R. (2010). *Linguistic imperialism continued.* New York: Routledge.
Skutnabb-Kangas, T. (2000). *Linguistic genocide in education—Or worldwide diversity and human rights?* Mahwah, NJ: Lawrence Erlbaum.
Smith, N. (2004). *Chomsky: Ideas and ideals.* Cambridge: Cambridge University Press.
Thiong'o, N. (1986). *Decolonizing the mind: The politics of language in African literature.* Portsmouth, NH: Heinemann.

THREE

Democracy, Schooling, and U.S. Foreign Policy

Noam Chomsky and Pierre Orelus in Dialogue

Context of Dialogue

This dialogue between Noam Chomsky and Pierre Orelus revolves around schooling, democracy, and U.S. foreign policy. Professor Chomsky critically analyzes the notion of democracy, arguing that it only works for the rich and big corporations and that people, especially ordinary people, are only given the illusion that they are living in a democratic society. He goes on to denounce the hypocrisy of the United States in imposing its form of democracy on other countries, when in fact there is no participatory democracy here. Professor Chomsky refers to countries such as Bolivia that have organized democratic elections and suggests that the United States should learn from that country instead of trying to export a prefabricated form of democracy to other countries. Chomsky also talks about the language issue, pointing out how it plays a role in the unequal power relations between those who speak languages historically constructed as dominant languages and those who speak the so-called subjugated languages. After critically analyzing the way that many forms of oppression manifest themselves, Chomsky contends that people need to organize so they can challenge those in power and fight for their human rights. Likewise, Chomsky encourages concerned citizens to use their agency to counter the corporatization of schools.

The Dialogue

Orelus: The United States has been trying for decades to impose its Western form of democracy on other countries, particularly on the so-called Third World countries. So what is your take on the U.S. definition of democracy, and how do you think this country has sold its form of democracy to other countries?

Chomsky: That's mostly mythology. It's ideology; it's just not a fact. In fact, this has been well studied by scholars here. So there are good studies of this so-called democracy promotion movement. The best studies are done by an interesting person, a man named Thomas Carothers, who's a well-known political figure and scholar. He was head of the law and democracy program at the Carnegie Endowment. And he's a neo-Reaganite. He was in the Reagan administration in the State Department in its democracy promotion programs. He wrote several books in which he studied programs that have been successful or have failed. And he thought it was a wonderful idea to promote democracy. But he finally concludes after having reviewed it from the Reagan years until today, that every U.S. leader is in fact a secret schizophrenic.

We support democracy if and only if it conforms to strategic and economic objectives. Which is another way of saying we don't support democracy at all. We support strategic and economic objectives if it happens that they can go along with formal democracy. Carothers does not seem to understand that; he thinks it's a paradox.

Democracy becomes now a great slogan. He said that during the Reagan administration U.S. involvement in countries was inversely related to their progress toward democracy. So in South America, there was real progress to democracy, which, he points out, the Reagan administration tried to block but had to tolerate. But in regions where the United States had more influence like the Caribbean and Central America, there was the least progress toward democracy. He's pretty frank about it. He said the United States would only tolerate forms of democracy that keep traditional structures in power, that is, dominance by elites that cooperated with the U.S. interest. This goes right to the Bush years and everything else. So this is just an ideological trap; it's like when Stalin said he was in favor of democracy.

Should we then say that democracy does not exist in this country?

That's a different question. With regard to supporting democracy abroad, there is no such thing. We should not even talk about it; the United States uses that word to pursue its strategic and economic interests. If it can be covered by formal democracy, that's fine. It looks better if you don't have to apologize for it. You can congratulate yourself for it; that's the objective. In fact, that's obvious, right?

There's a lot of talk about promoting democracy in the Middle East, right? The closest U.S. ally in the Arab Muslim world is Saudi Arabia, which is the most extreme fundamentalist dictatorship in the region, if not in the world. There was one free election in the Arab world, in January 2006, a real free election well monitored in Palestine. But it came out the wrong way. So the United States and Israel instantly turned to punishing the population for voting the wrong way in a free election.

Commentators, journalists, scholars, and others look at this and they can't see what's obvious, that is, the United States cares nothing about democracy. What it cares about is domination and control. If you can have democracy too, fine. Also, what is a U.S. model of democracy? We are what we call in Iran a guided democracy. In Iran the candidates for election are vetted by the ruling clerics. How do the candidates run for election here? They are vetted by the business community. Elections are largely bought. Unless you have a huge amount of funding, you can't participate. Obama defeated McCain mainly because the financial industries poured much more money in the Obama campaign than the McCain campaign.

Can you say more about the notion of a "guided democracy"?

It's a guided democracy because public opinion almost doesn't matter at all. Take the big issue right now: health care. When you read the polls, a large majority of the public continues to want a national health care system. This is not on the agenda. About 80 to 85% of the population is in favor of permitting the government to negotiate drug prices, using its purchasing power to negotiate drug prices, which is allowed in every other country but blocked here by law, that's 85% the latest polls reveal. A front-page story in *The New York Times* just a couple days ago said that Obama made a private deal with the drug companies to block it. Where's the democracy?

Professor Chomsky how do you see the link between the U.S. contested form of democracy and schooling?

Well, for one thing what's taught in the classroom is that the United States is a leading democracy and supports democracy everywhere. In fact, that's not just in the classroom; that's also taught in graduate school. And it's just not true. So one way in which it impacts the classroom is just by inculcating doctrinal fabrications, but also the structure of schooling tends to be pretty undemocratic. Let's take the *No Child Left Behind* legislation. That's just training children to be in the Marine Corps, that is, not to be creative and independent people. That's its nature.

You are referring to the No Child Left Behind Act, which is basically all about testing. Many teachers feel that they have to teach to the test; otherwise, they might run the danger of losing their jobs. Would you agree with this assertion?

That's right. The teachers are disciplined. They in turn have to discipline the students in order to regurgitate materials that they are supposed to memorize. That's not teaching. In places where there is a real effort to educate like, say, a graduate education in sciences program, you don't do that. Students are supposed to participate; they're supposed to challenge themselves and teachers; they're supposed to inquire. They don't repeat the lectures and tests. That should be true in some form from elementary school.

So in that case what role do you think citizens should play in building a democratic society?

It's up to citizens whether they want to accept the system and whether their opinions amount to essentially nothing while policies are determined by concentrations of private capital. They don't have to accept that. Just take what I just mentioned earlier about the health care system; citizens could mobilize, act, and insist that their own wishes be followed and legislated. This is a very atomized and depoliticized society, and people don't do anything. There are functioning democracies in the world. But we can't talk about them.

In the Western hemisphere, for example, probably the most advanced democracy is the poorest country in South America, Bolivia. There are real elections in which people participate. They know what the issues are; they elected someone from their own ranks, a poor farmer, who is in part at least pursuing policies that come from popular organizations. Voting isn't just a matter of showing up and pushing a button one day; it's a constant ongoing struggle for rights and justice; that's real democracy. Who in the United States could say: "We have to look to Bolivia as a model of democracy because we don't meet that standard." People, including scholars and academics, would look at you with a blank face.

How would you imagine citizens being active participants in decisions that affect their lives?

It's not magic. Take electoral primaries. In the United States, what happens is that a candidate announces that he is going to be in your town on May 15 or something. His advance team tries to organize people to come to a meeting and then the candidate comes in and tells the crowd, "I'm a wonderful guy, I love you all, here are all the wonderful things I'm going to do," and he goes home. Now, suppose it was a functioning democracy. Well, what would happen is that the citizens of that town would have gotten together and decided what kind of policies they want. And if some candidates say, "I'm coming to your town," they could say, "Well, you can come if you like. But if you come, you're going to sit there and we're going to tell you what we think, what'll be our programs, and if you don't accept them, then go home. If you do accept them, we may vote for you, but only as long as you do what we tell you to do." It's almost the opposite of what happens here; but it's not a pie in the sky. These are not utopian ideas.

What role do you think the media play in all of this?

The media basically play the role of instilling the faith. For example, when *The New York Times* published the front-page article about Obama making a secret deal with the drug companies, they didn't point out that he's undercutting the wishes of 85% of the population. This is a crucial issue because the problem with his health reform program that his opponents throw up is that it is going to cost too much. In cases like these, it's not the job of the newspapers to tell the truth. They instill systems of doctrine and the ideology of power, not entirely, you hear a criticism here and there, but overwhelmingly that's how it is. But it's not that they're misleading people; it doesn't ever occur to them.

In the case of Bush, the second Bush, when he invaded Iraq, if you look back at his rhetoric, he was very straightforward. As he, Colin Powell, and others kept saying, "There's a single question." "Will Saddam Hussein give up his weapons of mass destruction?" "That's the single question." They invaded; they looked very hard, and they couldn't find any weapons of mass destruction, so they needed another reason. Eight months later came along democracy promotion. Bush gave a very well-publicized speech at the National Endowment for Democracy, in which he talked about our love for democracy and explained that our invasion of Iraq was an effort to bring democracy to the world and so on. Well, instead of laughing, which is what they should have done, the newspapers just climbed on the bandwagon: "Oh yeah we're wonderful." "We're promoting democracy."

Do you foresee U.S. imperialism taking a different form or direction in the next decade or so?

It all depends on what the population is willing to do. It's not going to happen by itself. The government will continue to respond pretty much to the needs of those who concentrate power inside society. I don't mean to say that it's mechanical, but it's certainly an overwhelming tendency and a perfectly understandable one. And now unless citizens organize for different interests, that's what the government will do.

So the question becomes: Why is it citizens are not organized so they can collectively demand what they want from the government?

Well, that's a long story. This is very much a business-run society. And throughout its whole history, there's been a struggle, sometimes successful, by sectors of the general population who try to influence a policy and determine the shape of what takes place. But business is constantly fighting a bitter class war, and trying to undermine it, and in the last 6 years it has succeeded pretty well.

This is a depoliticized society; the organizations that constitute forces for democratic change, such as unions, have been attacked and severely weakened. There are no political parties; you can't be a member of a party here participating in policy formation. If you're a Democrat that just means you follow orders. The case of what the press calls "Obama's army" is revealing. Obama's army is supposed to be very exciting. After the election took place, the press asked people in the Obama administration: "OK, what are you going to do now that you've mobilized these people?" They say, "Well, we'll work out programs." It's the job of the army to push what they call "Brand Obama." That's more like a dictatorship, not a democracy.

It's a very depoliticized society. It's hard to get people together. It's a very rich country, so people have the right to expect a decent standard of living. Instead, they live difficult lives. The working hours are very high, far higher than Europe; you don't have much time; there are very limited benefits; there's a lot of insecurity—that is very high now, people are just driven to try to maintain their private lives.

During the presidential campaign, there were a lot of people who thought that under Obama's administration, the U.S. domestic and foreign policies would be different. Do you foresee any change in U.S. foreign and domestic policies under his administration?

First off, there wasn't ever any reason to expect any change. I'm not saying that in retrospect. I was writing before the primaries using his programs on his website. He's a centrist Democrat and really never pretended to be anything else. There's a little change because Bush was so far off the spectrum, especially in the first term. There is a spectrum of politics here. It's not monolithic. It's a pretty narrow spectrum, but there is a spectrum. Bush was way off at the extreme. That's why he came under such harsh criticism even within the establishment. So, yes there's a change back toward the center. But it's mostly a modification of Bush-style extremism of rhetoric and sometimes actions, which have gotten the country in a lot of trouble. There's a reason why the financial institutions, which are the most dominant element in the economy, supported Obama and not McCain. The Bush administration was really driving the country to disaster. They own the place, and they don't want it to be destroyed.

I want to change the subject a little bit. I'm going to move from what we've been talking about for the last 20 minutes to language issues. Do you see any link between language and Western imperialism?

Anything we do involves language. Of course, the terminology and the rhetoric is in language. It does reflect the ideology, power, and so on. For example, the last interview I had about an hour ago, it was a long interview on what are the right measures to use in responding and protecting the country from terrorism and combating terrorism. I spent probably the whole interview trying to explain that's just the wrong question.

If you want to stop terrorism, the first step is to stop participating in it. That's a simple way to reduce terrorism. Secondly, if it's the terrorism of others that you're worried about, then find out what the reasons for it are and deal with them. But if you just ask how to stop terrorism, it's as if the doctors said, "I'm going to inoculate you with poisons. Now how should I treat you after that?" That's not the right question. As the language is used, the word "terror" refers to what they do to us, not what we do to them, which is often much worse. And they don't ask about the sources of their terror, they just combat it with force either domestically or internationally. That's a way of saying we don't care about the problem. And it's the same for everything else, like democracy. It's nothing profound. Language is used in ways that reflect power interests.

Where does culture fit in? You were referring to how language has been used to lie and/or oppress people. What role does culture play in that?

Generally, there are aspects of the dominant culture that are largely sustained on the basis of power interests, although there are other factors that shape the way people think, the way they respond, the way they react, the way policies are made, and so on. How could it fail to be true? We could say more about it, but there is nothing profound to say about these topics. Intellectuals do produce complicated texts and polysyllabic words and so on, but basically what we understand, it's pretty straightforward. It can be said simply in ways that should be clear to everyone.

Let me ask you a question about the dominant aspect of the English language. As you know, there are some languages that are more valued than others. For example, the U.S. and the British English have been perceived as Standard English, whereas other Englishes spoken in other countries are seen as inferior. So as a linguist, where do you stand on this issue?

First of all, that's true now; it wasn't true a century ago. A century ago British English was the standard and American English was regarded as a kind of dialect. Well, what changed? Who was the most powerful country in the world a century ago? Who's the most powerful country in the world today? Then it was Britain, now it's the United States. Like I said there's nothing profound about these things. They're on the surface. English is the most dominant language because the United States is the richest and by far the most powerful country in the world. So sure, English is the dominant language, not Swahili.

So clearly there is a link between language and power. So whichever country has more power tends to use its language to dominate others.

Well, that's the way national languages are formed. Today people in Italy speak something like what was once a dialect of Florence, not the dozens of other Italian languages that are around. It's because of the process of state formation and the formation of the dominant culture and so on. You hear people talk a lot about endangered languages. Languages are dying all over the world, which is a serious problem. They talk mostly about indigenous languages dying, which is true; they are dying off very fast. But the same is true for languages in Europe. They are dying off very quickly just because of the establishment of a more powerful central state.

You were the one who coined the phrase "universal grammar," which I found fascinating. Would you add anything to that concept? Or do you think there's no need to add anything to it?

Well, frankly if I were starting over 50 years ago I never would have used the phrase. I had assumed that people would be rational enough to use the phrase as it was defined, and to pay attention to the fact that it does not have the same meaning as the traditional phrase although it's related to it. So it's like when a physicist uses the word *work* in a physics text, but they don't expect people to look up the employment statistics. They assume people are rational enough to know that this is an invented term, which has a loose relationship to the informal term *work*, but has its technical meaning. The same with energy, force, and everything else. So when you talk about force in a physics class, you're not talking about the number of military bases you have. You can easily get people to understand that in physics, but it's hard for them to grasp that in the human sciences.

The term *universal grammar* is radically misunderstood. I was just looking at the current issue of the journal *Language*, the journal of the Linguistic Society where there are a lot of tantrums about universal grammar, based on failure to comprehend these simple points. So I wouldn't have used the term universal grammar if I had recognized the irrationality of the likely reaction. The term "universal grammar," in the modern sense, my sense at least, is used to refer to whatever the genetic component of the language faculty is. That's universal grammar.

You said if you were to write about this, you would have chosen a different word. What word would that be then?

I would have picked some more technical term, which is less likely to be misunderstood. But there's no overcoming human irrationality. That's happened with other things too. I used to talk about knowledge of language but then I realized that, after years of commentary, philosophers are going to misunderstand it. They have a specific theory of knowledge, which has to do with *true belief* and so on. So, yes they interpret it in terms of warranted true belief and doctrines of philosophy. But it has to do with what we internally have represented in our minds—which actually accords better with informal usage. So I made up a new word and said, "OK. Let's call it competence, not knowledge." Then that got misinterpreted because some people are more competent than others. It's very hard in an irrational culture to do things that aren't going to be misinterpreted.

The French philosopher Michel Foucault talked about power and knowledge. How do you see the link between those two concepts?

If you have knowledge, it increases your power. The United States is now in a huge financial crisis. Who does the government turn to in order to fix it up? The people who have what's called knowledge of economics. It happens to be the very people who created the crisis. It doesn't matter if they have knowledge, know technical things about economics; they're the ones who are called upon to fix it. Again, knowledge is power. I don't really much appreciate his work to tell you the truth. He used fairly simple observations and restated them in complicated ways.

There are different types of knowledge. Why is it some knowledge is valued while others are not? For example, if I were to say something, they might not take it into consideration because I am not a powerful person; my words are not important. However, if it were someone serving under Obama right now, people would most likely listen to that person just because that person is in a powerful position.

Is that controversial or surprising? We understand it already. People who are powerful are in a position to influence and control what others do. That's power. Let's take this financial crisis that we've been through about 20 or 30 years due in no small part to extreme arrogance and confidence on the part of professional economists. Most of them, if not all, are still talking about the wonders of the markets, how markets are efficient, and the government shouldn't tamper with them. This led to a total disaster. It didn't mean that they knew what they were talking about. They didn't. But their ideas were very influential, because they happened to be in the short-term interest of people with real power like Goldman Sachs. Therefore, they were adopted. If someone came along and said, "Look! This is going to lead to disaster, so you guys had better cut back your risky loans and your bonuses to executives," would anybody pay attention? In fact, some did say that to economists but they ignored it. It did not contribute to the interest of the powerful. I don't frankly think that you're going to find anything in this domain that isn't fairly obvious on the face of it.

… FOUR …

Democracy and Language Rights of Minority Groups

Is democracy possible in a country where minority languages and cultures have been pushed to the margins, where citizens are merely spectators of educational, socioeconomic, and political decision-making processes affecting their lives, and where workers have been grossly exploited? This chapter aims to explore these questions. To this end, I begin by briefly reviewing major tenets of democracy as related to schooling. To further examine these tenets, I use excerpts of a dialogue in which I engaged Noam Chomsky about democracy and schooling. This dialogue is situated within the contemporary U.S. educational and neoliberal context, including the No Child Left Behind legislation. I go on to explore linguistic discrimination of minority students, including bilingual students, and how these students have faced barriers in schools and in society at large. I conclude this chapter by making an appeal for linguistic and cultural pluralism as a *sine qua non* for living in a participatory form of democracy.

Democracy: Whose Definition and Whose Interests Does It Serve?

It is important to note upfront that concepts such as economic democracy, ecological democracy, and democracy in the social realm, which are important aspects of direct democracy, are beyond the scope of this chapter. Broadly conceived, the concept of democracy has been at the center of many political debates and can be traced back as far as the time of Plato. This concept occupied a central role in

Plato's work, namely in his *Republic* (2008). However, despite the fact that the *Republic* is a groundbreaking text, it is well-documented that Plato, rather than a supporter of a participatory form of democracy, was a supporter of oligarchy, wherein the government is ruled by the enlightened few (Baird & Kaufmann, 2008).

Many scholars from various fields and with different foci, including education, philosophy, and political science, have challenged Plato's view of democracy and developed a much more progressive view of this concept (Carr, 2011; Chomsky, 1994, 2007; Denzin, 2009; Dewey, 1997; Giroux, 2003, 2007; Macedo, 2009). For example, John Dewey, the prominent American philosopher and educator, was a champion of a democratic school system. Specifically, through his book *Democracy and Education* (1997), Dewey advocated for democratic educational values and principles, which he argued should be the cornerstone of any progressive society. Furthermore, Dewey emphasized the great value and role of democracy in the construction of an equitable society, and he argued that embracing and implementing democratic values and principles in any given society can be conducive to the political stability of a country and the overall well-being of its citizens. Finally, unlike Plato, Dewey was against oligarchic and authoritarian forms of government in which the wealthy ruled at the expense of the poor (Greene, 2009).

With regard to schooling in particular, Dewey advocated the creation of democratic space within the U.S. school system, for he believed that such a space was essential for the creation of good citizenship. Finally, Dewey believed that students and professors should be allowed to discuss social and political issues in schools without the intrusion and infringement of the government. In other words, Dewey believed that students' and professors' voices should not be silenced if democracy is to exist. As Maxine Greene (2009) eloquently put it, "Without a Dewey, there would have been little concern for 'participatory democracy,' for 'consensus,' for the reconstitution of a public sphere" (p. 92).

Taking Dewey's view on democracy and schooling a few steps further, I argue that in order to have a democratic school system, students, including English-language learners and bilingual students, need to be allowed to voice their opinions about what kind of education they feel they should receive. Also, these students should be given the opportunity to actively participate in the co-construction of knowledge with their teachers (Orelus, 2010; Vygotsky, 1978). In my view, a school system within which students are expected to merely receive and regurgitate the information that their teachers pass on to them is not democratic. As the Brazilian educator Paulo Freire (1970) pointed out in his seminal work *Pedagogy of the Oppressed*, students should not be passive recipients of prefabricated knowledge that professors pour into their heads. Freire called this form of pedagogy a "banking" type of education. Freire explains what this form of education entails as follows:

1. the teacher teaches and the students are taught;

2. the teacher knows everything and the students know nothing;

3. the teacher thinks and the students are thought about;

4. the teacher talks and the students listen—meekly;

5. the teacher disciplines and the students are disciplined;

6. the teacher chooses and enforces his choice, and the students comply;

7. the teacher acts and the students have the illusion of acting through the action of the teacher;

8. the teacher chooses the program content, and the students (who are not consulted) adapt to it;

9. the teacher confuses the authority of knowledge with his or her own professional authority, which she and he sets in opposition to the freedom of the students;

10. the teacher is the subject of the learning process, while the pupils are mere objects. (p. 73)

Freire's notion of a banking form of education is unfortunately not an obsolete one. It has been a recurring practice in the U.S. school system, especially with the passage of the No Child Left Behind mandate. Because of this neoliberal educational reform, many teachers have been forced to "teach to the test" in the hope that their students would meet state and federal standardized test benchmarks (Linn, 2004; Lipman, 2004; Sleeter, 2005). To put it simply, the neoliberal agenda informing this type of educational reform has essentially dis-intellectualized teachers and led to the miseducation of students (Giroux, 2007; Orelus, 2010). That is, because of the neoliberal nature of this educational reform, the teaching practices of many public school teachers have been reduced to mostly rote and drill test practices, leaving limited time for creative and critical work conducive to student growth and learning (Au, 2008; Lipman, 2004; Sleeter, 2007).

School and politics are not two separate entities. Therefore, what is happening in school needs to be situated and configured within a country's political system. West (2004) and Chomsky (2007), among others, have been very critical of the U.S. political system and concur that in a democratic society, people—including students and teachers—should be able to assert their voices without any fear of governmental reprisal. These public intellectuals similarly argue that citizens should be allowed to actively participate in the political decision-making process, and that they should not merely be passive spectators to what happens to them. Critiquing the U.S. system of democracy, West (2004) stated:

> The American democratic experiment is unique in human history not because we are God's chosen people to lead the world, nor because we are a force for good in the world, but because of our refusal to acknowledge the deeply racist and imperial roots of our democratic project. We are exceptional because of our denial of the antidemocratic foundation stones of American democracy. (p. 41)

In a country where minority students, particularly bilingual students, have been forced to embrace and speak English at the expense of their native tongues (Crawford, 2008; Cummins, 2000; Macedo, Dendrinos, & Gounari, 2003; Valdés, 2001; Valdés, Capitelli, & Alvarez, 2010), where workers have been exploited and are put under surveillance so that they would revolt against their inhuman conditions (Aronowitz, 2006; McLaren, 2005), and where students have often been rewarded for being silent and compliant (Giroux, 2003), the concept of democracy becomes more of an illusion than a reality. Furthermore, one is dissuaded from talking about a progressive form of democracy in a country where a small group of wealthy people controls the information circulated through TV, newspapers, and radio stations that they own (Chomsky, 2002; Leistyna & Alper, 2007; Macedo & Steinberg, 2007). Likewise, there can't be democracy without the equal and representative voices and active participation of all citizens in political decisions concerning and affecting their lives. Moreover, democracy is an illusion in a capitalist, neoliberal state where profits are the priority, not the people (Chomsky, 2004; Klein, 2007; McLaren, 2005, 2008; Porfilio & Malott, 2008). Finally, as Alexander (2010) documented in her book *The New Jim Crow*, democracy is yet to become a reality for those—namely poor Blacks and Latino/as—who are unjustly and massively incarcerated and have been treated as the wretched of the earth (Fanon, 1963) in the U.S. prison system.

Unfortunately, this democracy myth has been ingrained in the minds of many people in many countries, including the United States, which has been dubiously called, and refers to itself, as the preeminent democratic country. Like Chomsky (2004) and West (2004), de Tocqueville and Grant (2000), and Myrdal (1944) had, decades earlier, already unveiled the contradictory nature of the U.S. political system. These authors observed that, while the United States has earned a democratic reputation worldwide, many groups, such as African Americans, Native Americans, Latino/as, and Arabs, among others, have historically suffered brutal forms of discrimination, including linguistic and racial discrimination. For example, while the grand narrative about democracy continues to shape public discourse and circulate in the mainstream media and in schools, historically marginalized groups have been forbidden to speak their languages. In fact, their languages have been attacked and relegated to an inferior status. Native American children, forcibly placed in reservations, were often reprimanded in government schools for speaking their native languages, which were perceived by their teachers as "uncivilized" (Churchill, 2004; Grande, 2004; Spring, 2009). Likewise, in Australia, aboriginal children were taken from their families and placed in boarding schools where they were prohibited from speaking their native tongues, and their names were changed to Anglo names (Olsen, 2003).

In his seminal book *How Europe Underdeveloped Africa*, Walter Rodney (1972) documented the way and the extent to which European colonizers imposed their languages on African children in order to maintain their linguistic, political, and socioeconomic domination. To achieve this goal, according to Rodney, the European colonizers hired submissive colonial teachers to teach European culture and history to African students in kindergarten and primary schools. Through this colonial form of schooling, African students were taught to value and embrace the language and culture of their colonizers at the expense of their own. Rodney stated:

> Schools of kindergarten and primary level for Africans in Portuguese colonies were nothing but agencies for the spread of the Portuguese language. Most schools were controlled by the Catholic Church, as a reflection of the unity of church and state in fascist Portugal. In the little-known Spanish colony of Guinea (Rio Muni), the small amount of education given to Africans was based on eliminating the use of local languages by the pupils and on instilling in their hearts the holy fear of God. (p. 249)

Finally, in the United States, other marginalized groups such as Latino/as have been prohibited from speaking Spanish in schools (Anzaldúa, 1990; Crawford, 1991, 2008; Cummins, 2000; Macedo et al., 2003). The colonial legacy continues to affect marginalized groups linguistically and culturally, especially with the rise of the English-only movement (Macedo et al., 2003). According to Macedo and his colleagues, in the United States, languages other than the hegemonic English have been attacked by conservative intellectuals such as E.D. Hirsch, Jr. (1987), who have fiercely rejected multiculturalism and bilingualism and advocated for a "common culture." Thus, one must ask: Who exactly has been benefiting from the Western form of democracy?

The noble idea of democracy needs to be a reality, not only for those who speak the so-called Standard English and who own the means of production and thus control the U.S. political apparatus, but also for those whose native languages have been attacked and whose voices have been silenced. As Chomsky (1994, 2007) contends, democracy is a mythology when a minority group in powerful positions has accumulated the wealth of a country and has used the corporate media and the police to manipulate and silence the voice of the majority so that they will not revolt against social injustice. These practices violate the core values and principles that shape and constitute the spirit of a democratic society. As Eric Williams (1993) pointed out, "Democracy means the obligation of the minority to recognize the right of the majority. Democracy means responsibility of the government to its citizens, the protection of the citizens from the exercise of arbitrary power and the violation of human freedoms and individual rights" (p. 266).

Williams's definition of democracy is yet to be meaningful to those who have been linguistically and racially discriminated and exploited in a capitalist, neoliberal state, where the wealthy, including CEOs of major corporations, have influenced institutions such as schools, the workplace, and the political apparatus. These issues are central to the arguments that Noam Chomsky made in a dialogue that I had with him more than a year ago. In this dialogue, Chomsky and I explored issues such as democracy, schooling, and U.S. domestic and foreign policies. To substantiate the points made throughout this chapter about language, schooling, and democracy, it is worth using some excerpts from the dialogue presented in the previous chapter.

* * *

Orelus: Do you see any link between language and the neoliberal agenda of the U.S. government?

Chomsky: Anything we do involves language. Of course the terminology and the rhetoric is in language. It does reflect the ideology, power, and so on. For example, the last interview I had about an hour ago, it was a long interview on what are the right measures to use in responding and protecting the country from terrorism and combating terrorism. I spent probably the whole interview trying to explain that's just the wrong question. If you want to stop terrorism, stop participating in it. That's the simple way to reduce terrorism. Second, if it's the terrorism of others that you're worried about, then find out what the reasons for it are and deal with them. But if you just ask, it's as if the doctors said, "I'm going to inoculate you with poisons. Now how should I treat you after that?" I mean you have to treat someone after they put poisons in their body, that's not the right question. All that is in language is the word *terror*, meaning what they do to us, not what we do to them, which is often much worse. And they don't ask about the sources of their terror, they just combat it with force either domestically or internationally. That's a way of saying we don't care about the problem. And it's the same for everything else like democracy. It's nothing profound. Language is used in ways that reflect the power interests.

Where does culture fit in? You were referring to how language has been used to lie and/or oppress people. What role does culture play in that?

Generally, cultural properties, which are largely sustained on the basis of power interest, although there are other factors, shape the way people think, the way they respond, the way they react, the way policies are made, and so on. How could it fail to be true? Well, we could say more about it, but there is nothing profound to say about these topics. I mean intellectuals do produce complicated texts and polysyllabic words and so on, but basically what we understand, it's pretty straightforward. It can be said simply where it's obvious to everyone.

Let me ask you a question about the dominant aspect of the English language. As you know, there are some languages that are more valued than others. For example, the U.S. and the British English have been perceived as Standard English, whereas other Englishes spoken in other countries are seen as inferior. So as a linguist, where do you stand on this issue?

First of all, that's true now; it wasn't true a century ago. A century ago British English was the standard and the American English was just a kind of dialect. Well, what changed? Who was the most powerful country in the world a century ago? Who's the most powerful country in the world today? Then it was Britain, now it's the United States. Like I said there's nothing profound about these things. They're on the surface. English is the most dominant language because the United States is the richest and by far the most powerful country in the world. So sure, English is the dominant language, not Swahili.

So clearly there is a link between language and power. So whichever country has more power tends to use its language to dominate others.

Well, that's the way national languages are formed. I saw people in Italy speak kind of what was once a dialect of Florence, not the dozens of other Italian languages that are around. It's because of the presence of state formation and the formation of the dominant culture and so on. I mean you hear people talk a lot about endangered languages. Languages are dying all over the world, which is a serious problem. They talk mostly about indigenous languages dying, which is true; they are dying off very fast. But the same is true for languages in Europe. I mean they are dying off very quickly just because of the establishment of a more powerful central state.

* * *

In the earler dialogue, Professor Chomsky critically analyzes the hegemonic aspect of language and illuminates the unequal power relations between dominant and subjugated languages. He also talks about the correlation between language and power. Specifically, Chomsky shows the way and the extent to which languages spoken by the dominant class in powerful countries such as the United States, Great Britain, and France tend to dominate languages perceived and treated as subaltern languages. Finally, in the dialogue Chomsky unveils the antidemocratic nature of the U.S. form of democracy, arguing that it only works for the rich and that people, especially ordinary people, are only given the illusion that they are living in a democratic society. Drawing on Chomsky's argument, it can be further argued that the U.S. government is very hypocritical in the sense that it has been trying to impose its form of electoral democracy on other countries when, in fact, there is no participatory democracy in the United States (Carr, 2011).

Toward a Democratic and a Linguistically Equitable Society

Drawing on the arguments articulated earlier, I ask: Isn't it ironic that despite the widespread belief that the United States is a melting pot and a democratic country, certain languages labeled as minority have been under attack and relegated to a subaltern position (Spivak, 1988)? Gloria Anzaldúa's (1990) linguistic and xenophobic experience with an Anglo teacher illustrates the persistent attack on minority languages by dominant groups, including teachers, who have embraced the ideology informing the English-only movement. Anzaldúa recounted her struggle with an Anglo teacher who forbade her from speaking Spanish in class.

> I remember being caught speaking Spanish at recess—that was good for three licks on the knuckles with a sharp ruler. I remember being sent to the corner of the classroom for "talking back" to the Anglo teacher when all I was trying to do was tell her how to pronounce my name. "If you want to be American, speak 'American.' If you don't like it, go back to Mexico where you belong." (p. 203)

Anzaldúa's experience with the Anglo teacher clearly illuminates how those who believe in and embrace the English-only movement have committed symbolic linguistic and cultural violence (Bourdieu, 1991) against marginalized groups by trying to silence their voices, prohibiting them from speaking their mother tongues (Phillipson, 1992, 2010; Skutnabb-Kangas, 2000). Moreover, her experience shows that language is not simply about uttering words but is intrinsically linked to ideology, culture, and power relations (Darder, 1991; Foucault, 1980; Gramsci, 1971).

Equally important, the linguistic discrimination that Anzaldúa faced in school calls into question the belief that the United States is a free and democratic country. In a country that has been called democratic and free, people should not be threatened and punished for speaking their native tongues. Prohibiting one from speaking one's language in a "democratic country" suggests that one is free in the "land of the free" only as long as one does not speak Spanish, Creole, or other subjugated languages. I argue that prohibiting people from speaking their native languages contradicts the belief that the United States is a democratic country.

Unfortunately, although Anzaldúa's experience with her Anglo teacher took place over 2 decades ago, it is still relevant, for minority students continue to experience linguistic discrimination in this so-called democratic country. Attacking minority native languages is not a simple matter, and I agree with Darder (1991), who stated: "Negating the native language and its potential benefits in the development of the student's voice constitutes a form of psychological violence and functions to perpetuate social control over subordinate language groups through various linguistic forms of cultural invasion" (p. 38). What Darder argues here speaks to a great extent to the problematic and divisive nature of the language issue in my native land, Haiti. For instance, French, the imposed language of the French colonizer, is valued over Haitian Creole, the native tongue of most Haitians like myself. Because of this colonial legacy, those who speak only Creole (the vast majority of whom tend to be the poor, dark-skinned Haitians) are looked down upon and have very limited access, if any, to sociopolitical mobility in Haiti. By contrast, the middle- and upper-class Haitians who have embraced and mastered the French language have historically been the ones dominating Haiti's economic and political systems (Orelus, 2011).

Along the same lines, it is worth noting that the French spoken by poor, working-class Haitians does not hold the same social-class status as the French spoken by those who belong to the upper-middle and upper classes, especially those who have been privileged enough to study abroad in French-speaking countries such as France and Belgium (Orelus, 2011). To further complicate the language issue in Haiti, it is equally important to mention that linguistic discrimination based on accents sometimes takes place among poor urban and rural working-class Haitians. Depending on the regions they're from, their French or Creole accent may be different. Those who believe they speak French or French Creole with the "right accent"—meaning close to the Parisian accent—sometimes assume they are linguistically superior to, or more sophisticated than, those who do not (Orelus, 2011). I use these examples to show that, as in the United States and elsewhere, there is a serious language and class divide in Haiti.

Conclusion

In closing, I contend that democracy, particularly a participatory form of democracy, is worth fighting for so that people can live in a society where their languages, cultures, and "funds of knowledge" (Moll, 1988) are respected and incorporated into the school curriculum; where workers would not be brutally exploited; and, most important, where ordinary citizens would be part of the political decision-making processes affecting their lives, rather than being passive spectators of these processes. Unless these necessary conditions are fully met, the concept of democracy would merely remain an illusion created by those in power, who have historically used empty rhetoric to gain the consent of, and give false hope to, the masses in order to maintain the status quo (Gramsci, 1971; Marx, 1994).

References

Alexander, M. (2010). *The new Jim Crow: Mass incarceration in the age of colorblindness*. New York: New Press.

Anzaldúa, G. (1990). How to tame a wild tongue. In R. Ferguson, M. Gever, T. Minh-Ha, & C. West (Eds.), *Out there: Marginalization and contemporary cultures* (pp. 24–44). Cambridge, MA: MIT Press.

Aronowitz, S. (2006). *Left turn: Forging a new political future*. Boulder, CO: Paradigm.

Au, W. (2008). *Unequal by design: High-stakes testing and the standardization of inequality*. New York: Routledge.
Baird, F., & Kaufmann, K. (2008). *From Plato to Derrida*. Upper Saddle River, NJ: Pearson Prentice Hall.
Bourdieu, P. (1991). *Language and symbolic power*. Cambridge: Polity Press.
Carr, P. (2011). The quest for a critical pedagogy of democracy. In C. Malott & B. Porfilio (Eds.), *Critical pedagogy in the twenty-first century: A new generation of scholars* (pp. 187–210). Charlotte, NC: Information Age.
Chomsky, N. (1994). *Secrets, lies and democracy*. Berkeley, CA: Odonian Press.
Chomsky, N. (2002). *Media control: The spectacular achievements of propaganda*. New York: Seven Stories.
Chomsky, N. (2004). *Hegemony or survival: America's quest for global dominance*. New York: Holt Paperbacks.
Chomsky, N. (2007). *Failed states: The abuse of power and the assault on democracy*. American Empire Project. New York: Holt.
Churchill, W. (2004). *Kill the Indian, save the man: The genocidal impact of American Indian residential schools*. San Francisco: City Lights.
Crawford, J. (1991). *Bilingual education: History, politics, theory and practice* (2nd ed.). Los Angeles: Bilingual Educational Services.
Crawford, J. (2008). *Advocating for English learners: Selected essays*. New York: Multilingual Matters.
Cummins, J. (2000). *Language, power and pedagogy: Bilingual children in the crossfire*. Tonawanda, NY: Multilingual Matters.
Darder, A. (1991). *Culture and power in the classroom: A critical foundation for bicultural education*. New York: Bergin & Garvey.
Denzin, N.K. (2009). Critical pedagogy and democratic life or a radical democratic pedagogy. *Cultural Studies—Critical Methodologies*, *9*(3), 379–397.
Dewey, J. (1997). *Democracy and education*. New York: Free Press.
Fanon, F. (1963). *The wretched of the earth*. New York: Grove Press.
Foucault, M. (1980). *Two lectures, power and knowledge: Selected writings and other interviews*. New York: Pantheon.
Freire, P. (1970). *Pedagogy of the oppressed*. New York: Continuum.
Giroux, H. (2003). *The abandoned generation: Democracy beyond the culture of fear*. New York: Palgrave Macmillan.
Giroux, H. (2007). Democracy, education, and the politics of critical pedagogy. In P. McLaren & J. Kincheloe (Eds.), *Critical pedagogy: Where are you now?* (pp. 1–5). New York: Peter Lang.
Gramsci, A. (1971). *Selections from the prison notebooks*. New York: International.
Grande, S. (2004). *Red pedagogy: Native American social and political thought*. Lanham, MD: Rowman & Littlefield.
Greene, M. (2009). In search of a critical pedagogy. In A. Darder, M.P. Baltodana, & R.D. Torres (Eds.), *The critical pedagogy reader* (2nd ed., pp. 84–96). New York: Routledge.
Hirsch, E.D., Jr. (1987). *Cultural literacy: What every American needs to know*. New York: Vintage.
Klein, N. (2007). *The shock doctrine: The rise of disaster capitalism*. New York: Metropolitan Books.
Leistyna, P., & Alper, L. (2007). Critical media literacy for the 21st century: Taking our entertainment seriously. In S. Steinberg & D. Macedo (Eds.), *Media literacy: A reader* (pp. 54–78). New York: Peter Lang.
Linn, R.L. (2004). Rethinking the No Child Left Behind Act accountability system. www.cep-dc.org/pubs/Forum28July2004/
Lipman, P. (2004). *High stakes education: Inequality, globalization, and urban school reform*. New York: Routledge.

Macedo, D. (2009). Unmasking prepackaged democracy. In S. Macrine (Ed.), *Critical pedagogy in uncertain times: Hopes and possibilities* (pp. 79–96). New York: Palgrave Macmillan.

Macedo, D., Dendrinos, B., & Gounari, P. (2003). *The hegemony of English*. Boulder, CO: Paradigm.

Macedo, D., & Steinberg, S. (2007). *Media literacy: A reader*. New York: Peter Lang.

Marx, K. (1994). *The eighteenth brumaire of Louis Bonaparte*. New York: International.

McLaren, P. (2005). *Capitalists and conquerors: A critical pedagogy against empire*. Lanham, MD: Rowman & Littlefield.

McLaren, P. (2008). Capitalism's bestiary: Rebuilding urban education. In B. Porfilio & C. Malott (Eds.), *The destructive path of neo-liberalism: An international examination of urban education* (pp. vii–xv). Rotterdam, The Netherlands: Sense.

Moll, L. (1988). Some key issues in teaching Latino students. *Language Arts, 65*(5), 465–472.

Myrdal, G. (1944). *An American dilemma: The Negro problem and modern democracy*. New York: Harper & Brothers.

Olsen, R. (2003). *Rabbit proof fence* [movie]. NTSC, Import.

Orelus, P. (2010). *Academic achievers: Whose definition? An ethnographic study examining the literacy [under] development of English language learners in the era of high-stakes tests*. Rotterdam, The Netherlands: Sense.

Orelus, P. (2011). *Courageous voices of immigrants and transnationals of color: Counter-narratives against discrimination in schools and beyond*. New York: Peter Lang.

Phillipson, R. (1992). *Linguistic imperialism*. New York: Oxford University Press.

Phillipson, R. (2010). *Linguistic imperialism continued*. New York: Routledge.

Plato. (2008). *Republic* (Robin Waterfield, Trans.). New York: Oxford University Press.

Porfilio, B., & Malott, C. (2008). *The destructive path of neo-liberalism: An international examination of urban education*. Rotterdam, The Netherlands: Sense.

Rodney, W. (1972). *How Europe underdeveloped Africa*. Washington, DC: Howard University Press.

Skutnabb-Kangas, T. (2000). *Linguistic genocide in education—Or worldwide diversity and human rights?* Mahwah, NJ: Lawrence Erlbaum.

Sleeter, C.E. (2005). *Un-standardizing curriculum: Multicultural teaching in the standardized-based classroom*. New York: Routledge.

Sleeter, C.E. (2007). *Facing accountability in education: Democracy & equity at risk*. New York: Teachers College Press.

Spivak, G. (1988). Can the subaltern speak? In C. Nelson & L. Grossberg (Eds.), *Marxism and the interpretation of culture* (pp. 23–45). Chicago: University of Illinois Press.

Spring, J. (2009). *Deculturalization and the struggle for equality: A brief history of the education of dominated cultures in the United States* (6th ed.). New York: McGraw-Hill Humanities/Social Sciences/Languages.

Tocqueville, A. de, & Grant, S. (2000). *Democracy in America*. Indianapolis, IN: Hackett.

Valdés, G. (2001). *Learning and not learning English: Latino students in American schools*. New York: Teachers College Press.

Valdés, G., Capitelli, S., & Alvarez, L. (2010). *Latino children learning English: Steps in the journey*. New York: Teachers College Press.

Vygotsky, L. (1978). *Mind in society*. Cambridge, MA: Harvard University Press.

West, C. (2004). *Democracy matters: Winning the fight against imperialism*. New York: Penguin.

Williams, E. (1993). *History of the people of Trinidad and Tobago*. Brooklyn, NY: A&B.

FIVE

Neoliberalism: The Rich Over the Poor

Noam Chomsky and Pierre Orelus in Dialogue

Context of Dialogue

In this dialogue, Noam Chomsky paints for us the dark side of the Western neoliberal and imperialist agenda and its impact on impoverished countries such as India and Haiti. Challenging the notion that neoliberalism has emerged simultaneously from the West and developing countries, Chomsky maintains that the elite in Third World countries may have welcomed the Western neoliberal agenda, because such an agenda works for them. However, they are not major players, and the poor in these countries have suffered the most from the implementation of neoliberal economic policy. Refusing to use a language of complete despair to talk about the desperate economic situation many developing countries have found themselves in as a result of Western neoliberal and imperial foreign policies, Professor Chomsky states that ordinary people could use their agency to organize and stand up against the madness and greed of those who have oppressed them, and demand real socioeconomic and political changes designed to ameliorate their plight. Equally important, Chomsky contends that neoliberal policy has also affected the poor in Western countries, including the United States, which has a high rate of unemployment, is in debt, and has a health care system that does not work for the poor.

The Dialogue

Orelus: Professor Noam Chomsky, your recent book is entitled Hopes and Prospects. *So are you hopeful that the U.S. neoliberal agenda will have a lesser negative impact on the economic development of Third World countries?*

Chomsky: I certainly hope so. But the prospects don't look pretty good. Hopes mentioned in that book are mostly about Latin America, where there has been real progress and real steps forward, and it's quite significant. It's 500 years of colonization that are suddenly being changed. This is not a small event in world affairs. Lots of things are happening in Brazil. But in the United States itself things in many ways are getting more reactionary and aggressive. After all, we are occupying two countries in the Middle East, and right on the borders of Iran we still have a credible military system. Military spending in the United States is roughly as much as the rest of the world combined. Logistically, we're much more advanced of futuristic means of destruction. We have hundreds of military bases. Maybe 800 or so naval forces are deployed everywhere around the world. It's a very aggressive posture. The threats against Iran are quiet severe. There's no sign of that retracting, which is quite traumatic because there are serious internal problems in the United States. The United States is facing serious economic, debt crisis. Meanwhile, military spending is increasing. The other issue is the dysfunctional health care system. That is not being touched. But it's still there. The potential welfare and strength of the county is not being modified in any significant way. In fact, in some ways that's the way the game works. Obama's deficit commission is basically committed to cutting social spending for the poor and the general population, but not cutting back on the causes and the sources of the crisis by taxing the rich. So the situation looks very good internally. But there's a lot of anger, fear, and frustration in the country. It's understandable. For about 30 years, real wages have pretty much stagnated for the majority of the population. There's a lot of wealth being created going into very few pockets. That's quite visible. People can see the banks that caused the crisis. The direct cause of the crisis is that the rich are getting richer and more powerful than ever. The government pays off their bonuses and this makes people very angry. I think the anger is exhibiting itself within extremely self-destructive ways, but there is no denying that the anger is the cause of such actions.

In a recent conversation with a professor from India about the damaging effects of neoliberalism on Third World countries, he stated that when we're talking about neoliberalism we should not only refer to the West because, according to him, neoliberalism doesn't only emerge from the West but also from the South, from Third World countries like India. Would you share this view?

Yeah, but these countries are not big actors in world affairs. They're victims, not agents. Of course the elites of those countries have accommodated to it. But in many respects the South African population, for example, is worse off than under apartheid. And it's partly the result of the elite accepting neoliberal principles. They're not the initiators and the agents of these principles. As far as India is concerned, it's a more complex story. They have instituted what they called reforms, neoliberal reforms, but at the same time they have maintained control over finances. India didn't suffer from the financial crises the way the neoliberal countries did. So it's been a kind of a mixed story, but their development model is very precarious. I mean a section of the population is doing magnificently. For those that were storming around Obama, that's less true. There are probably 700 or 800 million people whose standard of living has actually declined after the neoliberal reforms. That's not a small fact. How are they going to deal with this? We don't know. The rate of peasants' suicide is going up about as fast as the number of billionaires. You can read in *The New York Times* stories about some multibillionaire whose houses are incredible, indescribable mansions, but you do not find much about the peasants' suicide cases in neighboring areas where agricultural resources have been taken away from them. No support for them. You're not reading about the fact that absolute consumption of food has declined by a considerable amount for most of the population. That's the other side of it.

One of the arguments that have been made about neoliberalism is that it is a new form of colonialism disguised with a different mask. Would you agree with this statement?

I think it's basically correct. We should notice that where neoliberal policies have been adopted, including in the West, they have been harmful to most of the population. To some extent the neoliberal policies have been applied in the United States. In fact, that's the nature of the economic stagnation for much of the population that's taken place over 30 years with the deregulation of the economy and the hollowing out of domestic production. These are pretty standard neoliberal proposals. The population has been getting by with debt and asset inflation, like the housing bubble, which is substantially the result of kind of a deep loss of regulation linked to neoliberal prescriptions. On the other hand, the rich and the powerful are protected. They don't subject themselves to market pressures. So they're doing fine by and large, including the rich in the Third World. These polices don't have much of a future. They have just been too harmful. And the countries that are developing didn't abide by them. East Asia developed an economic model essentially rejecting the neoliberal principals. If they accepted them like the financial deregulation, this would lead very quickly to financial crises.

Basically, what you're saying is that neoliberalism has failed, as far as the poor and developing countries are concerned. In other words, it may have been a success for the rich, but for the poor it has been a disaster.

But that isn't a failure. I mean that's a success. It did what it was intended to achieve. That was the goal.

Well, that's been a double discourse on this issue. For example, through their hegemonic discourse, proponents of neoliberalism have tried to make the poor believe that they can benefit from it. However, as historically demonstrated, the neoliberal agenda of Western countries, like that of the United States, has impoverished the poor even more. So what would you say about the hegemonic neoliberal discourse of the United States and other Western countries about helping the poor in developing countries?

The elite discourse is always believed. You go back to the worst monsters in Japanese fascism, those in power were just full of uplifting rhetoric about how they were going to bestow on the people of China and so on. They probably believed it. From their point of view of liberation, they were going to turn China into an earthly paradise. They probably believed it. It's true of dominant groups throughout history.

But how do you explain that some Third World leaders still believe that neoliberalism might work in Third World countries?

Because it's working fine for them. Go to almost any Third World country; there's a sector of wealth and privilege, which is astonishing beyond what you see here. It's doing fine for them. It may not be working for the population, but that's a different question.

Some Third World leaders appear to be progressive, for example Michael Manley.

Look at what happened to him.

In some way, he embraced some aspect of neoliberalism. How do you explain that?

He was forced to do so.

Yes, he was forced to, but he could have chosen otherwise. That was a choice he made nevertheless. For example, Aristide could have chosen not to return to Haiti in 1994, declining the deal former President Bill Clinton made with him. Bill Clinton agreed to help Aristide return to Haiti with the expectation that he would implement Clinton's neoliberal agenda in Haiti.

Okay, but then he would be out.

Yes, but he chose to agree with Clinton's dictate. He refused to implement Clinton's new liberal agenda, so he was overthrown in 1994. How do you explain someone like Aristide who has some very progressive views but allowed himself to be fooled by, to be lied to by a Western imperial president?

I don't know in the case of Manley. It seems to me that he probably made a realistic assessment that he either accepted these rules or he's out. It's not much of a choice. Maybe his choice was based on the assumption, "Well, if I accommodate and stay in, this would be better than other alternatives." That's usually the argument given whether you like it or dislike it. It's not much of a choice. There're others who just sell out. For example, in South Africa some elements of the ANC took over power and simply enriched themselves.

If you were a consultant to some Third World leaders who wanted to make some effectual change in their countries, and you knew that neoliberalism has failed the poor, what advice would you give them?

Well, first of all it would be extremely arrogant and improper to give any advice at all without knowing the details of their society. There's no magic principle that applies to every country. You have to know what's happening in that country and what the options are. You have to have detailed information about it. Part of the reason for the human failure of neoliberalism was that it was basically a one-size-fits-all policy. We work something out of the World Bank of the IMF, we impose it on you whatever the circumstance are. And of course that's not going to work, except for the rich. So I wouldn't presume to give any advice without really knowing about the society. However, the one piece of advice, which is general, is to look at the cases that worked. I mean draw some conclusions from the cases that worked in economic development. The rich countries were once poor. For example, England, the United States, Germany, and France and so on are prime examples. Of course you don't want to replicate slavery and conquest and so on, but that's not the whole story. There was internal development as well. In East Asia there has been development. Take South Korea as an example. Fifty years ago, it was at the level of a poor African country. Now it's one of the leading industrial powers. Again you don't want to replicate that system of strong authoritarian violence and repression for a long period. But pick the elements of it that did work. If you look over these cases there are some uniformities. For one thing, it was almost invariably a state-led development. There were market elements, but they were under substantial control and supplemented by major state initiatives. I think that's true of every developing country.

Maybe Hong Kong is an exception. Any serious developing country tells you something after you coordinate industrial policies and planning and so on, which can be involved market elements. But it can't simply be applied to the market.

That's disastrous. No developing country has ever done that. So that's a general prescription, and there are other general prescriptions. But I think you really have to ask what the opportunities are for the country. We can see cases where extremely bad choices were made. I mean bad from the point of view of the people. The United States was able to impose its policies mostly on countries that were weaker, like Haiti. Of course Haiti had no choice, so the United States could impose forced policies on it. This has resulted in total destruction. I mean this destroyed the Haitian agricultural system. Remember, these policies as recently as the 1990s were reported to be very advanced and progressive. But they were so destructive that the country may not have survived for a generation. But that's the extreme case where they couldn't resist the imposition of the policies. There are plenty of lessons to learn from economic history. How you adapt them to your own situation is a delicate question. It depends on many factors. South Latin American countries, for example, Brazil, Chile, and so on, are growing fast. Now their development is precarious. Chile is going to run out of copper.

As you know, Obama just finished a trip in South Asia. Recently, he was in India and then from there he went to Indonesia. I know you have been writing about these countries, especially Indonesia. Do you think that Obama will do something different in terms of U.S. relations with these countries than those presidents who preceded him, like George Bush?

There are some differences. I mean circumstances have changed. There's a different rhetoric but I don't see very much of substance. Actually, Bush's foreign policies with regard to the South were not terrible by traditional standards. For example, in Africa he did some good things. His support for anti-AIDS programs, for example, were good programs. In the case of Sudan, the United States played a somewhat constructive role in leading to a temporary peace agreement between North and South. In Latin America he mostly left it alone, which was a good thing. They're better off when they are left alone. That's one of the reasons, I think, why South America at least was able to make this rather dramatic move toward independence. I mean he's criticized for not having paid attention to Latin America. It's probably the best thing that happened to them, because when the United States pays attention, it's always for its own interest, not for the interest of the people. The United States is particularly bad as a great power. It is the same with Britain, France, Germany, Japan, and anyone else.

You mentioned Haiti as you were talking about how many governments were forced to somewhat embrace the U.S. new world agenda. As you know, after the earthquake that took place in Haiti, President Obama chose two former U.S. presidents, Bill Clinton and George Bush, to supposedly facilitate the recovery effort in Haiti. As you may recall, when both Bill Clinton and George Bush were in power, they destroyed Haiti with the implementation of their foreign policies. What does that say about Barack Obama as a president?

I think that simply shows what should have been obvious in the first place, that Obama is a centrist democrat of the Clinton style, or the new Democrat, essentially the moderate—what used to be a moderate Republican. He never really pretended to be anything else. People decided to clothe him with illusions but they weren't there. So, sure, he's following their policies. Maybe it's a nicer rhetoric than the others, but it was never anything to be excited about. I mean it was a good thing just symbolically—just to have a black family in the White House. That's significant for the black community pride and so on. But as far as policy is concerned, there was nothing. There is no reason to anticipate anything. He was very vague about his policies. Just slogans, and he has no record to speak of, his actual record as a senator. There was nothing very impressive on foreign policy issues. It was often terrible. So he was welcomed into the world because they were infuriated with the aggressive, contemptuous rhetorical stance of the Bush administration, which basically just told the world get lost. Foreign leaders don't like that. They liked it better when Obama comes and says we're your partner. But there was nothing much behind his words, and you can see right through it. Take his speech in Cairo. His famous speech opening to the rest of the world, and what was in it? Nothing. He talked about his perpetual love for Israel. Nothing was offered to the Palestinians. In fact, his policies were total illusion. I was arguing with friends there at the time. The disillusionment with Obama is so extreme that now the majority of people in the Arab world say that they support Iran's development of nuclear weapons. I doubt that they really do, but I think that's a sign of fury at U.S. policy under Obama. If you wanted to blind yourself, you could. On his way to Cairo, he was asked at a press conference, are you going to say anything about repression in Egypt? The regime of brutal dictatorship, torture, and suppression. He said, "Mubarak is a good person, he is doing good things. I don't like to use labels with folks." In other words, if Mubarak wants to torture and kill, that's just fine. He's our ally. That's on the way to Cairo to make his conciliatory speech. How can anyone take his policy seriously?

U.S. imperialism has caused much economic and political damage to the world, particularly to developing countries. Should these countries and others try to function independently from the United States as far as their foreign policies are concerned?

Other countries have to follow their own path. I think the path that has been taken by the South American countries is by and large feasible. People may have made all kind of criticisms about it, but I think the general drift of it has been hopeful and proper. They're disentangling themselves from the grip of great power of control, including U.S. control, and it's a good thing. The same is true in Turkey. For example, the Turkish policy of opening its door to the East, beyond even Iran, is a sensible policy. Countries have to take their own path. Europe in my view ought to move further into independence, and be less subservient to the United States. They ought to and maybe they will. In the United States itself, what are needed are significant internal changes, very serious ones. I mean the United States is now a major threat to the world in a lot of respects. Let's take, say, last Tuesday's election. The Republican candidates who were elected will take over the House now. I don't think there is a single one of them who believes that, as humans, we have contributed to global warming. It's like a death knell for the species. If the United States isn't going to do anything, nobody else will. If these people are so off the planet that they decide to deny basic elementary scientific facts for the purpose of private short-term profits, then the world is in real trouble. Now that's a big problem here, and it's not the only one.

Should we stop focusing only on the United States because there are some emerging powers such as China and India that may be considered imperial powers in some context? For example, China has had a strong influence on Africa. Should we pay attention to these countries as well when we're talking about neoliberalism? If we only focus on the United States, don't you think we may lose sight of the fact that some developing countries can also oppress other developing countries with their foreign policies?

They can, but first of all let's be realistic. GDP per capita in China is about 5%. That's probably an underestimated number. It's like 10%. They've got a long way to go. China has incredible internal problems. Developed countries don't have a high level of poverty. There's an enormous ecological problem and a lack of democracy there, which is already under internal criticism. There's labor repression. I mean the share of GDP on the part of labor has declined more in China than almost anywhere in the world. Now those are major internal problems. If you calculate growth properly you have to take into account costs. And there are serious costs in the economic growth that have to be repaid. You can put them off, but they are there like the ecological consequence. Also, Chinese growth is seriously miscalculated. We have a huge trade deficit with China. But if you calculate it properly as some economists have started to do, the trade deficit with China goes down about 25%. Likewise, the trade deficit with Japan, South Korea, Taiwan, and Singapore goes up by about 25%. China is becoming an assembly plant for the high technology advanced industrial economies on its periphery, including the United States. They all supply parts, components, advanced technology to China where the cheap labor force assembles them. It doesn't add that much value, so the estimate of Chinese growth is significantly distorted. It's a serious issue that most foreign reserves and exchanges in the world are big powers unwilling to be pushed around. They are following their own policies.

Now let's take, for example, Africa. China is all over there. But it's not conquering Africa. As far as I can tell its policies are essentially commercial and developmental, building railroads, and these African countries want China to do it for their own reasons. It may not be good for Africa. They probably do not follow a developing model according to some experts. But China is not forcing them to do it. It's inducing the leadership to do it. So, sure, we have to keep our eyes on it. India has less of a foreign outreach. I mean India has tremendous internal problems of its own. As I mentioned, a considerable majority of the population is in real trouble. India has some of the worst social statistics in the world. It's worse than southern Africa. Also, a large part of the country is in rebellion. Kashmir, the occupied part of India, is in rebellion. Indian forces have a horrible record of repression, torture, and killing. They claim now to have nuclear weapons with the yield of those of the major superpowers, which is very dangerous. They're toying with space militarization, which could be quite dangerous. A U.S.–Indian alliance is forming, which, in my view, is pretty ominous. You can see the shared interests in opposition to the rest of the world. Things are quite unhealthy. However, they don't have imperial outreach very much. I mean a very limited amount. So, sure, we have to pay attention to them because they're important powers, and they're certainly growing and will be even more significant in the future. But right now I don't think that they are a significant part of the global imperial system.

How about Russia?

Russia was a major industrial society. It's now becoming kind of a Third World society. It's got tremendous internal mineral and other resources like oil, and it has kind of been living off those resources. But the society is in pretty poor shape. It's got a big military, which it still maintains. Throughout modern history Russia has been essentially a Third World country with a huge military. Under the Czar, for example, it was an impoverished country we call now a Third World country, but has always had a big military force. It was semi-colonized by Western Europe. The French built railways and France culturally had a great influence on this country. In his novels, Tolstoy talks a lot about France.

If you don't mind, let's shift the discussion about the catastrophe that recently occurred in Haiti. Since the earthquake that partially destroyed Haiti, there's been a whole discourse of reconstruction. But we know behind this discourse, there is always a hidden neoliberal agenda by the West aiming to protect its economic and geo-political interests. So what is your take on the whole discourse of the reconstruction of Haiti?

It's painful to discuss. I mean it's just savage. For example, there was just a report about aid to Haiti by the Council on Hemispheric Affairs that just came out. A lot of aid was promised by many governments, but a tiny fraction of it came through. The United States made fairly substantial promises. I forget the percentage. A small percentage has been given to Haiti. Right now there is one very influential Republican Senator, Tom Coburn, sitting on the aid. He has refused to allow it to be released. This is a country that we have destroyed. It's now suffered a terrible catastrophe largely because of what we did to it. He's now sitting on the aid and says we can't give it to them. I don't even know how to describe that. You can't talk about agendas; it's just pure savagery, and it's not being discussed. I can't find anything about it in the newspapers.

Given what has been happening to Haiti, in terms of cruel attitude and actions of many American pundits toward Haiti, the country seems to be in a very hopeless situation. Is this a fair statement to make?

I don't think it's hopeless, but I think it's going to take a real awakening in the United States for people to know about this. I think if people knew about it they would be outraged. But who knows? If they take a poll in the streets, nobody will know. Take a poll in the faculty clubs, nobody will know.

As you know, the United States has destroyed Haiti with its neoliberal agenda and foreign policy. But Haiti has often been forced to turn to this country. This has become evident since the earthquake. Other countries like Venezuela wanted to help Haiti, but they were prevented from doing so by the U.S. imperial power. Should Haitians look for other alternatives?

They should look for whatever alternative there is. Take as an example the cholera epidemic, which has now been traced to the multinational forces. This is pretty ugly in itself. As soon as the cholera news spread, Cuban doctors immediately showed up to help. I mean it was some kind of reaction from the world but nothing like from Cuba. Can Haiti turn things around for the best? That's been true in the past. Cuban doctors have played a big role, but they can't turn to Cuba. Cuba is a poor country, and they have been attacked by the hemispheric superpower. So they can't do much. Venezuela has its own problems though it's a major oil producer. It's a potentially quite rich country but they can't play a basic role because the United States stands in the way. The Latin America community could if, for example, the Latin American and Caribbean union actually begins to function. They could be an alternative, but that's just something in progress. It's not really there. Haiti can't realistically turn to this union at this point. The traditional torturers of Haiti, France and the United States, are playing the same awful role they always have. Take, for example, France's role in destroying Haiti. It's grotesque. A lot of France's wealth historically comes from Haiti. When Haiti politely asked for some reparations for the huge debt, that is, the indemnity that France imposed on Haiti, it was dismissed with contempt. I was in Paris not long ago and talked about this, and nobody even cared. Basically, the rhetoric is that we can't start repaying debts to former colonies like Haiti. If we do, what are we going to do in Africa and all the places we've destroyed? Haiti is the problem, but not the superpowers that have destroyed it, kidnapped and kicked out the elected president, and so on. No concern whatsoever for the poor Haitians.

So the question becomes, what is the alternative if Haiti cannot turn to Latin American and Caribbean countries for help because they have their own socioeconomic and political problems to deal with, and the United States has refused to help this country it has in many ways impoverished? What do you think Haitians should do? Should they try to rely on themselves when in fact they don't have too many resources to do so?

It's not very easy. I mean they did have a chance after the 1990 election. It was a hopeful period but that lasted only seven months. After the 2000 election, they had a chance but it was crushed. They can try to build on the ground to the extent it is possible, setting up an agricultural cooperative to do some construction from the damage. They can reach out to other parts of the world, like for example Latin America or the United States, because they are in a very weak position. The country has been so destroyed that there are just very few options.

Do you mind going back to the new issue that we just touched upon? We know that neoliberalism has failed, grossly failed, in announced goals. So should we seek another solution? Specifically, should we try to come up with some kind of socialist agenda?

I don't know exactly know what you mean. We have never accepted neoliberalism, so it's not a matter of giving it up and turning to something else. The people who criticized it from the beginning don't have to give it up. We should think about other agendas, but we haven't been doing it all along. There are other forms of development that I think are much more positive and hopeful. And to the extent that we can do something, we should educate and help the population here in the United States to have an understanding of what has happened, why it's happened, and what should be done. But who are we? We're only a couple of people. I think we should try to encourage them to look more carefully at the facts. There's nothing else we can do. I mean I'm not going to tell an African leader you can't do this. You can say, "Look. Why don't you take a look at the record and see if you can draw some lessons from it?" But I think that's the most we can do.

You're one of the most prolific and prominent scholars that the world has produced. You have written over 100 books. Which one of your scholarly works are you most proud of?

I am proud that people like you are picking up the mantle and going on. I can't do it forever. So it's good to see you doing it. I don't know if I feel proud about it. I feel happy about it.

All of us on this earth will be gone someday. What would you like to be remembered for when your day comes?

There are things that impress me personally and by which I feel emotionally moved. This summer, I went to Southern Colombia to visit some remote and endangered agricultural villages, which are trying to protect themselves and their resources, both from military attack, which is constant, but also from the predatory attack of multinational mining corporations and the Colombian government, which is trying to privatize their water and so on and so forth. It was pretty inspiring to watch. I mean it happened to be a personal connection. They were dedicating a forest to the memory of my late wife. Which is the immediate reason I went down there. That was really a moving experience. These are the kind of things that stick with me. There are a lot of things like that around the world.

⁌ SIX ⁍

Market Democracy in a Neoliberal Order

Doctrines and Reality

Excerpted from the annual Davie Memorial Lecture delivered by Noam Chomsky at the University of Cape Town, South Africa, May 1997

I have been asked to speak on some aspect of academic or human freedom, an invitation that offers many choices. I will keep to some simple ones. Freedom without opportunity is a devil's gift, and the refusal to provide such opportunities is criminal. The fate of the more vulnerable offers a sharper measure of the distance from here to something that might be called "civilization." While I am speaking, 1,000 children will die from easily preventable disease, and almost twice that many women will die or suffer serious disability in pregnancy or childbirth for lack of simple remedies and care.[1] UNICEF estimates that to overcome such tragedies, and to ensure universal access to basic social services, would require a quarter of the annual military expenditures of the "developing countries," about 10% of U.S. military spending. It is against the background of such realities as these that any serious discussion of human freedom should proceed.

It is widely held that the cure for such profound social maladies is within reach. The hope is not without foundation. The past few years have seen the fall of brutal tyrannies, the growth of scientific understanding that offers great promise, and many other reasons to look forward to a brighter future. The discourse of the privileged is marked by confidence and triumphalism: the way forward is known, and there is no other. The basic theme, articulated with force and clarity, is that "America's victory in the Cold War was a victory for a set of political and economic principles: democracy and the free market." These principles are "the wave of the future—a future for which America is both the gatekeeper and the model." I am quoting the chief political commentator of *The New York Times*, but the picture is conventional, widely repeated throughout much of the world, and accepted as generally accurate even by critics. It was also enunciated as the "Clinton Doctrine," which declared that our new mission is to "consolidate the victory of democracy and open markets" that had just been won.

There remains a range of disagreement: at one extreme "Wilsonian idealists" urge continued dedication to the traditional mission of benevolence, and at the other, "realists" counter that we may lack the means to conduct these crusades of "global meliorism," and should not neglect our own interests in the service of others. Within this range lies the path to a better world.[2]

Reality seems to me rather different. The current spectrum of public policy debate has as little relevance to policy as its numerous antecedents: neither the United States nor any other power has been guided by "global meliorism." Democracy is under attack worldwide, including the leading industrial countries, at least, democracy in a meaningful sense of the term, involving opportunities for people to manage their own collective and individual affairs. Something similar is true of markets. The assaults on democracy and markets are furthermore related. Their roots lie in the power of corporate entities that are increasingly interlinked and reliant on powerful states, and largely unaccountable to the public. Their immense power is growing as a result of social policy that is globalizing the structural model of the Third World, with sectors of enormous wealth and privilege alongside an increase in "the proportion of those who will labor under all the hardships of life, and secretly sigh for a more equal distribution of its blessings," as the leading framer of American democracy, James Madison, predicted 200 years ago.[3] These policy choices are most evident in the Anglo-American societies, but extend worldwide. They cannot be attributed to what "the free market has decided, in its infinite but mysterious wisdom,"[4] "the implacable sweep of the 'market revolution,'" "Reaganesque rugged individualism," or a "new orthodoxy" that "gives the market full sway." On the contrary, state intervention plays a decisive role, as in the past, and the basic outlines of policy are hardly novel. Current versions reflect "capital's clear subjugation of labor" for more than 15 years, in the words of the business press,[5] which often accurately reports the perceptions of a highly class-conscious business community, dedicated to class war.

If these perceptions are valid, then the path to a world that is more just and more free lies well outside the range set forth by privilege and power. I cannot hope to establish such conclusions here, but only to suggest that they are credible enough to consider with care. And to suggest further that prevailing doctrines could hardly survive were it not for their contribution to "regimenting the public mind every bit as much as an army regiments the bodies of its soldiers," to quote again from Edward Bernays while presenting to the business world the lessons that had been learned from wartime propaganda.

Quite strikingly, in both of the world's leading democracies there was a growing awareness of the need to "apply the lessons" of the highly successful propaganda systems of World War I "to the organization of political warfare," as the chairman of the British Conservative Party put the matter 70 years ago. Wilsonian liberals in the United States, including public intellectuals and prominent figures in the developing profession of political science, drew the same conclusions in the same years. In another corner of Western civilization, Adolf Hitler vowed that next time Germany would not be defeated in the propaganda war, and he also devised his own ways to apply the lessons of Anglo-American propaganda to political warfare at home.[6]

Meanwhile the business world warned of "the hazard facing industrialists" in "the newly realized political power of the masses," and the need to wage and win "the everlasting battle for the minds of men" and "indoctrinate citizens with the capitalist story" until "they are able to play back the story with remarkable fidelity," and so on, in an impressive flow, accompanied by even more impressive efforts.[7]

To discover the true meaning of the "political and economic principles" that are declared to be "the wave of the future," it is of course necessary to go beyond rhetorical flourishes and public pronouncements and to investigate actual practice and the internal documentary record. Close examination of particular cases is the most rewarding path, but these must be chosen carefully to give a fair picture. There are some natural guidelines. One reasonable approach is to take the examples chosen by the proponents of the doctrines themselves, as their "strongest case." Another is to investigate the record where influence is greatest and interference least, so that we see the operative principles in their purest form. If we want to determine what the Kremlin meant by "democracy" and "human rights," we will pay little heed to *Pravda*'s solemn denunciations of racism in the United States or state terror in its client regimes, even less to protestation of noble motives. Far more instructive is the state of affairs in the "people's democracies" of Eastern Europe. The point is elementary, and applies to the self-designated "gatekeeper and model" as well. Latin America is the obvious testing ground, particularly the Central America–Caribbean region. Here Washington has faced few external challenges for almost a century, so the guiding principles of policy, and of today's neoliberal "Washington consensus," are revealed most clearly when we examine the state of the region, and how that came about.

It is of some interest that the exercise is rarely undertaken, and if proposed, castigated as extremist or worse. I leave it as an "exercise for the reader," merely noting that the record teaches useful lessons about the political and economic principles that are to be "the wave of the future."

Washington's "crusade for democracy," as it is called, was waged with particular fervor during the Reagan years, with Latin America serving as the chosen terrain. The results are commonly offered as a prime illustration of how the United States became "the inspiration for the triumph of democracy in our time," to quote the editors of a leading intellectual journal of American liberalism.[8] The most recent scholarly study of democracy describes "the revival of democracy in Latin America" as "impressive" but not unproblematic; the "barriers to implementation" remain "formidable," but can perhaps be overcome through closer interrogation with the United States. The author, Sanford Lakoff, singles out the "historic North American Free Trade Agreement (NAFTA)" as a potential instrument of democratization. In the region of traditional U.S. influence, he writes, the countries are moving toward democracy, having "survived military intervention" and "vicious civil war."[9]

Let us begin by looking more closely at these recent cases, the natural ones given overwhelming U.S. influence, and the ones regularly selected to illustrate the achievement and promise of "America's mission."

The primary "barriers to implementation" of democracy, Lakoff suggests, are efforts to protect "domestic markets"—that is, to prevent foreign (mainly U.S.) corporations from gaining even greater control over the society. We are to understand, then, that democracy is enhanced as significant decision making shifts ever more into the hands of unaccountable private tyrannies, mostly foreign-based. Meanwhile the public arena is to shrink still further as the state is "minimized" in accordance with the neoliberal "political and economic principles" that have emerged triumphant. A study of the World Bank points out that the new orthodoxy represents "a dramatic shift away from a pluralist, participatory ideal of politics and toward an authoritarian and technocratic ideal...," one that is very much in accord with leading elements of twentieth century liberal and progressive thought, and in another variant, the Leninist model; the two are more similar than often recognized.[10]

Thinking through the background, we gain some useful insight into the concepts of democracy and markets, in the operative sense.

Lakoff does not look into the "revival of democracy" in Latin America, but he does cite a scholarly source that includes a contribution on Washington's crusade in the 1980s. The author is Thomas Carothers, who combines scholarship with an "insider's perspective," having worked on "democracy enhancement" programs in Reagan's State Department.[11] Carothers regards Washington's "impulse to promote democracy" as "sincere," but largely a failure. Furthermore, the failure was systematic: where Washington's influence was least, in South America, there was real progress toward democracy, which the Reagan administration generally opposed, later taking credit for it when the process proved irresistible. Where Washington's influence was greatest, progress was least, and where it occurred, the U.S. role was marginal or negative. His general conclusion is that the U.S. sought to maintain "the basic order of...quite undemocratic societies" and to avoid "populist-based change," "inevitably [seeking] only limited, top-down forms of democratic change that did not risk upsetting the traditional structures of power with which the United States has long been allied."

The last clause requires a gloss. The term "United States" is conventionally used to refer to structures of power within the United States; the "national interest" is the interest of these groups, which correlates only weakly with interests of the general population. So the conclusion is that Washington sought top-down forms of democracy that did not upset traditional structures of power with which the structures of power in the United States have long been allied. Not a very surprising fact, or much of a historical novelty.

Within the United States itself, "top-down democracy" is firmly rooted in the Constitutional system.[12] One may argue, as some historians do, that these principles lost their force as the national territory was conquered and settled. Whatever one's assessment of those years, by the late nineteenth century the founding doctrines took on a new and much more oppressive form. When James Madison spoke of "rights of persons," he meant humans. But the growth of the industrial economy, and the rise of corporate forms of economic enterprise, led to a completely new meaning of the term. In a current official document, "'Person' is broadly defined to include any individual, branch, partnership, associated group, association, estate, trust, corporation or other organization (whether or not organized under the laws of any State), or any government entity,"[13] a concept that doubtless would have shocked Madison and others with intellectual roots in the Enlightenment and classical liberalism.

These radical changes in the conception of human rights and democracy were introduced primarily not by legislation but by judicial decisions and intellectual commentary. Corporations, which previously had been considered artificial entities with no rights, were accorded all the rights of persons, and far more, since they are "immortal persons," and "persons" of extraordinary wealth and power. Furthermore, they were no longer bound to the specific purposes designated by State charter but could act as they chose, with few constraints.[14]

Conservative legal scholars bitterly opposed these innovations, recognizing that they undermine the traditional idea that rights inhere in individuals, and undermine market principles as well. But the new forms of authoritarian rule were institutionalized, and along with them the legitimation of wage labor, which was considered hardly better than slavery in mainstream American thought through much of the nineteenth century, not only by the rising labor movement but also by such figures as Abraham Lincoln, the Republican Party, and the establishment media.[15]

These are topics with enormous implication for understanding the nature of market democracy. Again, I can only mention them here. The material and ideological outcome helps explain the understanding that "democracy" abroad must reflect the model sought at home: "top-down" forms of control, with the public kept to a "spectator" role, not participating in the arena of decision making, which must exclude these "ignorant and meddlesome outsiders," according to the mainstream of modern democratic theory. But the general ideas are standard and have solid roots in the constitutional tradition, radically modified, however, in the new era of "collectivist legal entities."

Returning to the "victory of democracy" under U.S. guidance, neither Lakoff nor Carothers asks how Washington maintained the traditional power structure of highly undemocratic societies. Their topic is the terrorist wars that left tens of thousands of tortured and mutilated corpses, millions of refugees, and devastation perhaps beyond recovery—in large measure wars against the Church, which became an enemy when it adopted "the preferential option for the poor," trying to help suffering people to attain some measure of justice and democratic rights. It is more than symbolic that the terrible decade of the 1980s opened with the murder of an archbishop who had become "a voice for the voiceless," and closed with the assassination of six leading Jesuit intellectuals who had chosen the same path, in each case by terrorist forces armed and trained by the victors of the "crusade for democracy." One should take careful note of the fact that the leading Central American dissident intellectuals were doubly assassinated: both murdered and silenced. Their words, indeed their very existence, are scarcely known in the United States, unlike dissidents in enemy states, who are greatly honored and admired.

Such matters do not enter history as recounted by the victors. In Lakoff's study, which is not untypical in their regard, what survives are references to "military intervention" and "civil wars," with no external factor identified. These matters will not so quickly be put aside, however, by those who seek a better grasp of the principles that are to shape the future, if the structures of power have their way.

Particularly revealing is Lakoff's description of Nicaragua, again standard: "A civil war was ended following a democratic election, and a difficult effort is underway to create a more prosperous and self-governing society." In the real world, the superpower attacking Nicaragua escalated its assault *after* the country's first democratic election. The election of 1984 was closely monitored and recognized as legitimate by the professional association of Latin American scholars (LASA), Irish and British parliamentary delegations, and others, including a hostile Dutch government delegation that was remarkably supportive of Reaganite atrocities. The leading figure of Central American democracy, José Figueres of Costa Rica, also a critical observer, nevertheless regarded the elections as legitimate in this "invaded country," calling on Washington to allow the Sandinistas "to finish what they started in peace; they deserve it." The United States strongly opposed the holding of the elections and sought to undermine them, concerned that democratic elections might interfere with its terrorist war. But that concern was put to rest by the good behavior of the doctrinal system, which barred the reports with remarkable efficiency, reflexively adopting the state propaganda line that the elections were meaningless fraud.[16]

Overlooked as well is the fact that as the next election approached on schedule,[17] Washington left no doubt that unless the results came out the right way, Nicaragua would continue to endure the illegal economic warfare and "unlawful use of force" that the World Court had condemned and ordered terminated, of course in vain. This time the outcome was acceptable, and hailed in the United States with an outburst of exuberance that is highly informative.[18]

At the outer limits of critical independence, columnist Anthony Lewis of *The New York Times* was overcome with admiration for Washington's "experiment in peace and democracy," which showed that "we live in a romantic age." The experimental methods were no secret. Thus *Time* magazine, joining in the celebration as "democracy burst forth" in Nicaragua, outlined them frankly: to "wreck the economy and prosecute a long and deadly proxy war until the exhausted natives overthrow the unwanted government themselves," with a cost to us that is "minimal," leaving the victim "with wrecked bridges, sabotaged power stations, and ruined farms," and providing Washington's candidate with "a winning issue," ending the "impoverishment of the people of Nicaragua," not to speak of the continuing terror, better left unmentioned. To be sure, the cost to *them* was hardly "minimal": Carothers notes that the toll "in per capita terms was significantly higher than the number of U.S. persons killed in the U.S. Civil War and all the wars of the twentieth century *combined*."[19] The outcome was a "Victory for U.S. Fair Play," a headline in *The New York Times* exulted, leaving Americans "United in Joy," in the style of Albania and North Korea.

The methods of this "romantic age," and the reaction to them in enlightened circles, tell us more about the democratic principles that have emerged victorious. They also shed some light on why it is such a "difficult effort" to "create a more prosperous and self-governing society" in Nicaragua. It is true that the effort is now underway, and is meeting with some success for a privileged minority, while most of the population faces social and economic disaster, all in the familiar pattern of Western dependencies.[20] Note that it is this example that led the *New Republic* editors to laud themselves as "the inspiration for the triumph of democracy in our time," joining the enthusiastic chorus.

We learn more about the victorious principles by recalling that these same representative figures of liberal intellectual life had urged that Washington's wars must be waged mercilessly, with military support for "Latin-style fascists...regardless of how many are murdered," because "there are higher American priorities than Salvadoran human rights." Elaborating, *New Republic* editor Michael Kinsley, who represented the left in mainstream commentary and television debate, cautioned against unthinking criticism of Washington's official policy of attacking undefended civilian targets. Such international terrorist operations cause "vast civilian suffering," he acknowledged, but they may be "perfectly legitimate" if "cost-benefit analysis" shows that "the amount of blood and misery that will be poured in" yields "democracy," as the world rulers define it. Enlightened opinions insist that terror is not a value in itself, but must meet the pragmatic criterion. Kinsley later observed that the desired ends had been achieved: "Impoverishing the people of Nicaragua was precisely the point of the contra war and the parallel policy of economic embargo and veto of international development loans," which "wreck[ed] the economy" and "creat[ed] the economic disaster [that] was probably the victorious opposition's best election issue." He then joined in welcoming the "triumph of democracy" in the "free election" of 1990.[21]

Client states enjoy similar privileges. Thus, commenting on yet another of Israel's attacks on Lebanon, foreign editor H.D.S. Greenway of the *Boston Globe*, who had graphically reported the first major invasion 15 years earlier, commented that "if shelling Lebanese villages, even at the cost of lives, and driving civilian refugees north would secure Israel's border, weaken Hezbollah, and promote peace, I would say go to it, as would many Arabs and Israelis. But history has not been kind to Israeli adventures in Lebanon. They have solved very little and have almost always caused more problems." By the pragmatic criterion, then, the murder of many civilians, expulsion of hundreds of thousands of refugees, and devastation of southern Lebanon is a dubious proposition.[22]

Bear in mind that I am keeping to the dissident sector of tolerable opinion, what is called "the left," a fact that tells us more about the victorious principles and the intellectual culture within which they find their place.

Also revealing was the reaction to periodic Reagan administration allegations of Nicaraguan plans to obtain jet interceptors from the Soviet Union (the United States having coerced its allies into refusing to sell them). Hawks demanded that Nicaragua be bombed at once. Doves countered that the charges must first be verified, but if they were, the United States would have to bomb Nicaragua. Sane observers understood why Nicaragua might want jet interceptors: to protect its territory from the CIA over flights that were supplying the U.S. proxy forces and providing them with up-to-the-minute information so that they could follow the directive to attack undefended "soft targets." The tacit assumption is that no country has a right to defend civilians from U.S. attack, a doctrine that reigned virtually unchallenged in the mainstream.

The pretext for Washington's terrorist wars was self-defense, the standard official justification for just about any monstrous act, even the Nazi Holocaust. Indeed Ronald Reagan, finding "that the politics and actions of the government of Nicaragua constitute an unusual and extraordinary threat to the national security and foreign policy of the United States," declared "a national emergency to deal with that threat," arousing no ridicule.[23] By similar logic, the USSR had every right to attack Denmark, a far greater threat to its security, and surely Poland and Hungary when they took steps toward independence. The fact that such pleas can regularly be put forth is again an interesting comment on the intellectual culture of the victors, and another indication of what lies ahead.

Let us move on to NAFTA, the "historic" agreement that may help to advance U.S.-style democracy in Mexico, Lakoff suggests. A closer look is again informative. The NAFTA agreement was rammed through Congress over strenuous popular opposition but with overwhelming support from the business world and the media, which were full of joyous promises of benefits for all concerned, also confidentiality predicted by the U.S. International Trade Commission and leading economists equipped with the most up-to-date models (which had just failed miserably to predict the deleterious consequences of the U.S.–Canada Free Trade Agreement, but were somehow going to work in this case). Completely suppressed was the careful analysis by the Office of Technology Assessment (OTA; the research bureau of Congress), which concluded that the planned version of NAFTA would harm most of the population of North America, proposing modifications that could render the agreement beneficial beyond small circles of investment and finance. Still more instructive was the suppression of the official position of the U.S. labor movement, presented in a similar analysis. Meanwhile labor was bitterly condemned for its "backward, unenlightened" perspective and "crude threatening tactics," motivated by "fear of change and fear of foreigners"; I am again sampling only from the far left of the spectrum, in this case, Anthony Lewis. The charges were demonstrably false, but they were the only word that reached the public in this inspiring exercise of democracy. Further details are most illuminating, and reviewed in the dissident literature at the time and since, but kept from the public eye, and unlikely to enter approved history.[24]

By now, the tales about the wonders of NAFTA have quietly been shelved, as the facts have been coming in. One hears no more about the hundreds of thousands of new jobs and other great benefits in store for the people of the three countries. These good tidings have been replaced by the "distinctly benign economic viewpoint"—the "experts' view"—that NAFTA had *no* significant effects. *The Wall Street Journal* reports that "administration officials feel frustrated by their inability to convince voters that the threat doesn't hurt them" and that job loss is "much less than predicted by Ross Perot," who was allowed into mainstream discussion (unlike the OTA, the labor movement, economists who strayed from the party line, and of course dissident analysts) because his claims were sometimes extreme and easily ridiculed. Quoting the sad observation of an administration official, the *Journal* reports further that "'It's hard to fight the critics' by telling the truth—that the trade pact 'hasn't really done anything.'" Forgotten is what "the truth" was going to be when the impressive exercise in democracy was roaring full steam ahead.[25]

While the experts have downgraded NAFTA to "no significant effects," dispatching the earlier "experts' view" to the memory hole, a less than "distinctly benign economic viewpoint" comes into focus if the "national interest" is widened in scope to include the general population. Testifying before the Senate Banking Committee in February 1997, Federal Reserve Board Chair Alan Greenspan was highly optimistic about "sustainable economic expansion" thanks to "atypical restraint on compensation increases [which] appears to be mainly the consequence of greater worker insecurity"—an obvious desideratum for a just society. The February 1997 Economic Report of the President, taking pride in the administration's achievements, refers more obliquely to "changes in labor market institutions and practices" as a factor in the "significant wage restraint" that bolsters the health of the economy.

One reason for these benign changes is spelled out in a study commissioned by the NAFTA Labor Secretariat "on the effects of the sudden closing of the plant on the principle of freedom of association and the right of workers to organize in the three countries." The study was carried out under NAFTA rules in response to a complaint by telecommunications workers on illegal labor practices by Sprint. The complaint was upheld by the U.S. National Labor Relations Board, which ordered trivial penalties after years of delay, the standard procedure. The NAFTA study, by Cornell University Labor economist Kate Bronfenbrenner, was authorized for release by Canada and Mexico, but delayed by the Clinton administration. It reveals a significant impact of NAFTA on strikebreaking. About half of union organizing efforts are disrupted by employer threats to transfer production abroad; for example, by placing signs reading "Mexico Transfer Job" in front of a plant where there is an organizing drive. The threats are not idle: when such organizing drives nevertheless succeed, employers close the plant in whole or in part at triple the pre-NAFTA rate (about 15% of the time). Plant-closing threats are almost twice as high in more mobile industries (e.g., manufacturing vs. construction).

These and other practices reported in the study are illegal, but that is a technicality, on a par with violations of international law and trade agreements when outcomes are unacceptable. The Reagan administration had made it clear to the business world that their illegal anti-union activities would not be hampered by the criminal state, and successors have kept to this stand. There has been a substantial effect on destruction of unions—or in more polite words, "changes in labor market institutions and practices" that contribute to "significant wage restraint" within an economic model offered with great pride to a backward world that has not yet grasped the victorious principles that are to lead the way to freedom and justice.[26]

What was stressed outside the mainstream about the goals of NAFTA is also now quietly conceded: the real goal was to "lock Mexico in" to the "reforms" that had made it an "economic miracle," in the technical sense of this term: a "miracle" for U.S. investors and Mexican rich, while the population sank into misery. The Clinton administration "forgot that the underlying purpose of NAFTA was not to promote trade but to cement Mexico's economic reforms," *Newsweek* correspondent Marc Levinson loftily declares, failing only to add that the contrary was loudly proclaimed to ensure the passage of NAFTA while critics who pointed out this "underlying purpose" were largely excluded from the free market of ideas by its owners.

Perhaps someday the likely reasons will be conceded too. "Locking Mexico in" to these reforms, it was hoped, would deflect the danger detected by a Latin America Strategy Development Workshop in Washington in September 1990. It concluded that relations with the brutal Mexican dictatorship were fine, though there was a potential problem: "a 'democracy opening' in Mexico could test the special relationship by bringing into office a government more interested in challenging the U.S. on economic and nationalist grounds"—no longer a serious problem now that Mexico is "locked into the reforms" by treaty. The U.S. has the power to disregard treaty obligations at will, not Mexico.[27]

In brief, the threat is democracy, at home and abroad, as the chosen example again illustrates. Democracy is permissible, even welcome, but again, as judged by outcome, not process. NAFTA was considered to be an effective device to diminish the threat of democracy. It was implemented at home by effective subversion of the democratic process, and in Mexico by force, over substantial but vain public protest.[28] The results are now presented as a hopeful instrument to bring American-style democracy to benighted Mexicans. A cynical observer aware of the facts might agree.

Once again, the chosen illustrations of the triumph of democracy are natural ones, and are interesting and revealing as well, though not quite in the intended manner.

The announcement of the Clinton Doctrine was accompanied by a prize example to illustrate the victorious principles: the administration's achievement in Haiti. Since this is again offered as the strongest case, it is appropriate to look at it.

True, Haiti's elected president was allowed to return, but only after the popular organizations had been subjected to three years of terror by forces that retained close connections to Washington throughout; the Clinton administration still refuses to turn over to Haiti 160,000 pages of documents on state terror seized by U.S. military forces—"to avoid embarrassing revelations" about U.S. government involvement with the coup regime, according to Human Rights Watch.[29] It was also necessary to put President Aristide through "a crash course in democracy and capitalism," as his leading supporter in Washington described the process of civilizing the troublesome priest.

The device is not unknown elsewhere, as an unwelcome transition to formal democracy is contemplated.

As a condition on his return, Aristide was compelled to accept an economic program that directs the policies of the Haitian government to the needs of "Civil Society, especially the private sector, both national and foreign": U.S. investors are designated to be the core of Haitian civil society, along with wealthy Haitians who back the military coup, but not the Haitian peasants and slum dwellers who organized a civil society so lively and vibrant that they were even able to elect their own president against overwhelming odds, eliciting instant U.S. hostility and efforts to subvert Haiti's first democratic regime.[30]

The unacceptable acts of the "ignorant and meddlesome outsiders" in Haiti were reversed by violence, with direct U.S. complicity, not only through contracts with the state terrorists in charge. The Organization of American States declared an embargo. The Bush and Clinton administrations undermined it from the start by exempting U.S. firms, and also by secretly authorizing the Texaco Oil Company to supply the coup regime and its wealthy supporters in violation of the official sanctions, a crucial fact that was prominently revealed the day before U.S. troops landed to "restore democracy,"[31] but has yet to reach the public, and is another unlikely candidate for the historical record.

Now democracy has been restored. The new government has been forced to abandon the democratic and reformist programs that scandalized Washington, and to follow the policies of Washington's candidate in the 1990 election, in which he received 14% of the vote.

The background of this triumph provides no little insight into the "political and economic principles" that are to lead us to a glorious future. Haiti was one of the world's richest colonial prizes (along with Bengal) and the source of a good part of France's wealth. It has been largely under U.S. control and tutelage since Wilson's Marines invaded 80 years ago. By now the country is such a catastrophe that it may scarcely be habitable in the not-too-distant future. In 1981 a USAID-World Bank development strategy was initiated, based on assembly plants and agroexport, shifting land from food for local consumption. USAID forecast "a historic change toward deeper market interdependence with the United States" in what would become "the Taiwan of the Caribbean." The World Bank concurred, offering the usual prescriptions for "expansion of private enterprises" and minimization of "social objectives," thus increasing inequality and poverty and reducing health and educational levels. It may be noted, for what it is worth, that these standard prescriptions are offered side by side with sermons on the need to reduce inequality and poverty and improve health and education levels. In the Haitian case, the consequences were the usual ones: profits for U.S. manufacturers and the Haitian super-rich, and a decline of 56% in Haitian wages through the 1980s—in short, an "economic miracle." Haiti remained Haiti, not Taiwan, which had followed a radically different course, as advisors must surely know.

It was the effort of Haiti's first democratic government to alleviate the growing disaster that called forth Washington's hostility and the military coup and terror that followed. With "democracy restored," USAID is withholding aid to ensure that cement and flourmills are privatized for the benefit of wealthy Haitians and foreign investors (Haitian "Civil Society," according to the orders that accompanied the restoration of democracy), while barring expenditures for health and education. Agribusiness receives ample funding, but no resources are made available for peasant agriculture and handicrafts, which provide the income of the overwhelming majority of the population. Foreign-owned assembly plants that employ workers (mostly women) at well below subsistence pay under horrendous working conditions benefit from cheap electricity, subsidized by the generous supervisor. But for the Haitian poor—the general population—there can be no subsidies for electricity, fuel, water, or food; these are prohibited by IMF rules on the principled grounds that they constitute "price control."

Before the "reforms" were instituted, local rice production supplied virtually all domestic needs, with important linkages to the domestic economy. Thanks to one-sided "liberalization," it now provides only 50%, with the predictable effects on the economy. Haiti must "reform," eliminating tariffs in accord with the stern principles of economic science—which, by some miracle of logic, exempt U.S. agribusiness; it continues to receive huge public subsidies, increased by the Reagan administration to the point where they provided 40% of growers' incomes by 1987. The natural consequences are understood: a 1995 USAID report observes that the "export-driven trade and investment policy" that Washington mandates will "relentlessly squeeze the domestic rice farmer," who will be forced to turn to the more rational pursuit of agroexport for the benefit of U.S. investors, in accord with the principles of rational expectations theory.[32]

By such methods, the most impoverished country in the hemisphere has been turned into a leading purchaser of U.S.-produced rice, enriching publicly-subsidized U.S. enterprises. Those lucky enough to have received a good Western education can doubtless explain that the benefits will trickle down to Haitian peasants and slum dwellers—ultimately.

The prize example tells us more about the meaning and implications of the victory for "democracy and open markets."

Haitians seem to understand the lessons, even if doctrinal managers in the West prefer a different picture. Parliamentary elections in April 1997 brought forth "a dismal 5 percent" of voters, the press reported, thus raising the question, "Did Haiti Fail U.S. Hope?"[33] We have sacrificed so much to bring them democracy, but they are ungrateful and unworthy. One can see why "realists" urge that we stay aloof from crusades of "global meliorism."

Similar attitudes hold throughout the hemisphere. Polls show that in Central America, politics elicits "boredom," "distrust," and "indifference" in proportions far outdistancing "interest" or "enthusiasm" among "an apathetic public...which feels itself a spectator in its democratic system" and has "general pessimism about the future." The first Latin America survey, sponsored by the EU, found much the same: "the survey's most alarming message," the Brazilian coordinator commented, was "the popular perception that only the elite had benefited from the transition to democracy."[34] Latin American scholars observe that the recent wave of democratization coincided with neoliberal economic reforms, which have been harmful for most people, leading to a cynical appraisal of formal democratic procedures. The introduction of similar programs in the richest country in the world has had similar effects, as already discussed.

Let us return to the prevailing doctrine that "America's victory in the Cold War" was a victory for democracy and the free market. With regard to democracy, the doctrine is partially true, though we have to understand what is meant by "democracy": top-down control "to protect the minority of the opulent against the majority." What about the free market? Here too, we find that doctrine is far removed from reality, as the example of Haiti once again illustrates.

Consider again the case of NAFTA, an agreement intended to lock Mexico into an economic discipline that protects investors from the danger of a "democracy opening." It is not a "free trade agreement." Rather, it is highly protectionist, designed to impede East Asian and European competitors. Furthermore, it shares with the global agreements such anti-market principles as "intellectual property rights" restrictions of an extreme sort that rich societies never accepted during their period of development, but that they now intend to use to protect home-based corporations: to destroy the pharmaceutical industry in poorer countries, for example—and, incidentally, to block technological innovations, such as improved production processes for patented products allowed under the traditional patent regime. Progress is no more a desideratum than markets, unless it yields benefits for those who count.

There are also questions about the nature of "trade." Over half of U.S. trade with Mexico is reported to consist of intrafirm transactions, up about 15% since NAFTA. Already a decade ago, mostly U.S.-owned plants in northern Mexico, employing few workers and with virtually no linkages to the Mexican economy, produced more than 33% of the engine blocks used in U.S. cars, and 75% of other essential components. The post-NAFTA collapse of the Mexican economy in 1994, exempting only the very rich and U.S. investors (protected by U.S. government bailouts), led to an increase of U.S.–Mexico trade as the new crisis, driving the population to still deeper misery, "transformed Mexico into a cheap [i.e., even cheaper] source of manufactured goods, with industrial wages one-tenth of those in the U.S.," the business press reports. According to some specialists, half of U.S.

trade worldwide consists of such centrally managed transactions, and much the same is true of other industrial powers,[35] though one must treat with caution conclusions about institutions with limited public accountability. Some economists have plausibly described the world system as one of "corporate mercantilism," remote from the ideal of free trade. The OECD concludes that "oligopolistic competition and strategic interaction among firms and governments rather than the invisible hand of market forces condition today's competitive advantage and international division of labor in high-technology industries,"[36] implicitly adopting a similar view.

Even the basic structure of the domestic economy violates the neoliberal principles that are hailed. The main theme of the standard work on U.S. business history is that "modern business enterprise took the place of market mechanisms in coordinating the activities of the economy and allocating its resources," handling many transactions internally, another large departure from market principles.[37] There are many others. Consider, for example, the fate of Adam Smith's principle that the free movement of people—across borders, for example—is an essential component of free trade. When we move on to the world of transnational corporations, with strategic alliances and critical support from powerful states, the gap between doctrine and reality becomes substantial.

Public statements have to be interpreted in the light of these realities, among them Clinton's call for trade-not-aid for Africa, with a series of provisions that just happen to benefit U.S. investors and uplifting rhetoric that manages to avoid such matters as the long record of such approaches and the fact that the United States already had the most miserly aid program of any developed country even before the grand innovations. Or to take the obvious model, consider Chester Crocker's outline of Reagan administration plans for Africa in 1981: "We support open market opportunities, access to key resources, and expanding African and American economies," he said, and want to bring African countries "into the mainstream of the free market economy." The statement may seem to surpass cynicism, coming from the leaders of the "sustained assault" against the "free market economy."[38] But Crocker's rendition is fair enough, when it is passed through the prism of really existing market doctrine. The market opportunities and access to resources are for foreign investors and their local associates, and the economies are to expand in a specific way, protecting "the minority of the opulent against the majority." The opulent, meanwhile, merit state protection and public subsidy. How else can they flourish, for the benefit of all?

Of course, the United States is not alone in its conceptions of "free trade," even if its ideologies often lead the cynical chorus. The gap between rich and poor countries from 1960 is substantially attributable to protectionist measures of the rich, a UN development report concluded in 1992. The 1992 report concluded that "the industrial countries, by violating the principles of free trade, are costing the developing countries an estimated $50 billion a year—nearly equal to the total flow of foreign assistance"—much of it publicly subsidized export promotion.[39] The 1996 *Global Report* of the UN Industrial Development Organization estimates the disparity between the richest and poorest 20% of the world population increased by over 50% from 1960 to 1989, and predicts "growing world inequality resulting from the globalization process." That growing disparity holds within the rich societies as well, the United States leading the way, Britain not far behind. The business press exults in "spectacular" and "stunning" profit growth, applauding the extraordinary concentration of wealth among the top few percent of the population, while for the majority, conditions continue to stagnate or decline.

The corporate media, the Clinton administration, and the cheerleaders for the American Way proudly offer themselves as a model for the rest of the world; buried in the chorus of self-acclaim are the results of deliberate social policy of recent years, for example, the "basic indicators" just published by UNICEF,[40] revealing that the United States has the worst record among the industrial countries, ranking alongside Cuba—a poor Third World country under unremitting attack by the hemispheric superpower for almost 40 years—by such standards as mortality for children under 5. It also holds records for hunger, child poverty, and other basic social indicators.

All of this takes place in the richest country in the world, with unparalleled advantages and stable democratic institutions, but also under business rule, to an unusual extent. These are further auguries for the future, if the "dramatic shift away from a pluralist, participatory ideal of politics and toward an authoritarian and technocratic ideal" proceeds on course, worldwide.

It is worth noting that in secret, intentions are often spelled out honestly. For example, in the early post-World War II period, George Kennan, one of the most influential planners and considered a leading humanist, assigned each sector of the world its "function": Africa's function was to be "exploited" by Europe for its reconstruction, he observed, the United States having little interest in it. A year earlier, a high-level planning study had urged "that cooperative development of the cheap foodstuffs and raw material of northern Africa could help forge European unity and create an economic base for continental recovery," an interesting concept of "cooperation."[41] There is no record of suggestion that Africa might "exploit" the West for its recovery from the "global meliorism" of the past centuries.

In this review, I have tried to follow a reasonable methodological principle: to evaluate the praise for the "political and economic principles" of the world's dominant power by keeping primarily to illustrations selected by the advocates themselves, as their strongest cases. The review is brief and partial, and deals with matters that are obscure and not well understood. My own judgment, for what it is worth, is that the sample is fair enough, and that it yields a sobering picture of the operative principles as well as the likely "wave of the future" if they prevail unchallenged.

Even if accurate, the picture is seriously misleading, precisely because it is so partial: missing entirely are the achievements of those who really are committed to the fine principles proclaimed, and to principles of justice and freedom that reach far beyond. This is primarily a record of popular struggle seeking to erode and dismantle forms of oppression and domination, which sometimes are all too apparent but are often so deeply entrenched as to be virtually invisible, even to their victims. The record is rich and encouraging, and we have every reason to suppose that it can be carried forward. To do so requires a realistic assessment of existing circumstances and their historical origins, but that is of course only a bare beginning.

Skeptics who dismiss such hopes as utopian and naïve have only to cast their eyes on what has happened right here in South Africa in the last few years, a tribute to what the human spirit can accomplish, and its limitless prospects. The lessons of these remarkable achievements should be an inspiration to people everywhere, and should guide the next steps in the continuing struggle here too, as the people of South Africa, fresh from one great victory, turn to the still more difficult challenges that lie ahead.

Notes

1. UNICEF, *The State of the World's Children 1997* (Oxford: Oxford University Press, 1997); UNICEF, *The Progress of Nations 1996* (New York: UNICEF House, 1996).
2. Thomas Friedman, *The New York Times*, June 2, 1992; National Security Advisor Anthony Lake, *The New York Times*, September 26, 1993; historian David Fromkin, *New York Times Book Review*, May 4, 1997, summarizing recent work.
3. On the general picture and its historical origins, see, inter alia, Frederic Clairmont's classic study, *The Rise and Fall of Economic Liberalism* (Asia Publishing House, 1960), reprinted and updated (Penang and Goa: Third World Network, 1996); and Michel Chossudovsky, *The Globalisation of Poverty* (Penang: Third World Network, 1997). Clairmont was an UNCTAD (United Nations Commission on Trade and Development) economist for many years; Chossudovsky is professor of economics at the University of Ottawa.
4. John Cassidy, *New Yorker*, October 16, 1995. The sample is liberal-to-left, in some cases quite critical. The analysis is similar across the rest of the spectrum, but generally euphoric.
5. John Liscio, *Barron's*, April 15, 1996.
6. Richard Cockett, "The Party, Publicity, and the Media," in Anthony Seldon and Stuart Ball, eds., *Conservative Century: The Conservative Party Since 1900* (Oxford: Oxford University Press, 1994); Harold Lasswel, "Propaganda," *Encyclopaedia of the Social Sciences*, Vol. 12 (New York: Macmillan, 1933). For quotes and discussion, see "Intellectuals and the State" (1977), reprinted in Noam Chomsky, *Towards a New Cold War* (New York: Pantheon, 1982). Also available at last is some of the pioneering work on these topics by Alex Carey, collected in his *Taking the Risk out of Democracy* (Sidney: University of New South Wales Press, 1995, and Urbana: University of Illinois Press, 1997).

7. Ibid., and Elizabeth Fones-Wolf, *Selling Free Enterprise: The Business Assault on Labor and Liberalism, 1945–1960* (Urbana: University of Illinois Press, 1995). Also Stuart Ewen, *A Social History of SPIN* (New York: Basic Books, 1996). On the broader context, see Noam Chomsky, "Intellectuals and the State" and "Force and Opinion," reprinted in *Deterring Democracy* (London: Verso, 1991).
8. Editorial, *New Republic*, March 19, 1990.
9. Sanford Lakoff, *Democracy: History, Theory, Practice* (Boulder, CO: Westview, 1996), 262ff.
10. J. Toye, J. Harrigan, and P. Mosley, *Aid and Power* (London: Routledge, 1991), Vol. 1, 16. On the Leninist comparison, see my essays cited in note 7 and *For Reasons of State* (New York: Pantheon, 1973), Introduction.
11. Carothers, "The Reagan Years," in Abraham Lowenthal, ed., *Exporting Democracy* (Baltimore: The Johns Hopkins University Press, 1991). See also his *In the Name of Democracy* (Berkeley: University of California Press, 1991).
12. See Chapter 2 [In Noam Chomsky, *Profit over People: Neoliberalism and Global Order* (New York: Seven Stories Press, 1999)] and for further discussion and sources, Noam Chomsky, *Powers and Prospects* (Boston: South End, 1996), "'Consent Without Consent': Reflections on the Theory and Practice of Democracy," *Cleveland State Law Review*, 44(4) (1996).
13. *Survey of Current Business*, U.S. Dept. of Commerce, Vol. 76, no. 12 (December 1966).
14. Morton Horwitz, *The Transformation of American Law, 1870–1960* (Harvard University Press, 1992), Chapter 3. See also Charles Sellers, *The Market Revolution* (Oxford University Press, 1991).
15. Michael Sandel, *Democracy's Discontent* (Cambridge, MA: Harvard University Press, 1996), Chapter 6. His interpretation in terms of republicanism and civic virtue is too narrow, in my opinion, overlooking deeper roots in the Enlightenment and before. For some discussion, see among others Noam Chomsky, *Problems of Knowledge and Freedom* (New York: Pantheon, 1971), Chapter 1; several essays reprinted in James Peck, ed., *The Chomsky Reader* (New York: Pantheon, 1987); and Noam Chomsky, *Powers and Prospects* (Boston: South End, 1996), Chapter 4.
16. For details, see Noam Chomsky, *Turning the Tide* (Boston: South End, 1985), Chapter 6.3; and Noam Chomsky, *The Culture of Terrorism* (Boston: South End, 1988), Chapter 11 (and sources cited), including quotes from Figueres, whose exclusion from the media took considerable dedication. See my *Letters from Lexington* (Monroe, ME: Common Courage, 1993), Chapter 6, on the record, including the long obituary in *The New York Times* by its Central America specialist and the effusive accompanying editorial, which again succeeded in completely banning his views on Washington's "crusade for democracy." On media coverage of Nicaraguan and Salvadoran elections, see Edward Herman and Noam Chomsky, *Manufacturing Consent* (New York: Pantheon, 1988), Chapter 3. Even Carothers, who is careful with the facts, writes that the Sandinistas "refused to agree to elections" until 1990 (in Lowenthal, *op. cit.*).
17. Another standard falsification is that the long-planned elections took place only because of Washington's military and economic pressures, which are therefore retroactively justified.
18. On the elections and the reaction in Latin America and the United States, including sources for what follows, see Noam Chomsky, *Deterring Democracy*, Chapter 10. For a detailed review of the very successful subversion of diplomacy, hailed generally as a triumph of diplomacy, see Noam Chomsky, *Culture of Terrorism*, Chapter 7; and Noam Chomsky, *Necessary Illusions* (Boston: South End, 1989) appendix IV.5.
19. His emphasis, in Lowenthal, *op. cit.*
20. For details, see, inter alia, Richard Garfield, "Desocializing Health Care in a Developing Country," *Journal of the American Medical Association*, 270(8), August 25, 1993; and Noam Chomsky, *World Orders, Old and New* (New York: Columbia University Press, 1994), 131ff.

21. Michael Kinsley, *The Wall Street Journal*, March 26, 1987; *New Republic*, editorials, April 2, 1984, and March 19, 1990. For more on these and many similar examples, see Noam Chomsky, *Culture of Terrorism*, Chapter 5; Chomsky, *Deterring Democracy*, Chapters 10, 12.
22. H.D.S. Greenway, *Boston Globe*, July 29, 1993.
23. *The New York Times*, May 2, 1985.
24. See *World Orders*, 131ff. On the predictions and the outcome, see economist Melvin Burke, "NAFTA Integration: Unproductive Finance and Real Unemployment," *Proceedings from the Eighth Annual Labor Segmentation Conference*, April 1995, sponsored by Notre Dame and Indiana Universities. Also *Social Dimensions of North American Economic Integrations*, report prepared for the Department of Human Resources Development by the Canadian Labour Congress, 1996. On World Bank predictions for Africa, see Cheryl Payer, *Lent and Lost* (Atlantic Highlands, NJ: Zed, 1991) and John Mihevc, *The Market Tells Them So: The World Bank and Economic Fundamentalism in Africa* (Atlantic Highlands, NJ: Zed, 1995), also reviewing the grim effects of consistent failure—grim for the population, that is, not for the bank's actual constituency. That the record of prediction is poor, and understanding meager, is well-known to professional economists. See, e.g., Paul Krugman, "Cycles of Conventional Wisdom on Economic Development," *Internal Affairs*, 71(4), October 1995. See 25ff., above.
25. Helene Cooper, "Experts' View of NAFTA's Economic Impact: It's a Wash," *The Wall Street Journal*, June 17, 1997.
26. Editorial, "Class War in the USA," *Multinational Monitor*, March 1997. K. Bronfenbrenner, "We'll Close!," ibid., based on the study she directed: "Final Report: The Effects of Plant Closing or Threat of Plant Closing on the Right of Workers to Organize." The massive impact of Reaganite criminality is detailed in a report in *Business Week*, "The Workplace: Why America Needs Unions, But Not the Kind It Has Now," May 23, 1994.
27. Levinson, *Foreign Affairs*, March/April 1996. Workshop, September 26 & 27, 1990, Minutes, 3.
28. See next chapter. In the United States and particularly Canada (where there was far more open discussion), the population remained largely opposed, polls indicated.
29. Kenneth Roth, Executive, HRW, Letter, *The New York Times*, April 12, 1997.
30. See Paul Farmer, *The Uses of Haiti* (Monroe, ME: Common Courage, 1994); Chomsky, *World Orders*, 62ff.; Noam Chomsky, "Democracy Restored," *Z*, November 1994; North American Congress on Latin America (NACLA), *Haiti: Dangerous Crossroads* (Boston: South End, 1995).
31. Noam Chomsky, "Democracy Restored," citing John Solomon, AP, September 18, 1994 (lead story).
32. See my *Year 501* (Boston: South End, 1993), Chapter 8, and sources cited; Farmer, *op. cit.*, *Labor Rights in Haiti*, International Labor Rights Education and Research Fund, April 1989; *Haiti After the Coup*, National Labor Committee Education Fund (New York), April 1993; Lisa McGowan, *Democracy Undermined, Economic Justice Denied: Structural Adjustment and the Aid Juggernaut in Haiti* (Washington, DC: Development Gap, January 1997).
33. Nick Madigan, "Democracy in Inaction: Did Haiti Fail U.S. Hope?" *Christian Science Monitor*, April 8, 1997; See AP, *Boston Globe*, April 8, 1997, for more on the elections.
34. John McPhaul, *Tico Times* (Costa Rica), April 11; May 2, 1997.
35. Vincent Cable, *Daedalus* (Spring 1995), citing UN *World Investment Report 1993* (which, however, gives quite different figures, noting also that "relatively little data are available," 164ff.) For more detailed discussion, estimating intra-TNC trade at 40%, see Pete Cowhey and Jonathan Aronson, *Managing the World Economy* (New York: Council on Foreign Relations, 1993). On U.S.–Mexico, see David Barkin and Fred Rosen, "Why the Recovery Is Not a Recovery," *NACLA Report on the Americas*, January/February 1997; Leslie Crawford, "Legacy

of Shock Therapy," *Financial Times*, February 12, 1997 (subtitled "Mexico: A Healthier Outlook," the article reviews the increasing misery of the vast majority of the population, apart from "the very rich"). Post-NAFTA intrafirm transactions: William Grieder, *One World, Ready or Not* (New York: Simon & Schuster, 1997), 273, citing Mexican economist Carlos Heredia. Pre-NAFTA estimates intrafirm U.S. exports never entering Mexican markets passed 50%. Senator Ernest Hollings, *Foreign Policy*, Winter 1993–1994.

36. 1992 OECD study cited by Clinton's former chief economic advisor Laura Tyson in *Who's Bashing Whom?* (Washington, DC: Institute for International Economics, 1992).
37. Alfred Chandler, *The Visible Hand* (Cambridge, MA: Belknap Press, 1977).
38. Speech delivered by C.A. Crocker, Assistant Secretary of State for African Affairs, in Honolulu before the National Security Committee of the American Legion, August 1981. Cited by Hans Abrahamsson, *Hegemony, Region and Nation State: The Case of Mozambique* (Padrigu Peace and Development Research Institute, Gothenburg University, January 1996).
39. For discussion, see Eric Toussaint and Peter Drucker, eds., *IMF/World Bank/WTO, Notebooks for Study and Research* (Amsterdam: International Institute for Research and Education, 1995), 24/5.
40. UNICEF, *State of the World's Children 1997*.
41. George Kennan, PPS 23, February 24, 1948 (*Foreign Relations of the United States*, Vol. 1, 1948), 511. Michael Hogan, *The Marshall Plan* (Cambridge: Cambridge University Press, 1987), 41, paraphrasing the May 1947 Bonesteel Memorandum.

SEVEN

Third World Countries Under Western Siege

Noam Chomsky and Pierre Orelus in Dialogue

Context of the Dialogue

The dialogue that follows took place on March 18, 2005, at Noam Chomsky's office at the Massachusetts Institute of Technology. While writing some essays on the impact of globalization, imperialism, and the legacy of colonization on Third World countries, including Haiti, I felt that, besides my lived experience with and information excerpted from books about these issues, it was imperative that I have insights from critical theorists who have a keen understanding of how colonization, globalization, and Western imperialism have negatively impacted these countries' economic, political, and educational systems. To this end, I decided that I would interview Professor Chomsky who, throughout his scholarly and human rights activist work, has brilliantly unmasked the imperial and neocolonial actions of Western power against formerly colonized countries such as Haiti and India. Thanks to his intellectual generosity, Professor Chomsky agreed to share with me his insights on the colonial, neocolonial, and Western imperialist actions on Haiti and other Third World countries such as India and Nicaragua.

Professor Chomsky started by briefly talking about the history of colonialism and its negative impact on India and Haiti. He went on to talk about Western imperialist actions against these two countries. In the case of Haiti in particular, Chomsky talked about how the United States, through its neoliberal foreign policy, has politically destabilized and economically exploited that country since its independence. He provided concrete examples to illustrate how this has been done.

The Dialogue

Orelus: Can we begin by talking about the effect of colonization and neocolonization on formerly occupied countries such as India and Haiti?

Chomsky: They [British colonizers] created a rich Indian elite; they did not call themselves collaborators, but they were basically running the country, and the British didn't have many troops there. They were running the country with Indian Sepoys and tribesmen. And the usual technique was to move them around so you could use ethnic conflict and things like that; so the guys from one area would kill the people from the other area. It is typically the elites who came out of the British rule. And it is the same rhetoric. Actually there is a really good book on it if you have not seen it yet.

Who is the author?

Do you know Basil Davidson?

Yes, I do.

He's one of the leading historians of Africa and a very good one. He pays attention to Africa, and he has a book. I forget what it is called, but something like "Black Africa." It is about the postcolonial Black Africa. I mean he was really committed to the anticolonial movements, and he was involved with them. He was kind of on the left. He was then very disappointed by what came out, but he describes it very honestly and accurately, and he knows the history.

Let me see if I understand what you just said. Referring to the colonial legacy of colonization on Third World countries such as Haiti, and all the conflicts, division, killings, and exploitation that Haiti has, you know, gone through, would you say this is the end result of colonization?

It's not the end result; it is still going on. I mean Haiti is a particular, special case because the Haitian Revolution in 1804 just terrified everyone in the world. The British, if I recall correctly, sent more troops to Haiti than they sent to the American colonies to prevent the rebellion. In fact—I am sure you know the history—it was just a combined effort of every imperial country in the world, including the United States, then the former U.S. colonies, to crush the revolution because it was terrifying—the idea that a group of former slaves would galvanize the entire Western hemisphere. The French sent a huge army; the British sent a huge army; and Spain was involved. And it was particularly frightening for the United States, of course, because it was a slave society. Here's the first free country in the hemisphere. They could not tolerate that. Well, I don't want to go on with stuff you know perfectly well. You know the French imposed a huge indemnity on them [the Haitians] to pay the cost of having liberated themselves. The United States agreed. In fact, the United States did not recognize Haiti until 1862, while they recognized Liberia. They wanted to get rid of the slaves.

That was Abraham Lincoln's idea. That hideous history that goes right through to the present. I mean Clinton and the first Bush openly supported the military junta. I mean they were not reported here, but it was pretty obvious. They even went as far as authorizing illegal shipments of oil. They authorized Texaco to override presidential directives not to ship right in the middle of this war and while the CIA was testifying to Congress that no oil is being sent, well, you could see the ships in the harbor, building their oil platforms. They got leaked afterwards, but the press refused to report it. And right after President Bush number two canceled aid to Haiti.

It is obvious that imperialism and what I would call neocolonialism affects the political, social, and educational system of Haiti. But it seems to me people who are doing political analysis on Haiti don't seem to focus much on the educational aspect of this country. So would you agree that colonialism and neocolonialism affects the educational system of Haiti as much as its political, social, and economic system?

I think that is typical of colonialism. So take again the British and India, a classic case. I mean they revised the whole education system and the idea was to train them to be loyal subjects to the crown. And there were elements in the Indian elites which benefited from this: the guys who ran it. In fact, if you take a look at any Western country, a typical phenomenon is that there is a sector that lives in enormous wealth, way better than I do when I visit them. It's kind of mindboggling, but that's everywhere, and by now a lot of them are former revolutionaries. They let you know about that when you talk to them. I was in South Africa a couple years ago, in Cape Town.

You actually mentioned that in one of your talks.

Did I talk about it?

Yes, you did.

Did I talk about meeting with these guys who controlled the country?

Yes, you mentioned it.

That's typical in Nicaragua as well. I've been visiting there for a long time; my daughter lives there with grandchildren. The Sandinistas are the worst crooks around. And you can see why. I mean during the '80s, it was not entirely visible because they were in the government; you could not clearly distinguish how much they are just ripping off the population; but as soon as they were out of the government, it became apparent. My daughter's *compañero* [partner] that she lives with, his sister, poor woman, lives in a place right across the street from a huge walled estate. Nobody really knows what's inside, castles and baseball fields and so on. That's owned by Umberto Ortega. He doesn't even bother living there; he lives in Costa Rica since it is nicer down there. I mean they just ripped off the whole country. I mean that is the same in South Africa; it is the same just in any colonial country you go to. I cannot think of any exception to that.

As a Haitian immigrant living here, there is a question that has kept coming to me since I moved here. People who seemed to be curious to know about what is happening in Haiti have asked me, for example, why would the United States be interested in Haiti? Why would they want to be involved in the political affairs of a poor country like Haiti?

Now it's a poor country. But it was the richest colony in the world.

I am referring to the current political and economic situation of Haiti.

Look. For a long time, I mean as late as when Woodrow Wilson invaded it, it was still a potentially wealthy country. It was not like it was under the French. Maybe a lot of French wealth comes from Haiti, but it had lasted until the early twentieth century. I mean Wilson pretty much destroyed it. But even after Franklin Roosevelt destroyed a lot of Haitian agriculture to raise rubber because he needed rubber during the Second World War, it was perfectly capable of raising rubber. This was terrible for the population—they needed food. And after the war, they just destroyed all, and it went on until the 1980s. I mean USAID, the U.S. aid system, in the early 1980s had plans for converting Haiti into what they called "Taiwan of the Caribbean." They were going to make assembly plants for really cheap labor for American corporations and so on, and it goes into the Clinton years. Now it is not a rich country anymore: too much is destroyed by imperial violence. As late as the mid-'90s, when Clinton allowed Aristide to return, he insisted that Aristide accept the program and move out. The defeated U.S. candidate [Marc Bazin] in the 1990 election was supported by the United States, whose goal has been to destroy Haitian agriculture. I mean Haitian rice farmers are poor, but they were very efficient. Obviously they cannot compete with highly subsidized U.S. agriculture. Opening the doors of Haiti to the United States and wiping out its resources has been profitable for the United States. They even went to the extent of wiping out small industries. There were a couple of small industries that were functional in Haiti, like chicken parts, which were working, but the trouble is that American big corporations like Tyson, Clinton's friends, have a huge excess of dark meat and they wanted to dump it somewhere because Americans don't like dark meat. So they tried to dump it in Mexico and Canada, but they have laws. They have anti-dumping laws so they could not do it. However, Haiti under Clinton was forced to accept the condition on Aristide's return. There would be no conditions on imports, so his friends like Tyson could therefore dump chicken meat on Haiti and wipe out the chicken-parts industry, and the country was virtually affected by this. Actually the same thing is happening with NAFTA right now. I mean you read the *Boston Globe* and they'll tell you that this is just going to be marvelous for Central America, but what they don't tell you is what every development agency knows, including the NGOs, what the right-wing criticize to protect their interests. Published reports like OXFAM are saying that the first effect of NAFTA will be to drive tens of thousands of farmers off the field because it means that highly U.S.-subsidized agriculture is going to wipe out poor farmers.

I have a similar example to what you just pointed out. In the early- or mid-1980s, lots of indigenous pigs owned by Haitian farmers and peasants were killed by the Haitian government under the pretext that these pigs were contaminated.

That was incredible. But that was at the orders of the United States! I mean the United States ordered them to kill the pigs on the basis of a totally fraudulent claim about swine fever. But the point was to bring in pigs from Iowa, which are fat, elite pigs; they have to be fed special diets that no Haitian farmer could possibly afford. I mean that would be more than their entire annual income to feed these stupid pigs. But they were brought in, and of course they could not survive, and meanwhile the Haitian pig culture was destroyed, and it was more than just food; pigs were part of the culture, deeply embedded in the whole cultural system, and they were very hardy and resistant, and they were something the poor farmers could use, so they had to be killed. It's kind of comparable to destroying Social Security here. I mean anything that is useful for poor people, like 90% of the population, anything that works for them is useless, so it has to be destroyed. Here it happens to be Social Security; there in Haiti it was pigs. And in the 1990s it was rice farmers, so now Haiti cannot feed itself. Why? Because of Clinton's demands on Aristide's return.

It seems to me this is part of the Western globalization agenda.

Well, it is just an extension of Western imperialism. It goes all back; it takes different forms at different times, but fundamentally it's the same thing. I mean, take George Kennan, who just died yesterday. I was reading the obituaries today. You're not going to read in the obituaries what he actually said. When he was in power, he was a liberal icon. With regard to Latin America, he said that the United States should not hesitate before police repression by the governments because it is necessary to carry out police repression to bar the communists, like Haitian farmers, because we have to protect our resources, therefore they have to have police states. That is George Kennan, the liberal hero.

Do you think that poor Haitian, Somali, or Salvadorian farmers can benefit from globalization to a certain extent?

Globalization is a word we shouldn't even use. I mean globalization is a fine thing and everybody is in favor of it. The people who met at the World Social Forum at Porto Alegre are a perfect example of globalization. They are coming from all over the world; they are poor people, working people, *campesinos* [farmers], and activists; that's globalization. Globalization just for the people! What the West calls globalization is a particular version of industrial investor rights integration, so globalization means neoliberal economic policies, which are free-market policies. That is completely bullshit. They are highly protectionist in all sorts of ways, which many economists refuse to look at for ideological reasons, but it is a particular form of integration which benefits investors and banks. I mean we don't have to call that globalization. Globalization means just international integration. There are different forms of globalization—there would be a version of globalization which would be beneficial to people, but they are not going to consider it. It is the same with NAFTA. When NAFTA was instituted in 1994, the two major reports came out about NAFTA: one from the American Labor Movement, one from the Congress Research Bureau, the Office of Technology Assessment—they all said pretty much the same thing. They said this version of NAFTA is going to be harmful to working people and farmers in all three countries, but it will be beneficial for investors. However, we're in favor of a different version of NAFTA, one which would be oriented toward high growth, high wages, equality, productivity, and so on, and they laid out details. So they were not opposed to NAFTA; they didn't want the executive version.

The press refused to publish one single word about it. To this day, they have not reported it. Not even scholars report it because you're supposed to follow orders, and orders about globalization what the rich guys want and not what the people and farmers in the three countries want. NAFTA is maybe the first international agreement in modern times which was pretty much opposed strongly by the populations of all three countries, but 100% supported by elites. The population did not want it for good reasons. It has done exactly what the labor movement and the Congress Research Bureau predicted: it has led to low-wage, low-growth economies for all three countries, just like they predicted, but a lot of profit.

I'd like to shift from globalization to another topic that I am really interested in, that is, culture. As you know, culture defines who we are and are not. It also shapes how we see the larger world. However, it seems to me when individuals are talking about imperialism, invasion/occupation, they seem to put more emphasis on the sociopolitical body and the material resources of the country being invaded than on its cultural and linguistic resources. As a linguist and critical thinker, how do you understand that?

First of all, the imperial powers themselves are pretty conscious of it. Take the Indian classic case. The British instituted a system of education which was designed to destroy Indian culture—they did not care about most Indians, they cared about the top 5–10% of wealthy elites. They wanted to turn them into Englishmen, so they should get a class in English, pick up English manners so on and so forth and become Anglophiles, and they did! I mean to the extent that I find shocking when I am there. For example, the last time I was there, 3 years ago, I was in Calcutta, which happens to be run by the Communist Party; West Bengal is run by the Communist Party. What they call the Communist Party, it's kind of a European Social Democratic Party—it is the Communist Party in India with all these slogans.

Since we were guests of the government, we got special treatment. One day they insisted that we go to the Victoria Museum. So, I went and we were guided around by the head of the museum and 50 journalists taking pictures. It's a monument to British imperialism. When you walk toward it, there is a big statue of Clive, the conqueror of India. You go inside—the place is lined with paintings, hideous nineteenth-century paintings of British aristocrats beating Indians, who were lined at their feet. Finally, you get Queen Victoria's tearoom. They managed to get her piano or something. The point is that they were all treating this with veneration. One would have thought that as soon as you got independence they would have burned the place down. That it is the same throughout the whole cultural system. I've got honorary degrees at places that are ludicrous because they have all this pageantry, which goes back to the seventeenth century. They kind of laugh at it as they do it. I once got one in Delhi, and it was worse than England, except they did not laugh at it because they had internalized the English values, which is very typical of the colonial phenomenon. I mean the elite internalize the values of the colonial power; they sort of work for them. They are the ones who run the country and after some revolution or liberation or whatever they usually often take up the same patterns. That is sort of what you're describing here. [Here Chomsky referred to the essay where Pierre Orelus talked about the effect of colonialism and neocolonialism on Third World countries.]

Let's go back a little bit to Western neocolonialism.

Speaking of India, the educational system was geared toward the West, so the upper professional class is sort of Western. It doesn't reach about 85% of the population. In fact, something like 85% of the population is literally in the black or informal autonomy; they don't even count it as statistics. There's a good study of it.

But right now you read Thomas Friedman and others; these guys are just swooning about the marvelous, high-tech centers in Bangalore. Which is great—they are better than MIT. On the other hand, right near them is the highest suicide rate in India that is going way up. The reason why it is going up is because peasant farmers cannot survive neoliberal programs—the very same programs that are building the high-tech centers are also destroying hundreds of millions of people who cannot survive the import flow or they are being forced to agro-export. Instead of providing food, like Haiti, instead of providing food for the population, what they do is import stuff from big American agribusiness and grow export crops. The problem with export crops is that they are capital intensive. You want to grow cotton, specialized fruits, and so on, you got to put a lot of capital into it. Furthermore, the prices are fluctuating all over the place. I mean you are a big agribusiness and prices fall one year, you don't care. If you are a farmer and prices fall one year, your family starves to death. And that's what's happening. The other aspect of the neoliberal policies is that the government is supposed to leave people alone, which means they don't provide rural credit; which means you use huge amounts of money. They don't develop irrigation; they don't provide the rural technical stations used to aid farmers.

Speaking of farmers, it seems to me when people are talking about imperialism they don't seem to refer to issues related to land and geographical locations. To me, that is crucial. One should not talk about imperialism without linking it to those two issues.

The reason is that that involves just 90% of the population and nobody cares about them, so why worry about it? I mean there are people who do good work in India.

Can you say more about this?

A lot of studies by very good people—some of them British and some Indian—talk about what I was mentioning about India. Actually one of the best journalists in the world, maybe the best journalist, is an Indian journalist who has done fantastic work on the Indian rural economy, but he does it by living with the people. So for the last 15 years, he actually lives with people in the villages, and when they migrate he migrates with them. He writes detailed, extensive studies of what it is like to be the part of 80% of India and not the 10% that we hear about; so there is work. And they actually care about the land and the destruction of the land. One of the effects of high-tech agriculture is that ecologically it is very destructive, and that is going to matter to people.

Going back to Third World countries such as Haiti, what role do you think intellectuals from the West and Third World countries should play or must play in the fight against social inequality and cultural invasion of their countries?

The first thing they should do is to tell the truth. Instead of concealing everything that is going on, they should let people know what is going on. If other people know what is going on in the rich countries, they are not going to tolerate it. If people in the United States knew the truth about what the U.S. government is doing in Haiti, they would never tolerate it. That is why it has to be concealed. And that's why they have to lie all the time. That is why you have to praise ourselves for magnificent effort in democracy enhancement because after Clinton tortured the people enough, he sent in the Marines to restore Aristide, provided that he follow the platform of the defeated U.S. candidate who was going to destroy Haiti. But here that is called a noble, humanitarian effort to bring democracy to Haiti, which then became a failed state because they have bad genes. All right, if there were honest intellectuals, they would expose all this and the population would not tolerate it, and you have to change policy. The same is true of Western intellectuals. And of course there are some who do it. Take Jeff Sachs. He does it, but it's a scattering. Most intellectuals are servants of power. This goes way back. I mean history is very distorted. Who writes history? Intellectuals, so they make it look pretty; but if you take a look at the real history, you'll find that 95% of them are not as pretty.

What is wrong with the world? Maybe I should ask, what is wrong with the imperialist world?

What is wrong with patriarchal families—if you have systems of power and domination, there is something that is going to be wrong. It doesn't matter whether it is a family or an international system. When you have concentration of power somewhere, it is going to be used to oppress people, almost inevitably. That is what is wrong. It is true of interpersonal relations and it's true of international relations.

Do you think there should be a coalition between Western and Third World intellectuals in the fight against human oppression?

If there are people like, say, Paul Farmer, yes. If there are people like 95% of the people at the Harvard faculty, no. It doesn't just have to do with intellectuals.

Do you see any hope for the educational, political, and economic systems of Haiti?

Look. I mean Haiti did something unbelievable in 1990. Haiti had an election in 1990 of a kind that is just unimaginable in the United States, which has never had such a free election. I mean in Haiti the choice wasn't between two spoiled, rich guys who went to Yale and joined the same secret society and have rich people voting for them. In Haiti people were actually able to elect someone from their own choice. People had organized in the slums, in the hills, and had developed a real democratic society.

So are you referring to Aristide when he was elected in 1990?

Yes. The election in Haiti terrified the United States because it was a democratic election, and we don't tolerate that in the United States. In the United States, the population has to be excluded from the political process, and sometimes it becomes just like a comic strip, like the last election. It is the United States that is a failed state, not Haiti. Haiti achieved something fantastic and that is why it had to be destroyed. As soon as that happened, it set off alarm bells in the United States. You know what happened.

Given what has been happening in Haiti, what is the alternative—if there is any?

What they did is an amazing achievement. It's going to be harder now that the country has been devastated with war, but it is not impossible. If it can be done in collaboration, it has to be done in cooperation with people in the rich countries. I mean, they are the ones who have the guns. If they can be brought into the solidarity movements, I think a lot can be done. And it is needed here, too. Unlike Haiti, the United States is a rich country; nevertheless, it has gone through a period of economic history in the last 25 years which has no precedent. I mean for the last 25 years, for the majority of the population the real wages have stagnated or declined and benefits have declined, and people have to work harder and they are all in debt and so on. And it has got the worst health system in the industrial world. It [the United States] is not a disaster like Haiti because it is a far richer country, but structurally it is the same problem, and that means there is a very good reason for cooperation, but that has to break through the doctrinal system, which doesn't let people know anything crucial. The more educated you are, the less you know. So when you talk about these things in the Harvard faculty club, they say you're a radical. In the United States, the population simply doesn't know what's going on, and can't unless they are part of an activist organization which carries out research projects. But that can achieve something, and it has in the past.

EIGHT

Re-Envisioning Social Justice
Noam Chomsky and Pierre Orelus in Dialogue

Context of Dialogue

In this dialogue, Pierre Wilbert Orelus takes part in a heartfelt and politically engaged conversation with Noam Chomsky revolving around social justice, as broadly conceived. Chomsky begins by talking about the manner in which his work for the last several decades has been centered on social justice issues. He then goes on to denounce the abuse and exploitation of poor countries by powerful Western countries. In this dialogue Orelus and Chomsky explore a wide range of issues, including the negative effects of U.S. imperialism and the Western form of globalization on the poor living in Third World countries. Also central to this dialogue is their analysis of the violation of language rights of historically marginalized groups in different parts of the world, such as the Turks in Turkey, poor Haitians in Haiti, and Latino/as in the United States.

The Dialogue

Orelus: Let me begin by saying that the main focus of this dialogue is social justice. With that said, let me ask you the following question: In what way do you feel that social justice, as broadly defined, has informed your work?

Chomsky: It's the main thing I work on. Virtually everything I do in the activist social political realm is falling under the concept of social justice.

Can you tell me more about that?

Opposition to aggression, difference to protect human rights. Just about everything. I just came back from Gaza a couple of days ago; that's motivated by the first visit there; and the work I do is motivated by concern for the rights of the people; that's social justice. I stopped in Egypt on the way to Gaza and gave talks on situations in the Arab world; and that's again motivated by the idea that people should be able to have their legitimate rights. I can't think of anything that wouldn't fall under social justice.

You have written and spoken extensively about a wide range of issues such as Western imperialism, particularly U.S. imperialism. You have also talked about democracy and globalization. These are issues people should be concerned about. To what extent do you think these issues are connected to social justice?

They're all connected. For example, let's take democracy. A country is democratic to the extent that its population plays a role in determining policy. This is a good measure of democracy. And the role of the public, if it had a role, would be to promote their rights and justice and organize to have an accurate perception of the world. So the two are closely related. Imperialism is obviously domination and control to undermine social justice. As far as globalization is concerned, we have to be careful about what we're talking about. There are several versions of globalization. There is the kind of globalization symbolized by the simultaneous meetings for the last 10 years at Davos, Switzerland. People attending the World Social Forum in Brazil and India, where we happened to be meeting, are committed to globalization, but a different kind. The Davos meetings are the people who are sometimes called the Masters of the Universe. They are the investor class, the banks, the powerful states that cater to their interests and so on. This is a particular version of globalization, which is designed primarily to promote investor rights, corporate rights, power of the wealthy, and so on. That's what's called globalization because they are the dominant force. The World Social Forum is also concerned with globalization. It's sometimes called alternative globalization; they're concerned with the rights of people. And if you attend the World Social Forum meeting, you'll realize that it's drawn from people all over the world with different social classes and vocations; they are farmers, workers, and women, etc. They are concerned with trying to create a world system which will respond to the needs of people. That's another kind of globalization. Well, for the powerful and the elite, that's not called globalization because they don't run the international information system.

Noam, in your talks focusing on U.S. foreign policy, you have eloquently and critically talked about how certain countries, particularly developing countries, have been affected both economically and politically by U.S. foreign policy. So in your opinion, what are some of the long-term socioeconomic, educational, and political effects of this policy on the lives of marginalized groups living in developing countries?

Well, the United States essentially picked up where the European imperialism left off. Up to the Second World War the United States was the richest country in the world. It wasn't a major actor in world affairs. It was nearby, like in the Western hemisphere, but not globally. Britain was the major actor after the Second World War that changed for obvious reasons. The United States took over the effort to control the world in the interest of Western power. Britain became a junior partner, as they called themselves, and of course the consequences for the world are generally negative, not surprisingly. Powerful states act in the interest of their own internal sources of domestic power. And the effect on others is incidental sometimes; sometimes it may harm. But it certainly isn't designed to improve their interests. In fact, the whole First World and Third World divide traces back to early Western imperialism. In the eighteenth century the gap between what's now called the First and the Third World was not very great. By now it is, of course; it's huge. And that's a result of who has the guns.

So what would you propose be done, Noam, to counter the negative effects of U.S. imperialism on these countries?

Two things. First of all, they have to take their own fate into their own hands and move toward independence and some serious internal development. For example, Latin America has done that to an important extent in the last 10 years. That's a historically significant achievement. That's after 500 years of subordination to Western power. So partly it's internal and partly it has to be internal to the United States. The World Social Forum is a place where concerned citizens meet and work together. Together they offer more opportunities and freedom to people in the world to pursue their own concerns without foreign domination.

Speaking of domination, as I was going through many of your books that I have bought and have been reading for the last 10 years, I came across one that caught my attention: Hegemony or Survival. *So I'm curious to know what exactly do you mean by that? What prompted your decision to attribute this title to this book? What exactly do you mean by hegemony or survival?*

Hegemony is just the standard word for global domination in the interest of domestic power systems. That's one option we can pursue. There are serious questions of survival, including survival of the species. As discussed in that book there are two major threats to survival and a lot of minor ones. The major threats are environmental catastrophe and nuclear war. And they remain very serious threats. As long as U.S. policy is directed toward hegemony, it's going to threaten survival. So we have a choice. Which one is it going to be?

Well, it all depends on where one stands and whose interests are in danger. I'm going to shift from U.S. foreign policy to language issues. As you know, many bilingual and multilingual students continue to be punished in school for speaking their native tongues, especially with the abolishment of the bilingual program in the state where you're currently living, Massachusetts, as well as in Arizona, California, and so on. How do you explain this form of linguistic intolerance or, if I may, this form of linguistic apartheid? And what does that really say to you as a linguist in terms of the political nature of the U.S. school system?

Well, that's really not a linguistic question; it's a social justice question. People should have the right to speak their own language; to have their own culture; to help it become a flourishing culture, a lively language, and so on. And I think that's healthy for the society as a whole. However, there are very strong native entitlements that persist and take many forms, including racism. Anti-immigrant supporters have always tried to preserve their image of what's called a white Anglo-Saxon society. This runs right through American history for obvious reasons. Those supporting a white Anglo-Saxon society participated in the elimination of the indigenous population. The influx of immigrants pouring into the rich country from abroad has threatened those in power. They are going to be a minority of the population pretty soon. And this is causing a lot of hatred, fear, and anger. I'm sure a lot of the hysteria about Obama comes from that. It's not just the people dislike him. They're hysterical about it. The popular views about Obama's place of birth are unbelievable. I may have the figures wrong, but my recollection is that in the latest polls, 40% of Americans think that Obama was born in the United States. This is outlandish. A very small percentage, maybe a third or so percent of the population believe he's a Christian. About half of Republicans think that he intends to impose Islamic law not just on the United States but on the whole world. I mean that's actual lunacy. Actually, a quarter of Republicans think that he might be anti-Christ. These are views that you just can't find anywhere else in the world. But it's a large part of the U.S. culture. And it goes way back and in many ways is becoming more frightening as the society becomes more diverse and complex. The power and role of the traditional ruling sector is diminishing.

The gap between the so-called Standard English and languages such as Spanish, Haitian Creole, and Vietnamese is getting wider every day. So what would you propose be done to bridge this gap?

Usual story, political activism in some places. For example, I was in Arizona a while ago. Arizona, which basically I refer to as occupied Mexico. Texas, Arizona, Southwest, and generally the West Coast were just conquered territories, and there are plenty of Mexicans. That's why you have Spanish place names. San Diego, San Francisco, Santa Cruz, and so on are occupied Mexico. Plenty of

Mexicans are living there. Now there are Mexican Americans. While I was there, the Arizona legislature had just forced the closing of a very successful Chicano/a studies program. They had actually gone as far as banning books like *The Tempest*, because it has anti-colonial character to it; they banned Chicano history, historical work on Columbus. That's really pretty extreme but that's Arizona. Places like Massachusetts are doing other things like opposing bilingual education.

You are considered one of the world's leading linguists. In your opinion, Noam, to what degree have language studies contributed to improve the cultural, linguistic, and material conditions of the less fortunate or, if I may borrow Frantz Fanon's phrase, the wretched of the earth?

Well, it's different answers in different places. Take Haiti, for example, where the language of the people is Creole but the language of the elite is French. You know better than I do about this. Creole has been undermined in many ways through publications, official usage, and textbooks, all kinds of things. In fact, it is denounced as not really a language, which is ridiculous. It's as much of a language as French. Of course that's very harmful to the cultural and the socioeconomic life of the Haitian people. Take Turkey as another example. Right now there's been harsh oppression of Kurds for years, but it's picking up again. Kurds are a very large minority in Turkey, and they want the right to speak their own language, to have their own radio programs, their own schools, and to some degree their autonomy. This has been destroyed by a fear of massive violence. It was improving for a while but now it's getting worse—dozens of journalists and others are in jail. All of this is undermining the linguistic, cultural, and political rights of a very large segment of the population. These things are happening everywhere. Spain is another example. The debate over the use of Catalan is happening. Under the Franco dictatorship Catalan was banned. You couldn't have a street sign in Catalan. After Franco was finally kicked out and died, Catalan surfaced again. Of course people have already spoken it not just officially but also publicly. It's now the language of the region and it's moved on to the pressures of its revival; cultural practices, like dancing and singing are done in Catalan.

Given your descriptive and critical analysis of the language situation in Haiti, Turkey, and Spain, what would you propose be done in order to live in a society that is linguistically and socially just?

Too many things to enumerate. I mean we could make a long list of rights that ought to be recognized and secured for the entire population. In fact the Universal Declaration of Human Rights is a good start. That includes cultural rights. That's one third of it. It also includes socioeconomic rights and political rights. It's not perfect, but it's quite a good start.

You have referred to the Universal Declaration of Human Rights as a starting point. But from your own standpoint as a linguist and political activist, what would you propose be done to counteract these social wrongs?

I don't think there's a single answer for every situation. It depends on circumstances. In Haiti, Creole should be the national language. In Turkey, Kurdish should be an accepted, supported language, which people should be permitted to freely use. In the United States, the Spanish-speaking community should have a right to bilingual education in pursuit of Hispanic culture, if they want to. And there are different answers in different places.

What role should public intellectuals play in building a society where one language is respected and valued? What should we do as teachers, public intellectuals?

We should act like moral human beings recognizing that what makes us public intellectuals is not superiority in intelligence or special insight, but privileges. There's a reason why people like you and me are called public intellectuals, but not the janitor who cleans the floor; it's a matter of privilege and prestige. I don't think it should exist, but it does. Those that have more privileges have more responsibility, because the privilege grants it to them, and they should use that responsibility to achieve just and moral aims, like everybody should.

Well said. One last question, Professor Chomsky. Now we have two presidential candidates that are not different in terms of domestic and foreign policies and ideology. So what does it mean to the future of this country with respect to education, the economy, and social services that need to be much better than they are now?

I don't like either candidate. But I think the Republicans are extremely dangerous. They are an extremist party. They're not a traditional parliamentary party at this point. And the Democrats have moved to the right, filling the vacuum left by the moderate Republicans. So I don't like either of them. There's a lot of good political science work studying their policies. As it turns out, roughly they are about the same. Seventy percent of the population is basically disenfranchised. They have no influence on policy. If they did, the policies would be much more progressive—promoting social justice. But they are basically disenfranchised. As you move up the income ladder, influence grows, and the rich essentially get what they want. That's very anti-democratic. That is one of the things that should be overcome. This is one of the major problems that the country faces.

NINE

What Should Be the Role of Intellectuals in the Twenty-First Century?

If it is the responsibility of the intellectual to insist upon the truth, it is also his duty to see events in their historical perspective.
—Noam Chomsky, *The Chomsky Reader* (1987)

Are intellectuals an autonomous and independent social group, or does every social group have its own particular specialized category of intellectuals? The problem is a complex one, because of the forms to date by the real historical process of formation of the different categories of intellectuals.
—Antonio Gramsci, *Selections from the Prison Notebooks* (1971)

The job of the honest intellectual is to help out people who need help; to be part of the people who are struggling for rights and justice. That's what you should be doing. But of course, you don't expect to be rewarded for that.
—Chomsky, interviewed by Pepi Leistyna, *Presence of Mind* (1999)

Various forms of oppression, such as linguicism, neoliberalism, and U.S. imperialism, have been analyzed in the previous chapters. Many people, particularly members of marginalized groups, have been affected by this matrix of oppression. These are social justice issues that cannot and should not be ignored, because they have impacted everyone regardless of one's position in society. The question then becomes: What role should intellectuals, particularly progressive intellectuals, play in the fight against these forms of injustice? This chapter attempts to shed light on this question.

It is without question that intellectuals play an important role in society. Through their scholarly work, they influence how people think and act. While some challenge the status quo through progressive and radical ideas, others work to maintain it through their conservative thoughts and ideas. The goal of this chapter is to analyze what role Third World intellectuals and allies play or should play in the fight against the neocolonization of the Third World. The West by and large controls the wealth of the world, and this has enabled many Western intellectuals and scientists from privileged backgrounds to have access to resources that have allowed many of them to produce high-quality work. Prime examples are David Hume, John Locke, Adam Smith, the Marquis de Condorcet, the Baron de Montesquieu, Rousseau, and Voltaire.

For instance, The U.S., French, and Haitian legal systems have been greatly influenced by ideas that Montesquieu (1975) and Jean-Jacques Rousseau (1968) articulated in their books *The Spirit of the Laws* and *The Social Contract*, respectively. Moreover, Western intellectuals such as Voltaire, Hume, and Condorcet profoundly impacted the world, especially during and after the Enlightenment that took place in Europe, particularly in France. As Steven Seidman (1994) observes, "If the Enlighteners were not creators of the scientific revolution, they were its great popularizers and propagandists. Through their writing and speeches, they proved indispensable in spreading the word of science to educated Europeans" (p. 21). Through their scientific vision of the world as articulated in their scholarly work, these intellectuals challenged the Greco-Roman Christian tradition, which strongly influenced and shaped major institutions in society such as school, family, and even the state. To paraphrase Walter Rodney (1972), during the colonization era, the Greco-Roman Christian tradition was wrongly used by the European colonialist powers to enslave and dominate the "other." Using the Catholic religion as the symbol of salvation and purification, Christopher Columbus, the messenger of Queen Isabella of Spain, for example, duped, exploited, and murdered millions of indigenous people in Central America, South America, and the Caribbean (Zinn, 2003).

While his murderous legacy continues to cause economic, political, and psychological damage to indigenous people in these regions, Christopher Columbus, ironically, has been glorified as the brave discoverer of the so-called New World, which he exploited and destroyed. Similarly, within the Greco-Roman Christian Church in France, the clergy used religion to lie to people, monopolize power and wealth, and maintain social and economic inequalities (Seidman, 1994). As the powerful ambassador of the church, the clergy was able to influence the political power structure and the state apparatus of European countries such as France. And the clergy was not alone in using religion for its own imperial interest. As

Rodney (1972) pointed out in his classic book *How Europe Underdeveloped Africa*, colonial European countries such as France, Great Britain, and Portugal used religion as a weapon to justify and maintain colonization in Africa. Worst of all, religion was and continues to be used by the Roman Catholic Church as an ideological weapon to brainwash the minds of people, including students, so that they accept the status quo. In my view, the Catholic Church was and still is in a powerful position to do so because it is believed to be the source and the depository of canonical truth.

However, with the advent of the Enlightenment, the old world began to give way to a new world. The church was no longer seen as the legitimate and reliable source of truth. Its power was challenged and even weakened by the fresh, new, and revolutionary ideas that were articulated and propagated by the philosophers and scientists of the Enlightenment. It was no longer a question of believing blindly in the clergy, for people came to the realization that science—rather than unfettered religious faith—should guide their actions. Asymmetrical power relations that the Church supported and maintained between the powerful and the powerless were questioned and threatened by the revolutionary ideas and actions of Voltaire, Montesquieu, and Condorcet. Needless to say, the Enlighteners, with their novel ideas, opened up a new vista and shed some light on a world that was in the shadow of the concentrated power of the Roman Catholic Church.

It is undeniable that influential figures in the Enlightenment fought against the injustice and aristocracy inherent in the Catholic Church. They also held out for a better world informed by reason and the ideas of liberty, equality, and fraternity. While Montesquieu and Rousseau greatly contributed to and impacted the legal system worldwide, Voltaire and Condorcet produced an impressive body of social ideas that opened—and continue to open—people's eyes to the social injustice perpetuated by the dominant class in society. I personally have been strongly influenced by ideas that Rousseau, Montesquieu, and Voltaire articulated through their scholarly work. In fact, their ideas have helped me to better understand the world.

By reading the work of these thinkers, I have come to understand the world as a place where the powerful control the wealth at the expense of the powerless; a place where almost everything is falling apart because of educational, economic, social, and political inequalities; a place where a privileged, powerful minority often denies opportunity to certain groups of people based on their gender, race/ethnicity, social class, sexuality, national origin, and linguistic backgrounds; and, finally, a place where the voice of the powerful and the oppressors has been heard, whereas the voice of the powerless and the oppressed has been silenced. By making this argument, I do not mean that the world is not at the same time full of possibility and hope. My contention is that this hope has unfortunately been compromised by imperialism, neocolonialism, racism, sexism, classism, and ableism, while the possibilities are largely inaccessible to the poor.

Philosophers and critical theorists, including Jean Paul Sartre, were influenced and inspired by thinkers such as Voltaire, David Hume, and Montesquieu. Novel ideas that Enlightenment thinkers articulated through their scholarly work challenged members of the Frankfurt School, including Jurgen Habermas, Herbert Marcus, Theodor Adorno, and Max Horheimer, to see the world not through the eyes of religion but through reason and logic. Furthermore, through their scholarly work, the Enlighteners and succeeding Western intellectuals such as Rousseau, Montesquieu, and Thomas Jefferson, eloquently made an appeal for liberty and freedom and advocated for a world built upon the establishment of a legal system and a social contract that cherish and protect people's freedom, rights, and liberty. It goes without saying that the ideas of the Enlighteners have a universal human character attached to them. Consequently, one might be convinced that these intellectuals advocated for the benefits of all human beings on earth. However, what is problematic, contradictory, and hypocritical about the Enlighteners and their successors is that the same Voltaire, Thomas Jefferson, and David Hume—who fought for a scientific understanding of the world and made convincing appeals for the sacred, inalienable human rights such as liberty, equality, justice, and happiness—also fervently supported the enslavement of black people, whom they declared to be inferior and unintelligent. As Galeano (2000) observed:

> Voltaire, anticlerical writer, advocate of tolerance and reason, claims that Blacks are inferior to Europeans but superior to apes. Carolus Linnaeus, classifier of plants and animals, maintains that the Black is a vagabond, lazy, negligent, indolent, and dissolute morals. And David Hume, Master of human understanding, declares that the Black might develop certain attributes of human beings, the way a parrot manages to speak a few words [sic]. (p. 62)

Such a racist position directly excludes blacks from the social and political project for which the Enlighteners fought. It also clearly denies black people the human rights that these thinkers wrote about and stood for in their battle against the Catholic Church. Simply put, the black, the colonized, and the oppressed were not included in the agenda of these European intellectuals as they rebelled against the ignorance perpetuated by the aristocracy within the Catholic Church and the clergy in Europe. It seems their battle for a so-called better world free from oppression and ignorance was launched for the exclusive benefit of white Europeans, particularly the privileged ones. While Montesquieu and Voltaire were writing about the need to have a world free from oppression, subjugation, and control of the Roman Catholic Church, millions of Africans were being enslaved in Haiti. Yet nowhere in their work did these authors suggest that a stand should be taken against the inhuman condition of the slaves in Haiti. Nor did they write about or stand up for indigenous people's rights in South/Central/North America and the Caribbean who were murdered by the Spaniards.

Years later, during the French Revolution, house slaves in Haiti most certainly overheard French colonizers talking about justice and freedom. However, these words were meaningless to the imported African slaves in Haiti who were oppressed by the same country, France, where the battle for freedom, justice, equality, and a better world was taking place. Of course, one cannot and should not dismiss the work and effort of intellectuals of the Enlightenment who fought for a world that should be scientifically oriented, free from ignorance, superstition, and the concentrated power of the Catholic Church. However, given the class background and status of these French intellectuals, one might ask whether their underlying strategy in fighting against the Catholic Church was not to overthrow this institution, but rather to create for themselves the same access to power that the clergy had. In fact, this was the outcome of the French Revolution, which was influenced by the ideas of the Enlightenment. That is, the bourgeoisie that revolted against the noble and clerical classes turned out to be equally oppressive to the lower classes once they took power. To some degree they reproduced the asymmetrical power relation that the clergy maintained for centuries. This confirms the idea that social movements led by bureaucratic intellectuals usually fail to serve the interests of marginalized groups in society.

In the case of the Enlightenment, it is doubtful that it was intended to serve the interests of all humankind, given that non-Europeans—particularly people of color—were not part of the agenda of the Enlighteners. Rather, it was clearly a movement whose objective was solely to serve the interest of bourgeois Europeans. This is, in my view, the danger that lies in social movements led by the bourgeois class, which historically has not proven to be a revolutionary class, due to its selfish interest in maintaining the status quo. In this sense, Marx and Engels (1975) were right when they argued that only the proletarian class can truly be a revolutionary class, for this is a class that has nothing to lose and everything to gain. In his book *State and Revolution*, Lenin (1943) illustrated Marx and Engels's idea about the two opposing classes. He stated:

> The exploiting classes need political rule in order to maintain exploitation, i.e., in the selfish interests of an insignificant minority, and against the vast majority of the people. The exploited classes need political rule in order to completely abolish all exploitation, i.e., in the interests of the vast majority of the people, and against the insignificant minority consisting of the slave owners of modern times—the landlords and the capitalists. (p. 22)

Although the intellectual bourgeois who were the leading figures of the Enlightenment might not have been the exploiting class per se, they needed, as Lenin made clear, "political rule" in order to maintain the status quo. Thus, to echo Lenin (1943), "what is to be done" to unveil the hypocritical nature of the

Enlightenment and its negative impact on the Third World? Should progressive intellectuals and activists work together to challenge the scholarly works of influential European Enlighteners that have been used in both the "modern" and "postmodern" world? How would Western and Third World intellectuals support each other and work on an equal footing in this project? What role should intellectuals living in the Third World or the Western world play in countering the cultural, linguistic, economic, and political domination of the powerful Western countries of the world? It is the analysis of the role that Third World intellectuals and allies need to continuously play to change the sociopolitical and economic paradigm of such an "uneven world" (Radhakrishnan, 2003) to which I turn next.

The Role of Third World Intellectuals in a Neoliberal and Neocolonial Era

At the outset, it is worth making a clear distinction between territorial conservative intellectuals and borderless intellectuals. I argue that while territorial conservative intellectuals are often the servants of the dominant class, borderless intellectuals write about and speak against social, economic, and political inequalities perpetuated by this class. Their actions and political stances are radical and humanist by nature and thereby transcend the borders of their socioeconomic and political milieu. Critical thinkers such as Noam Chomsky, Antonio Gramsci, Edward Said, Antenor Firmin, Howard Zinn, bell hooks, Antonia Darder, Vandana Shiva, Walter Rodney, Paulo Freire, Peter McLaren, Robert Phillipson, Frantz Fanon, Amical Cabral, Aimé Césaire, Arundhati Roy, Tove Skutnabb-Kangas, Henry Giroux, Ngugi Wa Thiong'o, and Eqbal Ahmad, to name only a few, are borderless intellectuals par excellence. Their intellectual activism has transcended the borders of their native lands and impacted the entire international intellectual community. The legacy they left behind or will be leaving behind will teach humankind the following lesson: It takes love, courage, sacrifice, dedication, persistence, and consistency to be a borderless intellectual. In this context, it is worth alluding to Said's praise of the scholarly and activist work and legacy of Eqbal Ahmad, a borderless intellectual. The late Said, recognizing the undying contribution of Eqbal Ahmad to the world, cherishes his intellectual courage in the following terms:

> One of the remarkable things about him was that even though he crossed more borders and traversed more boundaries than most people, Eqbal was reassuringly himself in each new place, new situation, new context. This was not at all a matter of ethnic or religious identity, nor did it have much to do with the habitual stability we associate with solid citizens. Rather, Eqbal's special blend of intellectual brilliance and courage, supernally accurate analysis, and consistently humane and warm presence made of him, to paraphrase from Rudyard Kipling's Kim, a friend of the whole world. (cited in Ahmad, 2000, p. 25)

As Said's comments illustrate, borderless intellectuals like Ahmad are an inspiration to future borderless intellectuals. In fact, I argue that borderless intellectuals are a beacon to those who dare to transcend ethnic, linguistic, racial, and social boundaries surrounding their socioeconomic and political milieu in order to fight for a universal human cause. Borderless intellectuals have, of course, been strategic in their political acts in the sense that they know when to stand up and speak against social inequalities. They also have been proven to be courageous and determined when faced with multiple challenges and adversity in life. For example, Antonio Gramsci (1971) and Ngugi Wa Thiong'o (1986) never stopped writing about and fighting for what they believed in while they were incarcerated. They took risks that not only caused them to be incarcerated but also affected their families and ultimately, in the case of Gramsci, cost him his life. Ngugi Wa Thiong'o was jailed by the Kenyan government for his scholarly and activist work aimed at maintaining Kenyan native languages and culture by countering the cultural dominance of the English language imposed by the British colonial power on Kenyans. He narrated his experience in the following terms:

> It was in the same months of June and July 1982 that, as I was about to return to Kenya, I received frantic messages from different directions: orders were out for my arrest and detention without trial on arrival at the Jomo Kenyatta Airport in Nairobi. Should I not delay my return? I did and I have been telling the Kamirithu story wherever and whenever I have a chance. For on a personal level it has changed my life. It has led me in prison, yes; it got me banned from teaching at the University of Nairobi, yes; and it has now led me into exile. But as a writer it has also made me confront the whole question of the language of African theatre—which then led me to confront the language of African fiction. (p. 62)

Although daunting, I believe these risks are worth taking because intellectuals should not wait to be told why, when, and where to intervene while the evil forces of imperialism, linguicism, neoliberalism, neocolonialism, racism, and sexism are affecting humanity. In my view, this is what differentiates borderless intellectuals from other intellectuals and makes them unforgettable and immortal in the historical archive of the world.

Like Arundhati Roy, Vandana Shiva, Frantz Fanon, Paulo Freire, Antenor Firmin, Walter Rodney, Che Guevara, and Amilcar Cabral, other intellectuals in and from the Third World need to act as borderless intellectuals. My contention is that Third World intellectuals should not be the receptacles, transmitters, and executers of ideas articulated by conservative Western intellectuals. Rather, they should try to act as authentic intellectuals who challenge these ideas. Equally important, they should become involved in global political and social movements aimed at combating misrepresentation and servile cultural alienation of postcolonial subjects living in both the Third World and in the Diaspora. As Thomas Sankara (1984) contends:

They must understand that the battle for an ideology that serves the needs of the disinherited masses is not in vain. But they must understand, too, that they can only become credible on an international level by being genuinely creative by portraying a faithful image of their people, an image conducive to carrying out fundamental change in political and social conditions and to wrenching our countries from foreign domination and exploitation, which leave us no other perspective than bankruptcy. (p. 88)

As Sankara suggested, Third World intellectuals should act internationally as ambassadors of their native countries willing to engage in an ideological, political, and intellectual battle to represent and defend them. Nationally, they should play the role of intellectual vanguards tenaciously fighting against foreign cultural invasion. Both nationally and internationally, Third World intellectuals should work tirelessly to heighten and defend the national dignity and culture of their countries. Historically, one of the biggest challenges that countries with a historical burden of colonization have faced is salvaging their culture, which was and still is to a certain extent perceived as an alienating or a savage culture. It is therefore imperative that both Third World intellectuals and ordinary people who have lived under colonization and/or have had to deal with the aftermath of it redefine who they are, for the cultural image attributed to them by the colonizers and neocolonizers is one of savagery. This is well-captured by Arundhati Roy (2003), who maintains: "Fifty years after independence, India is still struggling with the legacy of colonialism, still flinching from the 'cultural insult.' As citizens we're still caught up in the business of 'disproving' the white world's definition of us" (p. 13).

As Roy's statement suggests, even though formerly Third World-colonized countries such as Haiti and India have gained their independence, they continue to face the challenge of making the West respect their culture, which is often looked down upon. The cultural autonomy and identity of many formerly colonized countries have been in jeopardy due, in some cases, to a lack of unshakable cultural resistance of intellectuals living in these countries to the cultural and "linguistic imperialism" (Phillipson, 1992) of the West. Having said that, I suggest that Third World intellectuals play the role of cultural vanguards in their intellectual fight against Western cultural invasion of their countries. But can they take on that role if their intellectual work has merely been reduced to teaching, writing, publishing, and lecturing at conferences?

The cultural vanguard role of Third World intellectuals, as I conceive it, should not be thusly limited to teaching, writing, publishing, and lecturing at conferences. It should also consist of reaching out to the masses and helping them to be better prepared ideologically for potential radical social changes. Third World intellectuals can start playing that cultural vanguard role by helping the masses organize cultural events where, collectively, they explore and discuss the important interconnections among nation, state, and culture. Moreover, through the sharing and exchange of ideas, cultural vanguard Third World intellectuals can guide and help the masses to use cultural artifacts, such as songs rooted in their culture and history, as a form of cultural and historical resistance to Western neocolonial cultural, economic, and political domination. Equally important, on a national level, cultural vanguard Third World intellectuals ought to make the effort to fight against obsolete cultural practices and social norms that contribute to the marginalization and oppression of certain groups of people in society such as gay men, lesbians, bisexuals, transgender individuals, and people who are physically, mentally, and emotionally challenged. My contention is that the fight against neocolonialism should also entail fighting against all other forms of oppression, starting with the ones that occur in one's home or native land.

I am fully aware that what I am articulating here might be a great challenge for Third World intellectuals, including myself, who have been educated in the West and immersed in Western discourse. Such intellectuals would need to "reinvent themselves," as Freire (1970) suggested, in order to play the cultural vanguard role. Otherwise they might end up regurgitating what they have been taught in Western universities in terms of Western discourse and ideology. Another huge challenge that awaits Western-educated Third World intellectuals is to find ways in which to make their language accessible to both students and the formally uneducated masses in the Third World.

By language, I do not mean simply words uttered, nor do I refer to syntactical and morphological aspects of it. Rather, I am referring to the ideological aspect of it, that is the values, beliefs, ideology, and norms embedded in languages like English and French, in which many Third World intellectuals have been educated. Eqbal Ahmad (2000) understood the ideological component and implications of language. In the case of the Algerian school system, Ahmad maintained:

> Higher education is supposed to have Arabized. The reality was, the Algerian independent state remained organically tied to France and to the international market. Therefore the local language, Arabic, was devalued. So you have a situation in which you have higher education without a language. You can't impart higher education without a consistent language policy. That contributed to a decline in education.
>
> Second, we all inherited a colonial system of higher education. These post-colonial governments had no will or desire to introduce an alternative system of education. The rhetoric and the structure they announced was that of independence. The reality was that of higher education based on colonial premises and systems. The educational system in this new setting of post-colonial statehood became increasingly dysfunctional because it came under opposing, contradictory pressures. (pp. 19–20)

Expanding upon Ahmad's argument, I contend that in order not to culturally alienate students by assimilating them into Western culture, it is imperative that Western-educated Third World intellectuals de-Westernize their language and knowledge so that they can be accessible to students and the uneducated masses in Third World countries. Furthermore, if Third World intellectuals both in the native land and abroad are serious about contributing to the linguistic, cultural, educational, and political advancement of their countries, they ought to take a stand against governments influenced by Western capitalist countries—governments that invest more in their national army than in school materials and resources such as computers, laboratories, and books.

All in all, Third World intellectuals have a twofold task to perform. On an international scale, they need to talk back to Western power that refuses to treat them on an equal footing despite their intellectual, academic, and professional achievements. While it is crucial that they continue striving for intellectual excellence, they should not lose sight of the importance of fighting against Western imperialism in order to ensure that the national and cultural dignity and political autonomy of Third World countries are respected. Such a noble but immense task might sound idealistic or utopian to Third World intellectuals who have allowed their voices to be silenced by the Western power structure in order to secure a tenured position at a university.

Those who choose to sell their intelligence, knowledge, and human dignity to huge Western capitalist corporations also might ridicule this proposal. Raising consciousness among this group of intellectuals can be a huge challenge, for they may have no interest in changing the status quo from which they have been profiting. In fact, these intellectuals often behave as the Third World version of Western colonialists, whose goal is to profit from the capitalist and neocolonial system apparatus. These intellectuals, as Sartre (1965) pointed out, "will change nothing and will serve no one, but will succeed only in finding moral comfort in malaise" (p. xi). However, one should not lose hope, for as Freire (1997) reminds us, "it is imperative that we maintain hope even when the harshness of reality may suggest the opposite" (p. 23). We should indeed maintain hope because there are still very few borderless intellectuals who, despite being marginalized by the bureaucracy of such institutions as universities, continue to engage in a fight to balance the power relations between the Western and the Third World. Unfortunately, these few intellectuals have not gotten enough recognition for their courageous political and intellectual stances.

On a national scale, Third World intellectuals should work tirelessly to influence and, if necessary, infiltrate the political body of the government they live under, for sometimes the strategic way to challenge the political power structure of a government is by penetrating it. As insiders in the political structure of the government, Third World intellectuals might be able to serve, in my view, four important purposes. First, they would be in a better position to challenge drastic economic and political decisions that governments in Third World countries make on behalf of the poor. Such decisions, if not challenged by intellectuals who possess or have a clear sense of "historical conscience" (Diop, 1991), might have ruinous consequences on the masses in the Third World. Cheick Anta Diop, the prominent Senegalese intellectual, eloquently explicates the significance of and vital role that historical conscience plays in the cultural protection of a people, as well as in the historical renaissance of a nation. Diop (1991) maintains:

> The historical conscience, through the feeling of cohesion that it creates, constitutes the safest and the most solid shield of cultural security for a people. This is why every people seeks only to know and to live their true history well, to transmit its memory to their descendents. The essential thing, for people, is to rediscover the thread that connects them to their most remote ancestral past. In the face of cultural aggression of all sorts, in the face of all disintegrating factors of the outside world, the most efficient cultural weapon with which a people can arm itself is this feeling of historical continuity. The erasing, the destruction of the historical conscience also has been since time began part of the techniques of colonization, enslavement, and debasement of peoples. (p. 212)

Second, as Diop suggests, by using a historical conscience as part of the political framework of their intellectual activism, Third World intellectuals would be well-equipped ideologically to counter the hegemonic, imperialist, political, and cultural attack of Western empires against their countries. Third, the Third World intellectuals who manage to infiltrate the government apparatus would be in a position to play an active role in any democratic and political process that leads to the liberation of the poor from the prison of poverty and inequality. Finally, by being at the center of the political debate of their country, Third World intellectuals can play a major role in fighting against any occupation of their native land by Western imperial powers. As Fanon (1963) observed: "The native intellectual nevertheless sooner or later will realize that you do not show proof of your nation from its culture but that you substantiate its existence in the fight which the people wage against the forces of occupation" (p. 223).

Building on Fanon's view, I argue that if Third World intellectuals are to earn a national reputation as cultural vanguards of their countries, they first need to be immersed in their own culture and to work hard to salvage it from Western cultural invasion. And to earn an international reputation as borderless intellectuals, they should not be afraid to take risks to tell dangerous truths about social, racial, economic, and political inequalities of Western neocolonizing powers. Nor should they be afraid of engaging in the defense of human rights wherever they happen to be violated. Until they have cultivated moral clarity and courage to do so, they would simply be "servants of power" (Chomsky as cited in Leistyna, 1999) who, throughout history, have been serving the corporate interests of Western imperial powers and that of a small, nationally dominant group that has monopolized the wealth of the Third World.

References

Ahmad, E. (2000). *Confronting empire*. Cambridge, MA: South End Press.

Diop, A.C. (1991). *Civilization or barbarism: An authentic anthropology.* New York: Lawrence Hill Books.
Fanon, F. (1963). *The wretched of the earth.* New York: Grove Press.
Freire, P. (1970). *Pedagogy of the oppressed.* New York: Seabury Press.
Freire, P. (1997). *Pedagogy of hope.* New York: Continuum.
Galeano, E. (2000). *Upside down.* New York: Henry Holt.
Gramsci, A. (1971). *Selections from the prison notebooks.* New York: International Publishers.
Leistyna, P. (1999). *Presence of mind: Education and the politics of deception.* Oxford: Westview Press.
Lenin, I.V. (1943). *State and revolution.* New York: International Publishers.
Marx, K., & Engels, F. (1975). *The German ideology.* In *Collected works* (Vol. 5). New York: Random House.
Montesquieu, B.D. (1975). *The spirit of the laws.* New York: Hafner Press.
Philipson, R. (1992). *Linguistic imperialism.* Oxford: Oxford University Press.
Radhakrishnan, R. (2003). *Theory in uneven world.* Malden, MA: Blackwell.
Rodney, W. (1972). *How Europe underdeveloped Africa.* Washington, DC: Howard University Press.
Roy, A. (2003). *War talk.* Cambridge, MA: South End Press.
Rousseau, J.-J. (1968). *The social contract.* New York: Penguin Books.
Sankara, T. (1984). *Thomas Sankara speaks.* New York: Pathfinder.
Sartre, J.P. (1965). Introduction. In A. Memmi, *The colonizer and the colonized.* Boston: Beacon Press.
Seidman, S. (1994). *Contested knowledge: Social theory in the postmodern era.* Malden, MA: Blackwell.
Thiong'o, N. (1986). *Decolonizing the mind: The politics of language in African literature.* London: James Currey.
Zinn, H. (2003). *A people's history of the United States.* New York: Harper & Row.

AFTERWORD

Passing the Torch

by Pepi Leistyna

"We are entering Israeli airspace, please fasten your seatbelt."

These are the words that come over the intercom from the flight attendant as you cross over into the Holy Land. It was my first trip to Israel and little did I realize that the seatbelt command would be both a warning and a metaphor as I was in for the ride of my life.

I should have been prepared for this particular venture, given that over the past three decades my research and activist work in social justice at home and abroad has brought me face-to-face with some of the world's worst human atrocities. Regardless of the injustice and suffering that I've witnessed over the years, this life that I've chosen and weathered and this path that I make as I go has also led to so many wonderful and often unexpected encounters; and along the way, I've been showered with intense beauty and the remarkable and unforgettable grace and dignity of people who regardless of their circumstances and hardships are giving and forgiving as they maintain an amazing and unyielding faith in the possibility of peace and justice in this world, and in dreams that can only be realized when the human heart acts in concert with others.

I've studied the geopolitics of the Middle East and I have learned a tremendous amount about this complex region from Noam Chomsky who has written extensively on the subject, as well as from the late Edward Said whose work on representational politics, especially as they pertain to western stereotypes of Arab cultures, has played a pivotal role in shaping my own scholarly endeavors as a student and a professor.¹ Both of these public intellectuals have fueled my ethical drive as a social justice activist.

I also learned a great deal about the history and dynamics of the Middle East while traveling with my wife Susan around Turkey in the summer of 2006. After I gave a talk on "Civil Society and the Global Justice Movement: New Challenges" at Bilgi University in Istanbul, Susan and I flew to and explored the central region of this vast, storied, and extraordinary country with its tapestry of vibrant twists and turns, richly layered history, delicate yet spicy flavors, and colorful and deeply soulful people. No matter how far we'd venture out by foot, car, camel, boat, plane, or hot air balloon, we always seemed to make it back to an outdoor café for a nargila filled with tasty apple tobacco, and some spicy and soothing hot tea and conversation with the locals. We'd settle in on the soft colorful pillows surrounded by beautiful rugs and tapestries, under these ancient trees that welcomed and embraced us each time with their cool and comforting shade. Amidst the blended scents of coffee, flavored teas and tobacco in the air—and when in Istanbul or down south, an added hint of salt from the Black Sea, the Bosporus, or the Mediterranean—were the gently swirling sounds of the tanbur lute, ney flute, kanun zither, and kudum drum; there was a tranquility that we'd never experienced before. With this ethereal glow about her, Suzy would take it all in and exhale this graceful beauty and serenity. I so often try to go back there in my mind to be with her in those fleeting moments that were free of the anxiety and grief that now so often take hold of me since her unexpected death in December of 2011. We didn't know that she had pancreatic cancer, and on the seventh day of feeling under the weather—typical during a hard New England winter around the holidays, she died in my arms at home.

Unfortunately, interwoven with life's offerings of beauty and tranquility are the trials and tribulations of human struggle: the paradoxical threads that join together at the seam the insufferable grief that inevitably accompanies deep love when death comes calling, as well as the unnecessary and unacceptable stains of callousness, greed, senseless violence, and war that so needlessly and yet ubiquitously taint human history. Both are sharp reminders that life is fragile.

The cafés offered a much needed moment of respite as it was a particularly stressful time while Susan and I were in Turkey because Israel had just invaded Lebanon as a swift and stern retaliation for Hezbollah's indiscriminate missile and rocket attacks in northern Israel—especially on the city of Haifa. During this crisis, the U.S. was making use of Incirlik Airbase just south of where we were, to evacuate Americans from Beirut as they were being transferred to the seaport city of Mersin, west of the Syrian border, along the Mediterranean.

The U.S. Army Corps of Engineers built this airbase near Adana in 1951 during the Cold War and it was strategically designed and positioned to keep an eye on the Soviets. It's now of particular strategic importance as it is located in striking distance of Syria, Iran, Pakistan, and some of the major oil and gas reserve regions of the Russian Federation and the Caspian Sea. While we were there, the Pentagon was making use of most of NATO's 24 bases.[2] But Incirlik was the main staging ground for U.S. assaults on Afghanistan and Iraq. Needless to say, these deadly and destructive military operations created a great deal of local resentment toward Americans. Muslim outrage was palpable and justified as it was abundantly clear to them as well as to the international community, that Washington's pretext for invading Iraq was based on fabricated evidence of weapons of mass destruction and Saddam Hussein's involvement with the events of 9/11—proof concocted by the George W. Bush administration with Secretary of Defense Donald Rumsfeld and Vice President Dick Cheney at the helm.

While the Turkish government largely supported the Bush administration's neoconservative 'War on Terror,' it was obvious to Susan and me that everyday-people there were by no means in favor of any military attacks on Afghanistan, Iraq, or Lebanon for that matter. Indeed, it was reported that over 70% of the population was opposed to the U.S. invasion of Afghanistan in 2001.[3] Meanwhile, the indiscriminate U.S. bombing of Iraqi and Afghani civilians, mosques, and other religious sites was infuriating the Turkish public. But their overwhelming dissent was systematically ignored by the state, which was busy making the necessary arrangements to ensure that protesters and human rights activists be summarily arrested and disappeared by government security forces. This is precisely what's happening at this very moment in Turkey: Accused by the public of being a dictator, Prime Minister Tayyip Erdogan, who has been in office since 2003, has ordered his security forces to crush the anti-government protests occurring all around the country, claiming that terrorists are behind the movement to overthrow his ruling Justice and Development Party—the AKP.

The U.S. price tag for the initial operations in 2003, and the subsequent insurgency and long-term occupation of Iraq, was over two trillion dollars; for the Iraqis, besides being bombed back into the Stone Age, the human cost was estimated at 134,000 civilian lives—650,000 *people in total if you include military personnel who were killed in combat;* lest we forget the estimates that over 100,000 Iraqi casualties occurred during the 1991 offensive—35,000 of which were civilians, mostly killed by the 120,000 air sorties that were credited with dropping more than 265,000 bombs during these operations.[4]

When President Barack Obama finally declared an end to U.S. military operations in Iraq in 2011, the bombing had been non-stop since the 1991 blitz of "Operation Desert Storm." During the 2003 invasion called "Operation Iraqi Freedom," with its "Shock and Awe" bombing campaign, 68% of the munitions used were precision-guided; only 6.5% were of such caliber back in 1991. A great deal of the ordinance unleashed during the relentless carpet-bombing over the years were cluster bombs, which are now illegal under international law because of their utterly devastating and inhumane effects.[5] The 2003 incursion included 29,200 air strikes, followed by an additional 3,900 deadly sorties over the next 8 years.

The fundamental principle of "Shock and Awe" is found in a 1996 publication by the National Defense University entitled "Shock & Awe: Achieving Rapid Dominance." Masterminded by Harlan Ullman of the National War College, the advisory report puts forth the argument that military victory is not enough—that you need to terrify the enemy by using brutal force in order to coerce them into complete and permanent submission. Describing "Shock and Awe" as "Massively destructive strikes directly at the public will…," Ullman writes:

> Intimidation and compliance are the outputs we seek to obtain. The intent here is to impose a regime of shock and awe through delivery of instant nearly incomprehensible levels of massive destruction directed at influencing society writ large. Through very selective, utterly brutal and ruthless and rapid application of force to intimidate, the aim is to affect the will, perception, and understanding of the adversary. Without senses, the adversary becomes impotent and entirely vulnerable.[6]

According to the U.S. Army manual the definition of "terrorism" is "the calculated use of violence or threat of violence to attain goals that are political, religious, or ideological in nature…through intimidation, coercion, or instilling fear" (U.S. Army Operational Concept for Terrorism Counteraction—TRADOC Pamphlet, pp. 525–537). If you compare this definition of terrorism to the idea of "Shock and Awe," they are one in the same.

The 1991 foray cost the U.S. $60 billion, and our partner in crime, Saudi Arabia, coughed up an additional $36 billion—all this to "liberate Kuwait," the tenth richest nation in the world that at the time wasn't, and still isn't, a democracy. Kuwait is a constitutional monarchy, or what's also referred to as a "constitutional hereditary emirate," where the Emir inherits his power and ultimately makes the final decisions on what the parliament can and can't do. While it is far more liberal than most Muslim states, Kuwait nonetheless has its own share of harsh human rights abuses. But the U.S. government and military have never really concerned themselves with such matters, at least not with any sincerity, including at this very moment when chemical warfare is being used by the Obama administration as the pretext for invading Syria.

What made Kuwait of particular interest and worthy of this beneficent rescue mission is that this tiny nation that borders Iraq and is in close proximity to Iran, permits the United States to use its 14 military bases, and more importantly, it is sitting on top of the world's fifth largest oil reserves. The UK and British Petroleum, our other partners in crime, still have major investments in the country. BP co-founded the Kuwaiti Oil Company in 1938 and has continued to play an advantageous managerial role in oil production there even after the government nationalized its petroleum industry in 1975. During the neoliberal scourge of

Margret Thatcher, BP was heading in the exact opposite direction as it was on its way to being completely privatized between 1979 and 1987—it is currently the world's fifth largest energy company. Under no circumstance were Kuwait's invaluable and lucrative resources to fall into the hands of Saddam Hussein.[7] The original name for the 2003 invasion was "Operation Iraqi Liberation," but the acronym O.I.L. was unintentionally far too revealing, and the masterminds of spin back in Arlington and Washington, just as soon as they realized their slipup in nomenclature, immediately fixed it.

Still vivid in the minds of the Turkish people and clearly present in the everyday chitchat that we experienced at the university and in the streets, cafes, and artisan workshops of small villages, towns, and cities, were stories of atrocities that were being committed by the U.S., such as the November 2005 Marine murders of 24 innocent people in Haditha—10 of the victims were women and children. This vicious act was followed in March, just three-and-a-half months before we arrived in Turkey, by the gruesome crime of U.S. soldiers of the 502nd infantry regiment who had killed an entire Iraqi family, including a 6-year-old child, after raping the 14-year-old daughter, Abee Hamza al-Janabi. In an attempt to hide any evidence of their heinous act, they burned her body in what is now referred to as the "Mahmudiyah Killings," for which four of the servicemen were eventually convicted of war crimes.

Just southeast of us in Iraq, there was a dramatic increase in sectarian violence in what the UN was describing as a "civil war-like situation"; meanwhile, there were heightened attacks on the coalition forces.[8] Back across the border in Turkey, the TAK—Kurdistan Freedom Falcons—said it was going to "turn Turkey into Hell" and true to its word, the extremist militant group was responsible for dozens of bombings that targeted the tourist industry throughout the country, including in Istanbul, Adana, Marmaris, Antalya, and Mersin. All that summer the PKK—the Kurdistan Workers Party—which publically denounced the TAK's use of violence against civilians, was battling with government counter-insurgency forces that were hell-bent on crushing the movement for a free and democratic Kurdistan. Any efforts to create an independent state had long been condemned by the Turkish government, and the PKK was labeled a "terrorist group." By September it was engaged in heavy combat with the Turkish military in Diyabakir, in which hundreds of lives were lost. Countless Kurds have been killed over the years in Turkey, especially in the 1990s when the extreme violence resulted in over one million refugees fleeing for their lives.

It's so twisted that we used oil-rich dictatorships such as Kuwait, Saudi Arabia, Qatar—the wealthiest country in the world, Bahrain, the Sultanate of Oman, the United Arab Emirates, Uzbekistan, and Turkmenistan, each of which is guilty of its own human rights atrocities, to invade a sovereign nation with the claim that we are there as a liberating force to bring freedom and democracy. It makes absolutely no sense unless you add in the fact that all these regimes have allowed the U.S. access to their military bases, they all buy our weapons in billion-dollar batches, and they all supply us with oil. Yemen, the poorest country in the region, was also our ally until the resignation of President Ali Abdullah Saleh in 2011, after 30 years of autocratic rule. Even a dictator like Saleh couldn't handle the tribal wars, a secessionist movement, and the ever-growing power of the jihadists of the former U.S.-backed Mujahideen, especially Al-Qaeda.

Sadly, Yemen has become the new Afghanistan and the Obama administration is using the impoverished country for drone target practice—nine in the last few weeks against suspected terrorists. But how is anyone to really know exactly who these people are, what they have done, and what evidence the government has against them? Instead of using civilized legal proceedings, the U.S. has chosen the unmitigated barbarism of assassination.[9] Obama is running a secret drone strike operation from the White House where on a regular basis he is presented with a "kill list" of potential terrorists, from which he and his advisors decide who lives and who dies. The president has kicked the Bush administration's use of black ops up a notch in his support of dirty wars, assassinations, secret detention and torture centers, and snatch and rendition operations all over the world—without abiding by any domestic or international legal codes or Congressional oversight.[10] This includes killing our own citizens, such as 16-year-old Abdulrahman al-Awlaki, who was born in Denver, Colorado and murdered in Yemen by a CIA-led drone strike from a CIA-built airbase in Saudi Arabia, as was his father Anwar al-Awalaki and Samir Khan in 2011 in Yemen, and Jude Kenan Mohammad in Pakistan—all Americans.[11]

It's important to remember that in the past, the U.S. has also supported a plethora of other Muslim dictatorships, including Suharto in Indonesia; Hassan II of Morocco; Muhammad Zia Ul-Haq, Mohammad Iyub Khan, and Pervez Musharraf of Pakistan; Abul Ibn Hussein of Jordan; Hosni Mubarak in Egypt; and Zine El Abidine Ben Ali of Tunisia; we have been courting the military-backed Bouteflika regime in Algeria since his rise to power in 1999—and now any political newcomers, as his government is on the verge of collapsing.

We also supported the Shah of Iran. On August 19, 1953 the CIA and the UK's MI6 orchestrated and financed a coup that overthrew the democratically elected government of Prime Minister Mohammad Mosaddegh—the first Muslim democratic administration in the history of the Middle East. Mosaddegh was a staunch nationalist, not a communist, who nationalized the oil industry while in office. This infuriated the Eisenhower administration and the AIOC: Anglo-Iranian Oil Company—what's now known as BP. Mosaddegh was put under house arrest and replaced by a monarchal military regime ruled by Mohammad Reza Shah Pahlavi. The Shah instantly handed over 40% of Iran's oil reserves to the U.S. and let the British maintain their power and influence in the country. The

Shah's puppet government, with its brutal secret police, would be overthrown in 1979, the year that the U.S. embassy was seized and the hostage crisis began. In retrospect, one can only imagine what 60 years of democratic rule in Iran would have done for the Middle East.

The U.S., which is the largest weapons producer and distributor in the world, is making money hand-over-fist from these Middle Eastern and Central Asian countries: "Overseas weapons sales by the United States totaled $66.3 billion… or more than three-quarters of the global arms market, valued at $85.3 billion in 2011."[12] The U.S. supplies more weapons to dictatorships around the world than China—the communist regime that has been allowed to buy up our national debt at the tune of 1.7 trillion dollars.[13] I wonder if weapons sales are helping to pay down our colossal international promissory note of $14.7 trillion. It's crazy: we take out massive loans from China so we can buy more of their cheap goods, pay for the $500 million interest that accrues each day on our national debt, and finance wars in countries that most people in the U.S. can't locate on a map, wars that probably wouldn't occur in the first place without our munitions.[14]

It's also important to point out that our symbiosis with China goes against the last 65 years of U.S. foreign policy that has been fundamentally anti-communist, certainly since the a Cold War. We have fought and/or supported costly military conflicts in Korea, Vietnam, and throughout Central and South America, Africa, and the Middle East in order to eradicate communist regimes. Of course, there is nothing communist about China, as it's a mix of state capitalism and totalitarianism—a system of elites that exploits labor on a grand scale, doesn't redistribute the wealth that is accumulated, controls the media, and has a harsh record of human rights abuses and crushing democratic movements;[15] it's like Dick Cheney's dream world order, only he and his neoconservative buddies would be in charge and would use the government and public taxes to protect and subsidize the rich with a massive defense department and police force—you know, to keep an eye on and arrest hundreds of Occupy Wall Street demonstrators that are simply practicing their Constitutional rights.

China has been diplomatically supporting the Assad regime in Syria at UN Security Council meetings—it will be interesting to see how they respond to a U.S. invasion; keep in mind that China and Russia—which also support Assad—have massive conventional military forces and a nuclear arsenal.

Obama's budget for the Department of Defense has risen to $533.8 billion. If you include monies allocated to overseas contingency operations—efforts to protect U.S. citizens, allies, and business interests from terrorists—and add in the costs for defense-related expenditures outside of the Pentagon, then the annual budget is well over one trillion dollars—more than what the entire world combined spends. And this does not include the aforementioned enormous costs for conducting military operations in the Middle East.[16]

There's no sincere desire for democracy and peace in this region by any of the governing parties, including the U.S. and Israel; in fact, quite the opposite is true: e.g., Saudi Arabia is among the most repressive regimes on the planet and has a glaring record of smashing democratic movements not only domestically, but all around the Persian Gulf—in March of 2011, the Saudi military played an important role in suppressing Bahrain's pro-democracy protests.

Not only is Saudi Arabia a totalitarian regime—an absolute hereditary monarchy with a well-documented record of human rights abuses, but it is also important to point out that 15 of the 19 hijackers on 9/11 were Saudi, as was Osama Bin Laden whose family has a multi-billion dollar construction company and close ties with the royals. George W. Bush acknowledged this fact some years later while visiting Saudi Arabia. When asked about the hijackers, he responded:

> There's a lot of really good people here. Look, you can't deny the fact that some, a majority of the terrorists came from Saudi, but you should not condemn an entire society based upon the actions of a handful of killers.[17]

And of course, as a prime example of George Orwell's notion of "double think," this comment is a blatant contradiction of Bush's own military actions in Afghanistan and Iraq.

Of the remaining four terrorists of 9/11: one was from Egypt, one from Lebanon, and the other two were from the United Arab Emirates. While you'd think that the idea of outsourcing and privatizing national security would be an insane proposition in this age when politicians are obsessed with international terrorism, the neoliberal Bush administration actually wanted to contract a United Arab Emirates-based company, Dubai Ports World, to provide port security here in the U.S.[18]

In 2005, Bush was seen greeting the future king of Saudi Arabia with a kiss on both cheeks when Prince Abdullah visited the Crawford ranch in Texas. The two men were negotiating oil production increases while strolling hand-in-hand through a garden of Blue Bonnet flowers. Likewise, in April of 2009, President Barack Obama, at the G-20 meeting in London, bowed to the very same man when they met. Accused of violating U.S. State Department protocol that the President of the United States bows to no one, the White House denied that Obama committed such an offense and retorted that it wasn't actually a bow, but rather a "stoop."

It's all so stupid, and yet there was a major uproar in mainstream U.S. media over these two incidents, with Republicans pitted against Democrats and vice-versa, but there was no substantive discussion of the fact that we're politically, economically, and militarily in bed with this tyrant who dictates over an abusive monarchy in what is among the richest countries on the planet as it holds the world hostage with its control of the oil tap. OPEC, which is largely under the influence of Saudi Arabia, has over 80% of the world's proven oil reserves. Who cares about these insignificant gestures and whether or not they are culturally or politically appropriate—one would expect Bush to kiss Abdullah's ass. What's of real importance is that the Obama administration neglected to publicly excoriate the Saudi king for human rights violations and his regime's role in smashing the pro-democracy movement in neighboring Bahrain. Obama's speech that addressed the Arab Spring of 2010—a whirlwind of uprisings, revolutionary demonstrations, and civil wars that have dramatically affected at least 17 Muslim nations, including Syria—didn't even mention Saudi Arabia. But behind the scenes, he did manage to negotiate a $60 billion arms deal with them—which is the largest single weapons sale in U.S. history.[19] So while Osama Bin Laden was from Saudi Arabia, as were 15 of the 19 hijackers on 9/11, we attacked Iraq in response—a country that was found by a UN inspections team led by Swedish diplomat Hans Blix to have no weapons of mass destruction as the U.S. so vociferously claimed; nor was there any evidence of Hussein's involvement with Al-Qaeda. In fact, the dictator was a secular Sunni who felt strongly that extreme Islamic protocol gravely endangered his own position of power and influence, and as such, he and Bin Laden despised each other.

Saddam Hussein was always a brutal despot, but when he was killing Iranians, Kurds, and Shia, it was perfectly fine with the U.S. who supplied him with economic, technological, and military support. He was a bastard, but he was our bastard. This is clearly evident in the photo of Donald Rumsfeld who was in Baghdad in 1983 as a special envoy of President Ronald Reagan and is smiling while shaking hands with Hussein.[20] In the Iran–Iraq war from 1980–1988, in which over 1.5 million people were killed, the U.S. played both sides of the fence and betrayed the Kurds caught in the middle—just as they would be in 1991. It's when Saddam turned on his benefactor that he became "Hitler revisited"—as both father and son Bush administrations so eagerly described him when he was no longer behaving.

What is particularly disturbing about the events of 9/11, besides the nearly 3,000 people who were murdered, is that the perpetrators—Osama Bin Laden and Al-Qaeda, were largely the creation of U.S. foreign policy; and yet only a handful of journalists and pundits of the mainstream media in the U.S. have been willing to seriously address this bitter fact.

The CIA, with the help of the Pakistani dictatorship led by President Mohammad Zia-ul-Haq, and subsequently by Ghulam Ishaq Khan in 1988 after Zia's death in a plane crash, funded, trained, and armed Muslim paramilitary groups to prepare for the 1979 Russian assault on Afghanistan. The plan was to ready these militant forces to carry out an insurgency—a jihad, against the "evil empire's" invading and occupying force. The Mujahideen was being trained in guerilla warfare, bomb making, sabotage, intelligence gathering, interrogation, and torture techniques. Many of its leaders were schooled at Camp Peary in Virginia—the facility known as "the farm" where the Special Activities Division of the National Clandestine Service of the CIA is educated.[21] SAD and its Paramilitary Operations Officers, led by Michael G. Vickers, would play a critical role in preparing and supporting the insurgents. British Intelligence's MI6 got involved in these training operations in Afghanistan and Pakistan from 1986–1992.[22]

This covert undertaking was called Operation Cyclone and lasted from 1979 through 1989 when the Soviets finally packed up and left Afghanistan. It is well-documented that Osama Bin Laden, the Saudi who had recently joined the resistance, got the full backing of the United States and would develop and fine-tune his techniques for networking and terrorist attacks during this period. President Jimmy Carter's National Security Advisor Zbigniew Brezinski told CNN in 1998 that his administration fully supported Bin Laden's forces and that on July 3, 1979, unbeknownst to the U.S. Congress, $500 million was funneled to the Muslim militants to start an Islamic movement throughout the region to destabilize the Soviets.[23] This support was greatly increased with the election of Ronald Reagan who in 1982 dedicated the upcoming flight of the Space Shuttle Columbia to the resistance fighters in Afghanistan; in 1985 he even entertained Mullah Omar and a delegation of the Mujahideen in the Oval Office. Reagan, the same guy who vetoed Congress's push to impose economic sanctions on the South African Apartheid regime, and rejected every piece of domestic civil rights legislation that came across his desk, enthusiastically referred to his guests as "freedom fighters" and added, "These gentlemen are the moral equivalents of America's Founding Fathers."[24]

Meanwhile, Reagan was deeply embroiled in the Iran-Contra scandal that by 1986 had been leaked to the public. His administration was caught red-handed secretly coordinating illegal weapons deals with the Ayatollah Khomeini regime in exchange for the release of American hostages and in order to fund the White House's covert wars throughout Central America, especially in Nicaragua.[25] Under the Boland Amendment passed by Congress, funding to the right-wing Contras was eliminated so Reagan's team found what it thought was a foolproof way around the sanctions that would allow them to continue to support the mission of removing the democratically-elected Sandinista government from power.[26] Israel would help with the weapons purchases from the Eastern bloc and deliveries to the Contras.[27]

Israel has a long and sordid past of supporting right-wing fascist movements and selling weapons throughout the Caribbean, and Central and South America—including in Haiti under Duvalier, in the Dominican Republic under Trujillo, in Chile under Pinochet, in Argentina during the junta (a country with a well-documented history of anti-Semitism),[28] and in Guatemala to assist the U.S.-backed Montt regime that was found guilty of genocide and crimes against humanity; talk about irony.[29]

Israel is currently the fourth largest arms dealer in the world with over $7 billion in exports—up 20% from 2011.[30] Over the past 5 years the Jewish state has even made equipment deals with Pakistan, Algeria, Egypt, Morocco, and the United Arab Emirates.[31]

When I was in Tel Aviv, I got a report that the Israeli Defense Ministry is providing additional support to the Mexican government to crush the Zapatista rebellion in Chiapas—in the form of weapons, technology, and advice on prisons and policing.[32] Israel has been providing Mexico with military aid since 1973 and military assistance in Chiapas since 1994 when NAFTA was signed into law and the insurrection began as a way for the indigenous people to defend themselves against the corporate annexation of their land through military force. The Zapatistas understand first-hand the global effects of neoliberalism, expansionism, racism, and dispossession, and have thus, regardless of the geographical distance, struggled in solidarity with the Palestinians.

The military occupation of Palestine, the longest occupation in the last 46 years, has been condemned by the International Court of Justice, the United Nations, the World Council of Churches, the European Union, the Red Cross, Amnesty International, Human Rights Watch, Machsom Watch, and countless other health and human rights associations and organizations that all agree that Israel is in violation of international territorial and humanitarian law under the Geneva Conventions.[33] Nonetheless, with virtual impunity Israel has rejected UN resolutions that demand that it put an immediate end to the occupation, the construction of the separation wall, and the expansion of settlements in the Gaza Strip, East Jerusalem, the West Bank, and the Golan Heights. During my 3-week stay in Israel and the occupied territories there were human rights abuses regularly perpetrated against the Bedouin and Palestinian people, including illegal property annexation; home invasions, evictions, and demolitions; unwarranted settler, police, and military brutality; and incarceration without charges or due process. Over 7,500 Palestinian children have been detained, interrogated, and imprisoned since the year 2000.[34] While I was there, 14 kids were taken into custody, or what the Palestinians more accurately describe as "were abducted." There have been reports of torturing children psychologically and physically, shackling them, putting them in solitary confinement, and keeping them from their families. The July 4, 2013 UN Convention on the Rights of the Child condemned Israel for its treatment of children.[35]

"Multiple laws, policies, and court rulings in Israel violate nearly every freedom enumerated in the First Amendment of the U.S. Constitution, including freedom of religion, freedom of speech, freedom of the press, and freedom of peaceable assembly."[36] And yet the U.S. has been giving Israel $3 billion in direct foreign aid each year, which now totals over $120 billion, and billions more in loan guarantees and preferential contracts.[37] Obama had promised $30 billion in additional assistance over the next 10 years.[38] Meanwhile people in the U.S. are facing a draconian sequester, have been losing their homes to foreclosure at the rate of one million a year, and public schools are being closed down all over the nation, especially in poor urban areas. The economic disparity between the rich and the poor is the largest it's been since the annual census was first taken in 1946. Over 48 million people are poor—up 2.6 million from 2011.[39] 3.9 million people are homeless—39% of which are children and over 200,000 are vets. 84 million people are without health insurance. There are currently 27 million people who are unemployed or underemployed,[40] and 47 million people who rely on food stamps—another social program that conservatives portray as a "hand out" that should be eliminated.[41] As the general population of the U.S. is falling deeper and deeper into debt, the top 20% of Americans who own 85% of the country's wealth are swimming in prosperity.

Obama is not only maintaining the tradition of class warfare here in the states, but he is also in step with supporting dictatorships in Central and South America.[42] In June of 2009, his administration assisted right-wing military forces in overthrowing President Manuel Zelaya in Honduras. And in 2010 there was a U.S.-backed coup attempt in Ecuador to remove President Rafael Correa who has categorically rejected neoliberalism and the United States' influence on the region and forced the closure of the U.S. Army base in his country. The Bolivian Alliance of the Americas (ALBA), a group of nations that is against U.S. imperialism and is working on economic independence and healthy relationships among Central and South American countries, has investigated and condemned the coups backed by Washington, USAID, and the National Endowment for Democracy. ALBA also holds the former Bush administration responsible for the attempt to oust Hugo Chavez in Venezuela in 2002, the call for his assassination, and funding right-wing opposition candidates in the nation's legislative elections.[43]

The CIA covert operation in Afghanistan in the 1980s proved to be the longest and most costly in U.S. history. It is estimated that up to $20 billion went to the Mujahideen over the years; and the weapons that were amply supplied to the militants included shoulder-fired anti-aircraft Stinger missiles. Once again, the Israelis would coordinate the deliveries of any non-U.S. weaponry—largely from China. Pakistan also received huge sums of economic support and weapons from the United States: over $7 billion and 40 F-16 fighter jets.

In 1982, Zia's military dictatorship in Pakistan assisted the U.S. in recruiting from the over three million refugees that had fled the fighting in Afghanistan and were finding safe-haven across the eastern border. Under the supervision of William Casey, the Director of the CIA from 1981–1987, the U.S. would be given the opportunity to hand pick extremist militants from other Muslim countries, that eventually totaled over 100,000 recruits.[44]

The CIA could be found on a regular basis at the headquarters of the Pakistani Inter-Services Intelligence in Peshawar, as the two agencies worked together to coordinate attack plans for the Mujahideen. Bin Laden and his fellow combatants would receive extensive satellite reconnaissance about Soviet positions and movements. The ISI and CIA also participated in leading guerilla fighters on undercover missions to bomb the infrastructure inside of Afghanistan, including airports. With the help of these two intelligence agencies, Bin Laden was able to recruit over 4,000 fighters and raise considerable funds back in Saudi Arabia. At the training and operation camps, militants from all over the world would meet for the very first time and were able to forge long-term relationships—and so Bin Laden's extensive global networking began. By 1988, while still assisting the U.S., he spawned Al-Qaeda. The name in English means "the base," and it has indeed been a centralizing force for coordinating terrorist cells all over the world. George H.W. Bush had just been elected president and Washington did nothing at the time to prevent this ominous development—thinking that there were bigger fish to fry. Richard Murphy, Assistant Secretary of State for Near East and South Asian Relations during the Reagan administration, admitted later:

> We did spawn a monster in Afghanistan. Once the Soviets were gone the people trained and/or funded by the U.S. were looking around for other targets, and Osama Bin Laden has settled on the United States as the source of all evil. Irony? Irony is all over the place.[45]

In the late 1980s, Prime Minister Benazir Bhutto of Pakistan told President Bush, "You are creating a Frankenstein."[46] Nonetheless, funding to the Mujahideed and Pakistan would continue even after the Soviets had called it quits. A civil war broke out after Russian forces had departed and the U.S. and Saudi Arabia wanted to make sure that their dog in the fight, now calling themselves the Northern Alliance, could hold its ground. But thousands of the former Mujahideen would return home after the war with Russia, to the many countries from whence they came, and begin their own campaigns of violence. The CIA essentially prepared forces for a global jihad; it wouldn't be long before they would turn on their benefactors.

U.S. congressional and senatorial representatives, the State Department, the Senate Foreign Relations Committee, and the CIA would also support the rise of the Taliban in the 1990s, regardless of their well-known extremism and disdain for democracy and human rights. American oil barons desperately needed a stabilizing government in place so that a pipeline could be built through Afghanistan and secured. The Taliban, which had been gaining power throughout the country during the civil war, seemed to be the optimal choice to back. As one U.S. diplomat was quoted as saying:

> The Taliban will probably develop like the Saudis. There will be Aramco [the consortium of oil companies that controlled Saudi oil], pipelines, an emir, no parliament and lots of Sharia law. We can live with that.[47]

A syndicate spearheaded by the U.S.-based Unocal Corporation masterminded a $4.5 billion plan to build a pipeline from the Caspian Sea through Turkmenistan, Afghanistan, Pakistan, and India, ending at the Arabian Sea. The Taliban would provide national stability and security, and thus received the support of the United States, all under the nose of the American people.

It wasn't until 1998 that the Taliban became a public concern for mainstream media when Washington was angered that the Afghan government wouldn't hand over Bin Laden after Al-Qaeda had bombed the U.S. embassies in Tanzania and Kenya. Over $10 billion had to go into ousting the very governing body that we had just spent billions to put in place, money that went directly into the pockets of the Northern Alliance to attack and bomb Kabul—something that they were really good at as their initial efforts during the early stages of the civil war had killed over 50,000 people.

Bin Laden believed that Muslims should take up arms against any enemy of Islam. He was angry with the U.S. for supporting Israel and their brutal treatment of the Palestinians during the decades-old illegal occupation of their lands. He despised U.S. foreign policy for being hostile toward Muslim countries—such as the military invasion in Somalia in the 1990s and the 1998 bombing of Sudan.[48] But mostly, Bin Laden was infuriated that the U.S. had military installations in what Muslims consider the holiest place on earth—Saudi Arabia, where Mecca and Medina are located. For Bin Laden, the Prophet Muhammad forbade the "permanent presence of infidels in Arabia." At one point in 1991, there were more than 550,000 U.S. troops stationed there, and many Muslims viewed the staggering size of this force as an occupation. Most Islamic countries were extremely upset with these U.S. military bases; in fact, 52% of Saudis themselves wanted the American soldiers out. The United States military finally wised up and packed up in September of 2003.

After the assassination of Bin Laden by U.S. Navy Seals on May 2, 2011 in Abbottab, Pakistan, the Pakistani government, who was kept out of the loop on Operation Neptune Spear, stopped sharing information with the Pentagon. Bear in mind that since 1984, Pakistan has possessed a nuclear arsenal. Many of its citizens hit the streets and expressed their anger by burning American flags. The Pakistani public has become more radicalized by U.S. policies and practices, especially Obama's current use of drone strikes in the region. It's a complex world out there to say the least.

I think that what all great educators like Edward Said and Noam Chomsky do, in what I call "passing the torch," is they encourage us to critically appropriate from existing explanations about how and why things work the way they do in order to help us actively theorize for ourselves the socio-political landscape that currently shapes our lives. In what I call a pedagogy of exposition and not imposition, critical pedgogues expose us to the important issues of the day and assist us in developing a language of critique that makes it possible to think about the political, economic, institutional, and cultural realities that surround us so as to be able to work toward realizing the kinds of social changes that we see fit. As Albert Einstein once said, "I don't teach my students, I create the conditions in which they can learn." These educators, among so many other awesome environmentalist, feminist, anti-racist, gay and lesbian, and anti-capitalist pedagogues, have passed the torch to countless people as they inspire us to go out into the world, experience it for ourselves, and make change.

So often, I hear from my graduate students or the audience during the Q&A session after a talk, "Academics only criticize, but they don't have any practical solutions, and they themselves don't do anything about the problem." This criticism is not without merit in that it is true that many progressive and radical leftist scholars often simply make a good living by weaving theoretical discourses that intellectualize oppression, but they couldn't be bothered with actually getting involved in remedying the very injustice that they speak, write, and teach about. In essence, they live off the backs of the oppressed.

I remember when I was a graduate student and I was left in charge of entertaining a bigwig critical pedagogue while he and his wife were in Boston. He's white and writes a lot about racism and the criminalization of the black male body, which is important work to be doing for sure, as the recent Trayvon Martins murder and disgraceful acquittal so glaringly reminds us 50 years after Martin Luther King, Jr.'s "I Have a Dream" speech. I brought this academic to Wally's, which is a tiny-little dive bar with cheap cold beers, a racially and economically mixed clientele, a sassy older African-American waitress, a few neighborhood old-timers in their favorite caps huddled up at the bar giggling amongst themselves, and good live tunes. It is among the oldest family-owned and operated jazz clubs in existence and is located on Massachusetts Avenue, just down the way from Berkley College of Music, the Christian Science building, the Boston Symphony, and just before the trendy South End. The police headquarters is down a block or two around the corner. Nonetheless, this guy was terrified and whispered in my ear that they wanted to leave immediately. I should have dropped them off in one of the beat down oppressed sections of Boston to add some authenticity and validity to his scholarship.

What's inspiring about educators like Said and Chomsky is that they embody the spirit of praxis. While each of them has published extensively and achieved international prominence, they don't just think, talk, teach, and write about the world in all of its abstract complexities—they actually leave the comforts and safety of their offices and lecture halls to put their lives on the line in solidarity with others to bring about justice, equity, and peace.

Edward Said certainly talked the talk and walked the walk until his untimely death in 2003 of leukemia at the age of 67. He was born in 1935 in Jerusalem during the British Mandate. His parents were Palestinian, Greek Orthodox Christians. Said's father had served in the U.S. Army during WWI and was granted U.S. citizenship in return. However, Edward spent much of his childhood in Cairo and Lebanon as he and his family were refugees after the Israelis had destroyed hundreds of villages, massacred Muslim civilians, appropriated Palestinian lands and homes, and orchestrated the forced exodus of nearly one million Arabs in 1948.

While he attended elite schools during his youth, Said was not fond of the ways in which traditional educational institutions dictated every aspect of his life and he resisted this conformity and was often reprimanded for his behavior. As a result, Said was sent to a private academy in the U.S., in Massachusetts. While he felt extremely isolated here, he nonetheless took great joy in learning and rose academically to the top of his class. He would complete his undergraduate education at Princeton and his master's and doctorate in English literature at Harvard. He was deeply influenced by the French poststructuralists—in particular the work of Michele Foucault, which offered up theoretical and empirical insights to understand how asymmetrical relations of power are inextricably linked to the ways in which culture is produced, maintained, and resisted. What was so important for Said was the fundamental idea that if oppressive practices are socio-historically constructed, then humans have the necessary agency, both personally and collectively, to change the world. In 1963, Said accepted a position in the Department of English and Comparative Literature at Columbia. His professional life would have him teaching in such elite institutions as Harvard, Stanford, and Johns Hopkins, but Said didn't let that get in the way of his political beliefs and activist efforts; by 1967 he was a voice to be reckoned with.

While he supported the right of Jews to have a safe haven, Said worked tirelessly to bring about a renewed Palestinian state and to counter racist representations of the Arab and Muslim world in Western literature, historical accounts, and corporate media. He was a member of the PNC, the Palestinian National Council, from 1977–1991. He left the organization because he disagreed with its support of the Oslo Accords—the Declaration of Principles on Interim Self-Government Arrangements that were being drawn up for the occupied territories. The Accords were eventually signed in 1993, much to Said's disapproval as he felt that they were fundamentally unfair and doomed to fail. He would push forward and focus his energy on alternative strategies for helping refugees and putting a stop to the illegal but ever-expanding Jewish settlements in the occupied territories.

In 1998, with his son by his side, and suffering with terminal leukemia, Said returned to Israel and the occupied territories to fight for Palestinians rights. A documentary was made of this journey called *In Search of Palestine*.[49] It has some very powerful scenes, including one in which Said confronts Israeli soldiers that were removing a family from their home before it was bulldozed. There is also a very moving moment during a visit with a family that lost their home many years back, and the father brings out the deed and a skeleton key that goes to the old front door that they keep in order to hold on to their dream that even though the structure is long gone, someday they or future generations will return to that place and rebuild their lives. I watched the documentary last night for the first time and it was a vivid reminder of what I saw on my trip to Israel and the occupied territories, as these injustices are not rare events, they are happening every day.

In 2000, Said was filmed throwing a stone across the Blue Line that separates Israel from Lebanon. As a result, conservatives in the U.S. and Israel referred to him as "the professor of terror," and reactionary students and alumni at Columbia University along with some influential members of the Anti-Defamation League were demanding that he be permanently removed from his academic position—a petition that was dismissed by the university provost.

In 2002, Said was awarded the *Prince of Asturias Concord Prize* in Spain for his efforts toward finding a lasting peace in the Middle East. The following year, fed up with the infighting among factions of the Palestinian Authority, he co-founded Al-Mubadara—the Palestinian National Initiative—as a way to open up other political avenues than those being offered by Fatah and Hamas.

Because of his activist efforts and associations with pro-Arab organizations, and his friendship with Noam Chomsky and Howard Zinn, the FBI, CIA, and Mossad kept close tabs on Said's movements, colleagues, and family. His surveillance records were filed under the header, "Foreign Counterintelligence/IS Middle East"—the "IS" standing for "Israel." The bureau was recently compelled to release 147 pages of his 238-page dossier. Edward's wife Mariam was quoted as saying: "We always knew that any political activity concerning the Palestinian issue is monitored and when talking on the phone we would say 'let the tappers hear this.'" Regardless of the non-stop surveillance and the frequent death threats that he received, Said continued his work for social justice and peace until the day he died. In honor of his life's work, the Michigan Peace Team established the annual *Edward Said Scholar/Activist Award*.

Noam Chomsky is also a beacon of light for those who wish to put theory into action. He was born in 1928 in Philadelphia; his parents were Ashkenazi Jews who fled from the Ukraine and came to the U.S. in 1913 just before WWI. His father was a schoolteacher and eventually became a professor of medieval Hebrew at Gratz College in Philly. Noam's early education in a Temple University experimental school—based on the ideas of John Dewey—allowed him to pursue his interests and creativity and by the age of 10 he was already researching and writing about the spread of fascism in Europe. He attended a public high school and like Said, he was dissatisfied with the conformity, control, and competition that permeated school life.

While his parents were democrats and fairly progressive, Chomsky would get the radical torch passed to him by some of his relatives who were socialists involved with the International Ladies' Garment Workers' Union. His uncle owned and operated a newsstand in New York City that made for a prime gathering spot for Jewish leftists to hang out and debate critical issues of the day. It was in New York City that Chomsky would bury himself in radical and anarchist bookstores where he would develop and sharpen his political ideas and voice.

In 1945, at the age of 16 Chomsky went to the University of Pennsylvania where he studied Arabic. As a way to help finance his education he taught Hebrew. During these years, he was heavily influenced by the work of anarcho-syndicalist Rudolf Rocker as well as democratic socialist George Orwell. Chomsky would go on to complete a research fellowship in linguistics at Harvard and his PhD at Penn in 1955. By the mid-1960s, given his breakthroughs in linguistic theory, he had developed an international reputation for himself.

Noam Chomsky's intellectual contributions and social activism span decades. In 1967, in solidarity with students who were protesting mandatory military service and the war in Vietnam, he was arrested for participating in a teach-in outside the Pentagon. Engendering what Italian theorist Antonio Gramsci called an "organic intellectual," Chomsky wasn't impressed with the elite leftist scholars of the time who were largely disconnected from reality; he preferred working with everyday activists and community organizations. As a result of his anti-war efforts, he was arrested on multiple occasions and President Nixon added him to his "Enemies List." At risk of losing the family livelihood and being incarcerated because of his political beliefs and actions, his wife Carol decided to go back to school and prepare for a career in case something drastic happened.

Leaving the comforts and security of MIT, Chomsky has traveled to some of the most oppressed and dangerous places in the world, to lend a hand of support. He was in Haiti at the peak of the terror in 1993, working with the late Father Gerard Jean-Juste who was in hiding from government forces. While there, he also met with labor leaders, many of whom had been detained and tortured.

Despite death threats, being told by MIT that he needed police security by his side at all times—which he turned down—and being relentlessly spied on by the FBI and CIA, Chomsky continued on with his political efforts. The Anti-Defamation League also placed surveillance on him as the organization has been in cahoots with Alan Dershowitz who has long been infuriated by Chomsky's anti-Israeli position on the Palestinian question—Chomsky is opposed to the establishment of a religious state and has long asserted that Israel's policies and human rights atrocities will ultimately destroy the country. On May 16, 2010, on his way to visit a university in the West Bank, he was detained for several hours by

Israeli border security after trying to cross over from Jordan, and denied entry by an Interior Ministry official.

Chomsky has vehemently protested against the Patriot Act and U.S. military detention centers around the world, in particular Bagram in Afghanistan and Abu Ghraib in Iraq where Army police sexually abused, tortured, and killed prisoners, as well as the Guantanamo Bay detention camp established by the George W. Bush administration in 2002 to interrogate "enemy-combatants" who are being held without due process and tortured—a direct violation of the Geneva Conventions and habeas corpus. There have been 41 suicide attempts since the camp was opened and Amnesty International has called Gitmo "the Gulag of our times."

For Chomsky, the Patriot Act, that was legislated in 2001 as a government response to the events of 9/11, violates civil liberties and Constitutional rights, especially the Fourth Amendment that protects against unlawful search and seizure, unwarranted roving wire taps and background checks on U.S. citizens, and surveillance of people with no ties to terrorists. In 2011, Obama signed a renewal of the Patriot Act, and the National Security Agency has thus been allowed to continue to tap our phones, access our records, and monitor Internet use and electronic communications without a legal warrant.

In January of 2012, Chomsky, along with Chris Hedges, Daniel Ellsberg, and four others, sued the federal government in the *Hedges v. Obama* case that resulted "in a permanent judicial injunction against the National Defense Authorization Act, 'which authorized the military to detain U.S. citizens indefinitely, strip them of due process, and hold them in military facilities, including offshore penal colonies.'"

In the spirit of collaboration, Chomsky would develop a long-lasting friendship with Howard Zinn and they worked together on the release of the controversial Gravel Edition of the *Pentagon Papers*.[50] In January of 1970, Daniel Ellsberg befriended the two and gave them a copy of the documents because nobody was talking about them publically, regardless of Ellsberg's efforts to expose their contents. He also released portions of the report to *The New York Times*, which resulted in him being tried for conspiracy, theft, and espionage. Zinn was called to testify for the defense. Reflecting on this experience, Howard said:

> I explained there was nothing in the papers of military significance that could be used to harm the defense of the United States, that the information in them was simply embarrassing to our government because what was revealed, in the government's own interoffice memos, was how it had lied to the American public. The secrets disclosed in the Pentagon Papers might embarrass politicians, might hurt the profits of corporations wanting tin, rubber, and oil in far-off places. But this was not the same as hurting the nation, the people.[51]

Like those progressive educators that passed the torch and inspired Howard Zinn along the way, as a scholar and activist he in turn encouraged countless students to think through and fight oppression in all of its forms:

> I wanted my writing of history and my teaching of history to be a part of social struggle. I wanted to be a part of history and not just a recorder and teacher of history. So that kind of attitude towards history, history itself as a political act, has always informed my writing and my teaching.[52]

Ellsberg, Zinn, and Chomsky's whistleblowing reminds me of what's happening today with Bradley Manning's leaks of more than 700,000 Pentagon documents, and Edward Snowden's exposure of British and U.S. domestic spy operations.

Manning, a low-level intelligence analyst for the U.S. Army in Iraq in 2010, was just sentenced to 35 years in prison for what's now considered the most extensive leak of classified information in U.S. history. The documents included information about the detainees in Guantanamo Bay, battlefield reports, and the details of a Reuters photojournalist being killed along with 11 others in a U.S. helicopter raid. Manning was arrested in May of 2010 and he has defended his actions by saying that he wants to provoke a public inquiry into U.S. military policies and practices that he views as having a total disregard for human life. In July of 2013, he was found guilty of most of the 22 charges held against him, including espionage and theft, but he was acquitted of aiding the enemy.

WikiLeaks creator Julian Assange also found himself in legal hot water because of the case. An activist and journalist from Australia, Assange wanted to design a place in cyberspace where people could be whistleblowers and anonymously submit information to the site, that he would edit and then post. The website was established in 2006. Manning felt ethically compelled to do what he did and later revealed, "I felt this sense of relief by them having it.... I felt I had accomplished something that allowed me to have a clear conscience."

Ex-CIA and former National Security contractor Edward Snowden, in May of 2013, leaked to the British paper, *The Guardian*, critical information about the U.S. and British governments' classified domestic surveillance programs. Snowden, who has been called everything from "a patriot" to "a traitor," has defended his actions by saying that he wants "to inform the public as to that which is done in their name and that which is done against them." This event has forced President Obama to try and reform these spy operations in order to regain the trust of the American people—as he ambiguously stated in his televised national speech. What the public was largely unaware of until Snowden stepped forward, is that since the passing of the Foreign Intelligence Surveillance Act of 1978, the FISA court system has allowed both post-9/11 administrations carte blanche to spy on Americans; the FISA court makes all the decisions on what is approved and the public has no access to this body or its decision-making process. Ironically, Snowden is currently hiding out in Russia.

It's important to note that the FBI, CIA, and Mossad don't spy on people like Said and Chomsky because they think they're buffoons: they keep close track of them because they know that they are on to the truth about crimes being committed against democracy and humanity and they are thus a threat to the right-wing agenda. Conservatives have no vested interest in telling the truth, as evident in George H.W. Bush's comment in *Newsweek* on August 15, 1988 while on the presidential campaign trail: "I will never apologize for the United States of America, ever. I don't care what the facts are!" On the contrary, when Noam was recently asked about "speaking truth to power," he responded as he always does when this subject comes up:

> That's actually a Quaker slogan, and I like the Quakers and I do a lot of things with them, but I don't agree with the slogan. First of all, you don't have to speak truth to power, because they know it already. And secondly, you don't speak truth to anybody, that's too arrogant. What you do is join with people and try to find the truth, so you listen to them and tell them what you think and so on, and you try to encourage people to think for themselves. The ones you are concerned with are the victims, not the powerful, so the slogan ought to be to engage with the powerless and help them and help yourself to find the truth. It's not an easy slogan to formulate in five words, but I think it's the right one.[53]

Years ago, Noam responded to my question about the role of the public intellectual in making substantive social change in the world:

> The job of the honest intellectual is to help out people who need help; to be part of the people who are struggling for rights and justice. That's what you should be doing. But of course, you don't expect to be rewarded for that.[54]

As a case and point, I had a graduate student named John who was brilliant and would read and take notes like there was no tomorrow. He was an inquisitive gentle giant with thick curly brown hair and the smile of a child who had just discovered something new. John had served in the U.S. Military and was stationed in Beirut, Lebanon. On October 23, 1983 the multinational military barracks were blown up by two Islamic Jihad truck bombs that killed, among others, 240 Americans, and injured 43—the worst single attack on U.S. Marines since the battle of Iwo Jima during WWII. John was one of the survivors of the First Battalion 8th Marines and he was placed in charge of watching over the dead before they could be transported back to the states. Needless to say, the experience of losing his friends and fellow soldiers and keeping watch over them day and night was deeply traumatizing. When he returned home, the Department of Defense got him a job as a tour guide for the Freedom Trail in Boston.

Well, John thought it proper to give the good visitors of Boston the truth about the American Revolution as he understood it from the extensive research that he had conducted—and believe me, when I say "extensive," I mean extensive! Much like Howard Zinn's book *A People's History of the United States,* John knew that the truth of the matter was that since the early colonial years, the U.S. has largely been built on the interests of the elite business classes, which needless to say have benefited greatly from a longstanding denial of the structural realities of a class system—as captured in the Pledge of Allegiance's closing phrase, "…one nation under God, indivisible, with liberty and justice for all." Their efforts may have been revolutionary against the King of England, but they were reactionary in creating an equitable society for the working class, women, indigenous populations, and enslaved Africans. So John added to the government-sanctioned script that was handed to him along with a uniform and hat, and he shared the little-known details with his guests. Until one day, when a Republican lawyer from Ohio was on the guided tour and was disgusted with what he was hearing. John told me with a giggle that he could see the man getting more and more agitated with what he was hearing as they moved from one historical site to the next. When he returned to Ohio, and probably still beet-red in the face, the man wrote a formal letter to Washington and to Beacon Hill demanding that John, who he described as "a disgrace" and "un-American," be removed from his post, which sadly and disgracefully he was.

For me, Chomsky's most inspirational political act was when he went to Turkey to defend his colleague against legal charges that were being brought against both of them by the government. In February of 2002, he and his Turkish publisher Fatih Tas were charged with crimes against the state. Tas had printed works by Chomsky in which comments were made about the U.S. support for the Turkish massacre of Kurds—which was described as "ethnic cleansing." A court in Istanbul had accused the two men of trying to subvert the unity of the country. When he became aware of the situation and the charges, Chomsky immediately flew to Istanbul to stand in solidarity with his friend. After their acquittal, Tas thanked Noam, who then jumped a plane for Kurdistan.

Throughout his career, Chomsky has been honored with a mountain of awards: He is twice winner of *The Orwell Award* granted by the National Council of Teachers of English for "Distinguished Contributions to Honesty and Clarity in Public Language"; he received the *A.E. Havens Center's Award for Lifetime Contribution to Critical Scholarship*; the *Thomas Merton Award* from the Thomas Merton Center for Peace and Social Justice; the *Sydney Peace Prize* for his "unfailing courage, critical analysis of power and promotion of human rights"; the *Dorothy Eldridge Peacemaker Award*; the *Global Exchange Human Rights Award,* U.S.; and the Peace Memorial's *Peace Prize*. The 2005 Global Intellectuals Poll conducted by the British magazine *Prospect,* voted him the "Leading Living Public Intellectual"; in 2006, *New Statesman* magazine placed him seventh on their list of "Heroes of Our Time."

Chomsky and Said are just two examples of educators who engage in praxis, but the reality is that in order to bring about social change, social justice activists have access to a rich theoretical and empirical history of different ways of thinking about the relations between intellectual and political practice. In fact, armed with a deep understanding of the synergy that exists among theory, research, and activism—a firm grasp of the multidirectional relationships within which each component influences and strengthens the other—people and organizations have long worked to secure human, economic, and political rights. At its foundation, the relationship among theory, research, and activism is relatively simple. As theory—through interpretation and explanation—begs empirical and practical questions and illuminates research findings and activist efforts, research not only puts theory to the test and provides the potential for its expansion, but it can also offer activists tangible models to critically appropriate from in order to address the specificities of their current predicaments. Meanwhile, activism can simultaneously push theory forward into uncharted territory and expand the horizons of empirical analysis. All of this ongoing interaction helps us better make sense of and act upon the world in far more informed, efficient, and effective ways. Making use of this synergy is of particular importance in this age of globalization—largely driven by changes in economics and interactive technologies—where social agency is taking on new forms. While many members of the global justice movement—that movement of many movements—have been making effective use of existing theory and research to inform their strategic maneuvers, their actions are simultaneously bringing into focus new questions for analysis and exploration.

In this respect, my trip to Israel and the occupied territories was extremely demanding. Now back home in the States, I am exhausted spiritually, emotionally, intellectually, politically, and physically. Fortunately, projects such as writing this afterword for Orelus and Chomsky's new book, and remembering the faces of the Palestinian children in the refugee camps in Jericho, reenergize me with hope that if we continue the good fight for peace, freedom, and justice, that substantive social, political, and institutional change is possible, and that if we continuously and unyieldingly pass the torch of knowledge, epistemological curiosity, and solidarity, we can leave this world a better place than we found it.

For the first leg of my journey, I was put in touch with a guide through a referral service at the hotel in Haifa. I needed a driver that could bring me into the Golan Heights and along the Lebanese border. Guides in Israel have to be licensed with the state. Yaacov, a Jewish man in his mid-'60s took great pride in his knowledge of the region. He told me twice that he had driven CNN's Senior International Correspondent Ben Wedeman around the northern region of Israel during the 2006 invasion of Lebanon—Wedeman's crew was doing a story on the medevac units of the Israeli military.

Over the next 6 days, we enjoyed each other's company—he was extremely bright and had this dry sense of humor that reminded me of Chomsky. I would often respond to his requests with an "OK dad…" as he was always worried about me wandering off in the villages with my camera, and especially around the minefields. He would nudge me in the ribs when I'd be taking pictures of security systems, armed soldiers, helicopters, gunboats, prison exteriors, military bases, and such, asking, "Are you a spy?" He was joking of course as I'm certain that he did a background check on me after our initial phone conversation when I shared with him that I am a professor and the kind of research that I planned on doing. He wanted to know that I wasn't just some 'conflict tourist' seeking a voyeuristic adventure in a war-torn area. The online profile check is how he knew about the extent of my research and publications and that I was the 2007 recipient of the *Studs Terkel Award for Media and Journalism*—Studs was an American-born author and journalist of Russian Jewish decent who is perhaps best known for his oral histories of everyday people, exactly what we were about to engage in.

Yaacov took me into the Golan Heights—occupied Syrian territory taken by Israel in 1967 in the Six Day War. The U.S. State Department had just released an advisory against going to the northern borders:

> Rocket attacks into Israel from Lebanon have occurred without warning along the Israeli–Lebanese border. Tensions have increased along portions of the Disengagement Zone with Syria in the Golan Heights as a result of the internal conflict occurring in that country. Sporadic gunfire has occurred along the border region. There have been several incidents of mortar shells and light arms fire impacting on the Israeli-controlled side of the zone as a result of spillover from the fighting in Syria. Travelers should be aware that cross-border gunfire could occur without warning. Furthermore, there are active landmines in areas of the Golan Heights, so visitors should walk only on established roads or trails. Due to the sporadic, unpredictable nature of the Syrian conflict in these areas, U.S. government personnel must notify the Embassy's Regional Security Office in advance if they plan to visit the Golan Heights.[55]

Part of my desire to go to the Golan was to see if Israel, given the economic and strategic importance of this territory, would ever return the land back to Syria—a prerequisite for a peace agreement for the Syrians. The annexed area is arguably between 440 and 589 square miles, depending upon whom you talk to. The Golan Heights look into Jordan to the south, Lebanon to the north, Israel to the west, and Syria to the east.

On July 17, 2013, the UN reported that over 93,000 people had been killed since the Syrian uprising began against Assad's repressive regime in March of 2011, and that 5,000 Syrians are now dying each month. It also estimates that 1.6 million people have fled the country and 1.2 million have been displaced internally. As the UN representative from Denmark that I met with in Jerusalem told me, "There are seemingly thousands of sectarian militia groups in Syria…

who do you support under these conditions?" He explained that there is a serious reluctance to arm the rebels, as there are Jihadists, even Al-Qaeda, among them.

On January 30, 2013, 10 Israeli jets bombed some trucks in Syria believed to be carrying Russian-made SA-17 anti-aircraft missiles to Lebanon. On May 5th, a little over a month before my arrival in Tel Aviv, Israel had bombed inside of Syria once again in an attempt to stop Hezbollah from getting a load of Iranian-made Fateh-110 guided missiles. Syria has claimed that the target was actually a research facility near the capital Damascus and that 42 soldiers were killed. In response to the attacks, and contemplating the possibility of retaliation against Israel, Syrian President Bashar Assad was quoted in the international press as saying that "Syria will respond in kind to any future Israeli airstrike on its territory." Ahmad Shalash, a member of the Syrian Parliament, added, "Let it all out, they want an open war, let it be an open war, we don't have a problem." Nonetheless, on July 5th the Israelis bombed what it said was a shipment of Russian-made Yakhont anti-ship missiles, killing several Syrian soldiers.

My travels through the Golan Heights took me from the border with Jordan up to the area near the small town of Katzrin. It is a Jewish settlement/moshavim with a population of 6,400 and it is considered the Israeli capital of the region because it is where the Golan Regional Council resides. There are 32 other settlements and 10 kibbutzim in the occupied territory that has a population of over 20,000 Jews and 20,000 Syrians who are mostly ethnic Druze.

At one point, I had to take a pee and Yaacov wanted me to wait in order to get past a landmine area. When he stopped the car next to a massive field of sunflowers and hay bales, he told me that the Israeli army had demined this particular section of land and the local Kibbutz is now able to cultivate it; and of course I provided the fertilizer. The settlements are on very fertile land that is prime for growing vegetables and fruit that the settlers and the Druze prosper from. There are vast orchards that produce the tastiest cherries and apples on earth, vineyards and wineries owned by conglomerates of kibbutzim, some luxury hotels, and even a ski resort in the northern mountains. Large stretches of land further northeast from us are littered with blown-out tanks from the warfare back in 1973. The vast plateau is also known for its potential oil and gas reserves that Israel has been working on exploiting.

The southwestern border of the Golan looks over the Jordan River and the Sea of Galilee—which is actually a large freshwater lake. Beyond the strategic military and agricultural value of this region, control of the water is of extreme importance. Yaacov explained to me that at one point the Syrians tried to dam up the Jordan River that flows from north to south to try and drain the Sea of Galilee in order to displace the Israelis living there. He proudly added, "Of course the air force immediately bombed the makeshift dam and that was that." I asked him if Israel had any plans on giving this land back to Syria and he responded with an emphatic "No! The bastards had it and they lost it…there are winners and losers in war and we are the winners." And war it was: the entire ridge to the southeast looking over the valley into Jordan, where we began our climb into the Golan, is littered with minefields, barbed wire, and bunkers where many soldiers died in the fighting back in 1967 and 1973.

Deeper into the heights, we drove past the Israeli drone training facility that looms above the Sea of Galilee—the very sea where Jesus was said to have fed 5,000 hungry people with fish and bread, walked on water, and calmed a threatening storm; I've always appreciated the bumper sticker, "Who would Jesus bomb?"

We drove through a number of abandoned Syrian villages that lay in ruin, engulfed by overgrown grass, thistle, and weeds. There are a lot of yellow, red, and black signs warning passersby of the landmines. Yaacov kept referring to such villages as "primitive." But when we'd pass by Jewish settlements and businesses, he would always comment, "These are vast improvements on what was here before." While such settlements are illegal under international law, the Israeli government has disregarded the demands of the international community and has actually promoted continued expansion. As a result, the Jewish population in the Golan has more than doubled since 1989.

The area south of Katzrin gave us a distant view into Quneitra, which sits on top of the disengagement line between Israel and Syria where there is intense fighting going on. This old capital dates back to the Ottoman Empire. High in the Golan Heights, the city was largely destroyed in the wars of '67 and '73 and is consequently virtually uninhabited. Since the ceasefire agreement on May 31, 1974, the United Nations Disengagement Observer Force has been monitoring the Golan. But the recent spillover of violence from the civil war in this border region has caused a number of UN forces to withdraw. In December 2012, two Austrian peacekeepers were wounded in a firefight between government and rebel forces. Given the growing instability, Japan made the decision to pull its personnel. On February 28, 2013, Croatia followed suit. On June 6th of 2013, during the fighting at Quneitra Crossing, a mortar shell that landed in the barracks of their border headquarters injured two U.N. peacekeepers. As a direct result, on June 11th, three days before I arrived in the area, Austria began withdrawing its 380 troops. A Reuters reporter said that Austria had already pulled out of Quneitra Crossing and moved into a UN base inside of the Israeli-occupied territories. A month earlier, four Filipino personnel had been held by rebel forces and were eventually released unharmed. A Filipino peacekeeper was one of the two people injured by mortar fire in early June and these two events prompted the Filipino government to contemplate a total withdraw as well. Meanwhile, Syrian civilians caught in the middle of this deadly mess were trying to get into Israeli-occupied territory, but the Israeli Defense Forces were turning them back. Russia offered to become part of the Golan monitoring team but the UN denied the request because President Vladimir Putin has been very vocal about backing the Assad regime and supplying his soldiers with weapons. In early July, Fiji agreed under specified conditions to add 380 troops to their already 182 personnel in the border region, which leaves India, the Philippines, and Fiji in charge of the UNDOF's mission to maintain the Israel–Syria ceasefire agreement.

By June 10th, the Quneitra Crossing, which is the only crossing between Syria and Israel, had been closed to all but the peacekeeping forces of the UN. The crossing's name means "the little bridge" in Arabic, and it is normally used by the Druze to transfer produce and go back and forth for work and school. The demilitarized zone, which is about 3.5 miles at its widest and 220 yards at its narrowest, was created in 1973 after Syria made a futile attempt to take back the land by force in what's known as the Yom Kippur War, which lasted 16 days.

In early June, just before I arrived in the area, Syrian tanks had crossed the border. Israel submitted a formal complaint to the United Nations and while we were there, IDF tanks were taking up positions along the demarcation on the Israeli-occupied side. It was readily apparent that the civil war in Syria was becoming a much larger regional and global conflict and Israel is slowly but surely getting drawn in as the northeastern tri-border area has increasing incidents of weapons smuggling, border clashes, refugees trying to cross into Israeli-occupied territory, and wildfires caused by the fighting that have been making their way across the border as well. There were reports when we got back to Haifa that some of the shelling that day had spilled over into Israel-occupied territory.

On the one hand, in Assad's favor, Russia is supplying weapons and diplomatic support, Iran's Revolutionary Guard is advising and protecting him, Iraqi Shia and Hezbollah are fighting on the ground for the regime, and China has been providing diplomatic support at UN Security Council meetings. On the other hand, funded by the U.S. the Islamic group Jabhat Al-Nusra, known to have fought along side Al-Qaeda in Iraq, is supporting the rebel insurgency; Al-Qaeda and the Egyptian Muslim Brotherhood are supporting them as well. The other NATO nations, including France and the UK, are favoring the rebels; and Saudi Arabia and Qatar support the effort to provide weapons to the insurgency.

Pakistan has yet to take a position in the conflict but surely will as the violence escalates. Jordan is leaning on the side of the insurgents and is currently providing a safe-haven for many of the refugees, as is Egypt. Turkey is also getting pulled into the conflict. In October of 2012, their military retaliated against Syrian mortar fire that landed across the border and killed five civilians. The Turkish artillery response killed 12 Syrian soldiers and destroyed two tanks. On June 22, 2012, Syrian air defenses shot down a Turkish F-4 Phantom fighter killing the two pilots. In addition, Syrian helicopters have violated Turkish airspace five times since the civil war began. Given these incidents, Prime Minister Endrogan had said with a threatening tone that the rules of engagement have changed.

The Kurds in Turkey, Iraq, and Syria are split on which side they support. Kurds make up the largest ethnic minority in Syria and are a little over 10% of the total population of 23 million people. Many of them are extremely poor and live in the northeastern regions of Hassakeh and Qamishli, just on the borders of Iraq and Turkey. It is possible that if the rebels win that Syria will be broken up into pieces and the Kurds may stake claim to the section that they currently live in. Given the tensions between Syria and Turkey, Erdogan has considered asking NATO to intervene in the civil war and he has expressed support for providing arms to the rebels. The Turkish government has also reached out to Syrian refugees by offering them safe haven in the border city of Gaziantep. Meanwhile, whether Erdogan is aware of it or not, Incirlik Airbase is being used by NATO as a headquarters for covert operations against Assad's regime.

CIA covert operations are now thought to be the reason behind the U.S. Embassy attack in Benghazi, Libya on September 11, 2012, killing the ambassador and three others.[56] The story is that the CIA was running weapons taken from Libyan arms depots to Syrian rebels.

Hezbollah has been playing a significant role in the Syrian civil war and is simultaneously drawing Israel into a confrontation over territorial claims to the Shebaa Farms and the village of Ghajar. The UN has attempted to keep the peace along the line of withdrawal established in 2000 between Israel and Lebanon. However, there is continued disagreement over the small area of Shebaa Farms (8.5 square miles): It is claimed by Lebanon but Israel insists that it is part of Syria and therefore is in the Golan and thus under their jurisdiction. Israel violates Lebabese airspace on a regular basis, and while the confusion over the border is often used as an excuse, it is clear that these flights are for surveillance purposes.

Amidst the chaos unfolding right in front of us on the Golan Heights, Yaacov looked at me and candidly said, "The Third-World War is going to begin here. His words came as Israel is scrambling to develop the Arrow III anti-nuclear defense system that they had tested just days earlier. The U.S. just funded and built a $25 million military base outside of Jerusalem as a home for this new defense system. And, Israel has already effectively tested the newest incarnation of the Jericho intercontinental ballistic missile capable of carrying a nuclear warhead.

Meanwhile, there is evidence of both sides of the Syrian conflict using chemical weapons, including Sarin nerve gas.[57] Given the most recent alleged chemical attacks that reportedly killed 1,400 civilians—including 400 children, the U.S. and Great Britain are on the verge of bombing and perhaps invading Syria.

The world is an incredibly complicated place, but sadly the general population in the United States is so politically and geographically illiterate that when the Boston Marathon bombers were said to be from Chechnya, social media were swamped with people in the U.S. who wanted to enact revenge on the Czech Republic, to the degree that the Czech Ambassador to the U.S. felt obligated to put a statement on his embassy's website: "The Czech Republic and Chechnya are two very different entities—the Czech Republic is a Central European country; Chechnya is a part of the Russian Federation." The Czech president subsequently made the following statement: "The Czech Republic is an active and reliable partner of the U.S. in the fight against terrorism. We stand side by side with our allies." This kind of ignorance is precisely what happens when people get their news from Fox's Bill O'Reilly, who got his start on E-Television, rather than from actual experts and scholars like Noam Chomsky, who has written countless books on international relations and U.S. foreign policy, and yet his presence is virtually nonexistent in primetime corporate-owned media.

While any act of bloodshed and savagery is abhorrent and unacceptable, more often than not there are complex historical, cultural, economic, and political reasons why they occur—reasons that need to be explored if peace here at home and abroad is at all thinkable let alone possible. I got a Facebook post a couple days after the Boston bombings that I think captures the spirit of the countless comments that people were making online; it said, "It's gonna be just another guy with some crazy cause that we'll forget about in two days or so and go back about our lives." While she intended this statement to be a "Fuck you" to the terrorists, sadly it also inadvertently revealed a glaring problem: This nation has yet to have an open and substantive dialogue about such traumatic events and why they happen. As with 9/11, the entire ordeal, once the dust had settled, should have provoked a larger public discussion about why terrorism exists, not to justify it or act as apologists, but rather to find ways to put an end to the violence that in one way or another affects us all.

What many people in the United States don't seem to realize is that violence like the Marathon bombings occurs on a regular basis in many other parts of the world, and if the U.S. is not directly involved, weapons that we've manufactured and sold usually are. Unfortunately, the public is not made aware of, or perhaps doesn't care about the brutality and tragedy that other human beings on this planet recurrently endure. So many people in the U.S. have a bumper sticker mentality of "God Bless America" and the hell with the rest. And those citizens who are concerned and exercise their Constitutional right to question and petition their government are marginalized throughout society.

When the mainstream media reports on international acts of violence, it often uses twisted language that obfuscates the true extent of the horror and quickly places the blame. As Beirut-based freelance writer Emily Dische-Becker commented about the news coverage of the car bomb that exploded in a southern suburb of the capital city of Lebanon today—August 16th, 2013 killing 22 people and injuring hundreds:

> The stock phrase employed by western mainstream media that the bomb struck a "stronghold of the militant Hezbollah group," to quote the *Washington Post*, belies the fact that

the area is dense and residential, and that the victims were civilians. This is akin to describing the September 11th attacks in Manhattan as striking 'a stronghold of American bankers.' It may be true symbolically, and also by crude motive of the bombers. But who are the victims and why were they targeted? They were civilians, overwhelmingly from the Shia sect, which make up Hezbollah's base of support in Lebanon. Curiously, despite the fact that civilians were indiscriminately targeted, U.S. mainstream media did not refer to the bombing as a 'terrorist attack.'[58]

This manipulation of language and representation is precisely what this new book, *On Language, Democracy, and Social Justice: Noam Chomsky's Critical Intervention* is all about. The dialogues herein explore the current state of democracy, U.S. foreign policy, and public education, and the ways in which racism, sexism, ethnocentrism, class warfare, imperialism, and neoliberalism are shaping the new world order. But what's facilitative rather than debilitating about this new book is that it doesn't only offer a language of critique, it simultaneously creates and encourages a collective praxis to make change in the world. This is particularly evident in the final chapter, "What Should Be the Role of Intellectuals in the Twenty-First Century?" I can remember when I first met Chomsky in the autumn of 1994 when I asked him this very same question.[59]

I was a doctoral student at the Harvard Graduate School of Education and a member of the editorial board of the *Harvard Educational Review*—both of which are historical accidents that I talk about in my book *Presence of Mind: Education and the Politics of Deception,* in the chapter "Veritas: The Fortunes of My Miseducation at Harvard."[60] HGSE maintains a powerful myth of being a liberal institution on the cutting edge of theory, research, and social change, when in fact it has worked to maintain the pillars of the republic by reinforcing reactionary educational policies in the guise of empirical innovation and progressive pedagogical practice that largely shun critical social theory.

The *Harvard Educational Review* was working on a special issue that we had proposed on youth violence. A buddy of mine, Steve Sherblom, and I thought it would be great to try and get a contribution from Chomsky, and we figured that since he was just up the street at MIT that it would be smooth sailing.

I was turned on to Chomsky's work back in the early 1980s when I took a course in Contemporary American History with Dean Albertson at the University of Massachusetts–Amherst, where I was an undergraduate. Dean's course flipped my sense of history and identity on its ass by exposing me to a radical critique of the glossy patriotic notions of American grandeur that I'd been inundated with all my life. Albertson had been a twentieth-century U.S. historian with a specialization in oral history at UMass since 1965. A veteran of the Second World War, he was interested throughout his career in new methods in conducting research and teaching history. His course covered a diversity of issues including anti-war movements, civil rights, anti-nuclear protests, welfare rights, riots, police brutality and incarceration. He encouraged his students to conduct interviews with social activists of the 1960s and early 1970s. I would go home to my parents' house up in the woods, away from the noise of the dorm, and bury myself in the course material and write extensively. Dean took a liking to my work and he asked me to be a teaching assistant for him. But his gracious invite came at an inopportune time as I was moving to France to continue my schooling. Sadly, we would never meet again. When I returned to the States to complete my degrees in French and Journalism with a minor in history, he was on leave after being diagnosed with cancer. He died on March 31, 1989 at the age of 68; I will never forget him or the impact that he continues to have on my life.

Steve and I presented the idea of including Chomsky in the special issue to the student-run editorial board. There was a great deal of resistance and it was clear from our formal discussion that the opposition wasn't coming from an informed critique of Chomsky's work, but rather centered on him being a political pariah and thus outside of what was considered to be the review's readership. This reminded me of when graduate students at the school of education would call me a "Marxist," but not to inspire an exchange of ideas: The label was being used as shock language to try and dismiss my contributions to classroom discussions and projects. If they had actually read Marx, they would have understood that my theoretical expansion of his economic base, with such critical issues as racism, sexism, heterosexism, and ethnocentrism, had moved far beyond his invaluable but limited model of social critique.

The editorial board would meet weekly in the Dean's Conference Room. In an attempt to use journal policy to try and bog down our plan of conducting and publishing an interview with Chomsky, the co-chairs asked me as part of the solicitation process—and I happened to be the Director of Solicitations—to get a copy of his CV. I burst out laughing but quickly pulled myself together so as to not sabotage the plan, and responded that I would surely need a wheelbarrow to carry it and that, as the most cited living intellectual on the planet, it may be insulting to request this as a precondition for publication given that he would be doing us a favor by offering his time. Funny that bourgeois protocol worked in my favor this time around as the majority agreed that it would be "improper"; but I compromised so as to appease the really conservative members of the board—one in particular who would go on to work with the George W. Bush administration to implement the abominable national education policy *No Child Left Behind*—by offering to bring in some of Chomsky's books to show people that he was more than qualified to speak on the issues at hand. Before the next board meeting and vote took place, I met with the general manger to strategize. She was extremely sharp and cool and agreed to express her support for the publication. The editorial board thus allowed Steve and me to do the interview that we eventually called

"Demystifying Democracy: A Dialogue with Noam Chomsky," but only under the condition that the following disclaimer front the publication:

> As participants in this dialogue, editors Sherblom and Leistyna acknowledge their understanding of violence as endemic to unequal and exclusionary economic and social structures. This understanding and their commitment to social transformation shaped both the flavor of the questions and the evolution of the discussion, and may not reflect the opinion of the full Board of the *Harvard Educational Review*.

Such a disclaimer had never been requested during my time on the board, nor ever to my knowledge.

On the way to Chomsky's office I frantically went over my questions. Noam invited us in with a smile just below those eyeglasses of his, and just above his worn out button-up shirt and a threadbare pair of jeans—he was just a regular guy hanging out in his office surrounded by piles of books, newspapers, and reports. I began the interview with a question that was phrased something like, "It appears that Republicans..." "It seems that....," and he stopped me midsentence and said, "That's like saying, 'It appears that Nazis were putting Jews on trains!'" In a matter of seconds, he taught me an important lesson about language—to use it with clarity and conviction. My undergraduate training in journalism had me trapped and suffocating in the myth of objectivity and Chomsky remedied that problem in a heartbeat. So I put down my list of questions, and that was the very moment that the interview turned into a dialogue—a much more participatory and critical interaction. This is precisely what the conversations between Pierre and Noam embody in this new book—a space where participation and dissent are welcome rather than conformity through coercion, which is so often the result of simply nodding to the big gun in the room.

I was searching through YouTube the other night and haphazardly came across a video called "A Pedagogy of the Oppressed: A Conversation with Noam Chomsky, Howard Gardner, and Bruno della Chiesa Askwith."[61] It was a forum held at HGSE on May 1, 2013 to celebrate the 45th anniversary of Paulo Freire's monumental book *Pedagogy of the Oppressed*. The forum took me by surprise, especially since I was told back in the day that given all the critical work that we were able to publish in the *Harvard Education Review*, that Howard Gardner, Mr. "Multiple Intelligences" himself, wrote a letter to the general manager—that was co-signed by a number of prominent faculty, stating that she should put an end to what was happening as we were destroying the integrity of the journal. I figured that critical consciousness was not on his list of intelligences.... Maybe this letter never existed and was just a rumour, as here he was commemorating Freire and sitting right beside Chomsky.

The forum opens with Gardner's brief introduction of the event and as he lays out the evening's agenda, he says:

I will then introduce Exhibit 'A' which I only discovered when I was boning up for this which is an amazing two pages out of the *Freire Reader* about the Harvard Grad school of Education. How many of you know that on page 4 and 5 of this book the Ed school gets excoriated? [Chomsky laughs].

He continued, "We're trying to figure out the origin of this evening and none of us was successful in doing this." There was no mention of the anniversary of *Pedagogy of the Oppressed* and that the forum happened to be held on May Day. As Gardner introduces the guests and the topic at hand, he struggles with pronouncing Freire's name and says, "whose name I'm not used to pronouncing"; a person in the audience corrected him, and he continued:

As I was doing my homework I have to admit that I was shocked when I picked up the *Paulo Freire Reader* and discovered that as early as page 4 of the introduction the whipping boy was the Harvard Graduate School of Education, and so I want to read a few quotations; Noam was here at the time and his wife was teaching, so they may have some context and it's possible somebody else in the audience does as well. So it begins by describing a professor who is not named, commenting on a graduate student's paper [me] and the comment is [he hesitates] critical especially mentioning quote unquote Freire.

I was amazed that after all these years, "Veritas: The Fortunes of My Miseducation at Harvard" had finally surfaced as a topic for public discussion at Harvard. After I had written the piece back in the late 1990s, I waited to publish it so that I could graduate, but once it was in print, a colleague photocopied it and put a copy in the mailboxes of everyone at the Ed School, including faculty. But the behind-the-scenes conversations that surrounded the publication and its campus circulation were never made public as Harvard leadership is smart enough to know that if you acknowledge something you bring it to center stage for public debate, so it's best to just ignore it all together—that's exercising power. So my hair rose up when I heard Howard Gardner, after all these years, reading quotes from the *Freire Reader* and realized that some of the substance of what was being said was derived from my experience and critique of HGSE.

Gardner read from the introduction:

How else can one explain a culture that pontificates about intellectual rigor and yet allows a graduate course titled "Politics of Literacy" to be taught without any reference to Freire? [Gardner interjects, "I had to chuckle at this last comment here."] What can you expect from a culture where a professor commented on Freire's death, [which was in 1997], Freire's coming to Harvard would have made 20 students happy while making the rest of the students very unhappy.

Gardner looked around the stage perplexed and deferred to Chomsky, "So can you help us understand why this reader begins with this, is Harvard a metonym here?" I would have been more than happy to answer his question. While I'm cited in the introduction, and Gardner repeatedly asks for contextualization of these comments, no effort was made to contact me just across the river at UMass, Boston where I've been since 1994—I graduated from the Ed School in 1998.

Chomsky goes on to explain that it's the entire system and he uses May Day as an example:

> It's a day of supporting the struggle of American workers for an eight hour day…that's May Day everywhere in the world except for the United States…Our Labor Day is when people go back to work, that's Labor Day, not the day in which they struggle for their rights…the number of things we don't learn is amazing.

Gardner interjects, "I was one of the people who knew Piaget and not Freire…. I don't think that there was any conspiracy not to teach him here; is there anybody here who could provide any additional context? Or we'll put it aside." Again, I find it interesting that HGSE contacts me several times a year for charitable contributions and to join the faculty club for a fee but I wasn't invited to this event to at the very least sit among the audience,[62] not only because the introduction that Gardner read from was largely based on my experience, but also because I worked with Freire, we published dialogues together, I was among the students who helped bring him to HGSE in the mid-1990s where he visited classrooms and gave an open lecture, and I helped to get the Paulo Freire Social Justice School in Holyoke, Massachusetts approved by the state this past year and am on its advisory board. Gardner asked the guests and the audience if they had ever witnessed a Freirian-based pedagogy in action.

A student from India got up and talked about how back home she was exposed to Freire in her formal education, and explained that the lack of exposure to him here is because of the way in which the curriculum is framed within the larger neoliberal context. Gardner responded:

> I think we should all feel a little bad that in India this was not a foreign infecting agent; I'm not going to give an exposition on this school, but I think that we could do well to be much more alert to intellectual currents including ones that might make us uncomfortable. You [Bruno] teach here after all, nobody tells you what to teach (laughs).

Bruno was in the process of mentioning how critical theory and pedagogy is discarded as dangerous in the states, and Gardner jumped in, "I'm going to interrupt here for a second because I think the notion would not be that it's 'dangerous', the notion would be that it's irrelevant, that's equally damning, but it's very different." Chomsky comes back and says:

> I would slightly disagree with the distinction between 'dangerous' and 'irrelevant', I think they're the same thing: these things are irrelevant because they're dangerous; if people think about them they're going to go after the throats, symbolically, of those with power; they'll ask for their rights too and that's much too dangerous…all of this is part of the system of indoctrination, which in Freire's terms provides the culture of submission…

When it came time for the Q&A session, Gardner gathered the questions from the audience and then read through each one. When it came to the question, "Why is there no Freire at HGSE, is it fear?" he says, "I'm going to actually take that one and my answer I think will surprise you." When it was his turn, he explained:

> I should mention that MIT is somewhat more open to confrontation, there's a certain gentility at Harvard that's less directly confrontational in many ways; I said I was going to say something about Freire at the Ed School, I don't believe for a minute that there was any censoring.

He goes on to say that there needs to be someone that can effectively translate Freire's work and he alludes to the idea that the reason that his work is not taken up is because it's foreign in nature and that his methodology is exclusively intended for adults. This is silly as there are tons of people in the U.S. that have reinvented Freire's adult education framework to fit the specificities of the K–12 classroom in the U.S. The comment also shows that Gardner misses the entire point about what Chomsky called "the system of indoctrination" and when he subsequently referred to Freire's notion of "a culture of submission": as Chomsky has argued for a long time in reference to the media and journalists: you don't need to censor them as they have already been through the proper channels and know for themselves what's appropriate and what isn't.

As a generous public intellectual and tireless activist, Chomsky has continued to work with us at the University of Massachusetts–Boston. He comes and speaks for free at public events we've arranged. We founded a Human Rights Working Group on campus, and he agreed to give the keynote, pro bono, for "Colombia: A Human Rights Disaster," where he spoke alongside Columbian labor activists about U.S. oppression in the region. Perhaps my favorite Chomsky story is when an older woman, an ex-nun, who was studying with us as she had started a small language school in the city, had some questions for Chomsky about his linguistic theories. I told her to give him a ring. So she called his office and Noam decided that it was best that he come to her class and address her questions with the entire group, which he did.

I've tried over the past two decades at UMass to have my graduate students make meaning for themselves, to expose them to the issues and let them begin to theorize the world for themselves to inform their own praxis. I did the same for years as an adult education, ESL teacher in community-based programs. What for me is critical in passing the torch is having students recognize the important relationship between theorizing and cultural activism. *Theory* embodies existing ways in which people have interpreted, analyzed, and made generalizations about *why* the world works the way that it does. It is the *why* and *how* of what has been happening around us and not simply a focus on *what* is occurring and how to effectively respond. A crucial part of any democratizing project is to realize that theory needs to be flexible. While understanding the ways in which existing theories explain social reality is enormously important, *theorizing* is the ability to actively engage bodies of knowledge and human practices for the logics and socio-historical conditions that inform them so that they can be reworked. It encourages individuals to evaluate, based on their own experiences, expertise, and insight, the strengths and weaknesses of any conceptual and practical movement and recontextualize and reinvent its possibilities for one's own predicaments, while extending, when possible, its geographical reach. It is important to emphasize that as we engage in the exploratory and creative process that theorizing offers, one's own subject position should always be held in a critical light, not only for the purposes of continued self-actualization, but also, as action-based research has long pointed out, so that the ethical stances that are taken on an issue allow a person to speak *to* particular problems and *in* solidarity *with* others rather than *for* people from different backgrounds. In this way, theory does not have a monopoly on understanding; rather it reveals much about how we relate to the world and the assumptions that guide our political actions. As Cornelius Castoriadis argued:

> More than in any other area, here the idea of pure theory is an incoherent fiction. There exists no place, no point of view outside of history and society, or 'logically prior' to them, where one could be placed in order to construct the theory of them.[63]

As an integral part of any political project, theorizing presents a constant challenge to imagine and materialize alternative political spaces and identities and more just and equitable economic, social, and cultural relations. It makes possible consciousness raising, coalition building, resistance, activism, and structural change.

Likewise, research has to maintain methodological flexibility in order for it to provide a lifeline to theory and what Raymond Williams referred to throughout his work as "knowable communities" engaged in cultural and political reflection and struggle. While the idea of 'knowable communities', as it pertains to political projects, is both appealing and useful, it does not aspire to essentialize geographies and identities by assuming that there are biologically-determined or culturally-fixed thoughts and practices at play that are easily identifiable, readily accessible, and necessarily indicative of what other groups are experiencing and how they are responding. A central goal is to explore and begin to build upon some of the infinite ways in which concerned individuals and groups from diverse geopolitical locations have worked toward critical awareness and more just and effective responses to current unjust and debilitating economic and sociopolitical conditions.

Whether it's action research, applied research, social movement research, or any other paradigm dedicated to political insight and social change, advocates of such exploratory processes need to learn to do research *with* others rather than *on* them, and thus speaking *with* rather than *to* people engaged in eradicating injustice. Making use of any and all methodological approaches—even creating new ones to address a specific set of conditions, researchers can help create the self-empowering conditions within which people can conduct their own studies, forge democratic organizational structures and decision-making processes, and work toward generative learning, social networking, and personal and social transformation through praxis.

It was in this pedagogical spirit that Pierre Orelus and I met. He was a poet from Haiti and a student in my *Cross-Cultural Perspectives* graduate course. I can still remember him all those years ago sitting there wide-eyed and eager to develop a critical language to make sense of and articulate his experiences with issues of race, class, gender, capitalism, and imperialism. I thought how awful it must be to live, study, and work in a country so deeply implicated in the colonization of his native culture, as the U.S. supported the dictatorships of Francois Duvalier (1967–1971), Jean-Claude Duvalier (1971–1978), and the military junta from 1991--1994. People with any sense of history should have been disgusted that President Obama called together Clinton and George W. Bush to help the Haitians after the devastating earthquake in 2010, and for his blanket statements that we are a caring and generous nation that responds swiftly to human suffering. Tell that to the long list of countries that have experienced the brutality of U.S. foreign policy—the United States has invaded 152 countries since 1850—let alone to the survivors of Hurricane Katrina back in 2005 who were neglected for days after the storm, and 8 years after the disaster still live in temporary mobile homes and under bridges. Clinton and Bush are some of the very people, and not mother nature or God—right-wing evangelical Pat Robertson, the same guy who called for the assassination of Hugo Chavez,[64] blamed the quake on Haitians making a pact with the devil—that have supported a colonial ideology in Haiti through economic and foreign policy initiatives that have backed oppressive regimes, supported U.S. occupation of the country, reinforced the oppression of workers—including children—and helped maintain its status of being among the poorest nations in the Western hemisphere. Of course most people in the U.S. don't know anything about this history: As Chomsky argued at the Harvard forum, it's not taught in schools or widely circulated in public culture; or controversies and crimes are quickly disappeared from public memory in what Gore Vidal has called "the United States of amnesia."

I turned Pierre and his classmates on to Chomsky along with other critical educators such as Ngugi wa Thiong'o, Gloria Anzaldua, Paulo Freire, Edward Said, Chardra Mohanty, and bell hooks. He took the torch and ran like the wind with it, on to do his doctorate and subsequently to accept a faculty position in the College of Education at New Mexico State University, where he has already compiled an enormous body of work for such a young scholar, and has become a force to be reckoned with. Back when Pierre was a graduate student, he invited me to give a keynote speech at Greenfield Community College and I was deeply moved when he introduced me as a person who had inspired and pushed him to read deeper into the world to make a difference.

All those years ago, Noam answered my question about what we can do to make change:

> As everyone has always known, the best way to defend civil liberties is to collectively build a movement for social change that has broad-based appeal, that encourages free and open discussion, and offers a wide range of possibilities for social agency. The potential for such a movement surely exists. Many positive changes have taken place in the last thirty years as the result of popular movements organized around such issues as civil rights, peace, feminism, and the environment. If this struggle ever becomes a mass movement of the oppressed and exploited on an international level, the impulse to contribute to it may intensify, growing both from moral pressure and the desire for self-fulfillment in a decent and humane society. The systems of private tyranny—totalitarian in character—are also not there by natural law, but by human decisions. They can be dismantled and democratized. What concentrated privilege can't live with is sustained pressure that keeps building, organizations that keep doing things, people that keep learning lessons from the last time and doing it better the next time. Students and others with similar privilege—and it is privilege—can also do their own research by going back to original sources in public libraries. Real research and inquiry is always a collective activity. Such efforts can make a large contribution to changing consciousness, increasing insight and understanding, and leading to constructive action.[65]

What struck me about this response, and still hits home, is the emphasis that he places on social change as a collective event in which forging relationships is the key to creating a more just and peaceful world. Ultimately, social change is about healthy relationships, as Pierre articulates in Chapter One of this new book, "Professional and Personal Encounters with Noam Chomsky: A Critical Self-Reflection." If we all continue to pass the torch then the world will be a more enlightened place and it is only through seeing the light, through dialogue, that social justice is possible.

Five months after Susan's death, my first trip out of the house was to go and give a plenary talk at the University of Calgary, thanks to the support of my dear friend Shirley Steinberg, who had lost her beloved partner Joe Kincheloe on December 19, 2008. Feeling the weight of my unspeakable grief, she said to me over the phone, "Get out of bed, get up here, or I'm going to kick your ass!" Shirley and Joe had a major impact on me as a student and published my very first book in their series. I wasn't sure if I could muster the strength to make the journey back out into the world, but when I thought of Shirley, and I thought of Noam losing his wife Carol to cancer after 59 years together on the very same day that Joe passed away back in 2008, and how they have had the courage to carry on, I gathered myself together as best I could and went to Canada. Pierre was also invited to speak, and he gave a shout-out to me in the crowd, "That's Pepi, my teacher!" I can't say with words what this did for me at a time when my spirits were so low and I wasn't sure if I could do this work any longer. When it was my turn to speak, I talked about how we need a radical passion for the work that we do, and most importantly, to never forget to express our deep love and appreciation for those who have supported and fought beside us—I never could have done what I've accomplished in life without Susan and I carry her in my heart and feel her in everything that is beautiful along the way and will keep climbing until I find her again.

I gave a shout out to Shirley who was on stage as the moderator, to thank her for putting some wind back in my sails, and to Pierre in the audience for carrying the torch.

When Paulo Freire passed the torch to me as a graduate student, I asked him, "When you spoke earlier of dialoguing among cultural groups, you mentioned the need for love. Both you and Che Guevara have discussed the role of love in leadership, and you have certainly expressed the importance of love in the classroom."[66] And Paulo responded:

> First of all, I understand the process of teaching as an act of love. I mean, it is not an act of love in the formal sense, and never in the bureaucratic sense. It is an act of love as an expression of good care, a need to love, first of what you do. Can you imagine how painful it is to do anything without passion, to do everything mechanically.... Second, in loving the very teaching process I cannot exclude loving those I work with when teaching, and those whom I teach. Lovingness, however, as part of the process of educational practice, does not exclude moments of anger. I feel this anger exactly because I love. I do not need to hide this anger. But I also need to understand the anger of the students. They also have this very right to be angry. Teachers working in coordination with the ideology of most formal institutions of schooling often forbid the students to expose their anger, frustration, and disappointment with the teacher and the institution itself.... Both teachers and students have this right. To not be angry when you are a victim of violent oppression constitutes a form of complicity with the very conditions that oppress you...You can't bring this kind of joy to life and you can't involve yourself with joy if you don't have the possibility of experiencing love and anger...I think that love, anger, rigor, and struggle are part of the constitution of joy.

In great big bold white letters painted just below the massive armed tower of the wall in Bethlehem separating Israel from Palestine, it says in protest and with hope that the world can come together and celebrate unity in diversity, "Love Wins."

When I was in Jerusalem I made my way to the top of Mount of Olives where the Jews believe the Messiah will come and raise the dead, and where Christians believe that Jesus ascended to heaven after the resurrection and where he will return. I put a precious touch of Susan's life into the warm breeze passing through the Kidron Valley. It is my belief that her kind, gentle, giving, and forgiving spirit that now looks over all of Jerusalem from the mountain will help bring peace to this war-torn region. The rest is up to us.

Susan and I were in Cambodia back in 2010. We were at the hotel bar across the street from the U.S. Embassy talking with the bartender about the interviews I was doing with survivors of genocide and my research on how public consciousness is constructed to commit such atrocities—an extension of work I had done in Poland at Auschwitz. We had just returned from a long day in the Killing Fields and at the S-21 detention/torture center that was a former schoolhouse. The men sitting next to us overheard our conversation. They had just come across the border from Thailand. I knew that there were extensive protests going on there led by Thailand's Red Shirt anti-government movement. They were demanding new elections in support of the former Prime Minister Thaksin Shinawatra, who was forced from power in a military coup in 2006. The protestors had assembled peacefully but when pushed, took the parliament building, and as a result the Prime Minister Abhisit Vejjajiva declared a state of emergency and gave power to the military and security forces to crush the opposition and pull the plug on their TV station. Six soldiers and over 80 civilians were killed during the initial clashes, and more than 2,100 people were injured before the opposition was eventually forced to retreat. My comment to the men at the bar, "I'd like to see a good working-class movement in action," was met with some serious anger as these guys turned out to be U.S. Special Forces. The older man closest to me said with a patronizing smirk on his face, "That's not what's going on!" They had also overhead my earlier comment to the bartender about the U.S.'s illegal bombings of Cambodia in the 1960s and '70s—that there were 8 times more bombs dropped on Vietnam, Cambodia, and Laos than all the bombs used during WWII and that over 300,000 Cambodians were killed as a result. The youngest of the bunch, who was maybe 25 at the most, waived his finger in my face and said, "Have you ever served your country!" Feeling Susan's grip on my leg under the bar, as she was always my voice of reason—and we both knew this guy could kill me with the callous digit he was aiming and waiving in front of me—I thought to myself, "First of all we're in Cambodia…," and then I responded, "Yea, as a matter of fact I have, I'm a teacher and I serve my country everyday." Dumbfounded by the response they wandered off into the night.

Noam Chomsky is now 84 years old, and Einstein, Zinn, Terkel, Albertson, Said, Freire, Vidal, Williams, Kincheloe, and Castoriadis have all passed away, but they have left an immutable flame that those of us with enough courage and conviction can carry onward to inspire others to work together for justice and peace. This book embodies such spirit, so take it for a ride, but as the flight attendant warned, be sure and fasten your seatbelt.

In loving memory of Susan Kubik (4/4/68 – 12/29/11)
In life and in death your love has and will always inspire me.

Notes

1. I was especially moved by his books: *Orientalism, The Question of Palestine, Culture and Imperialism,* and *Covering Islam: How the Media and Experts Determine How We See the Rest of the World.*
2. Global Research (2011). "NATO's Eastern Anchor: 24 NATO Bases in Turkey." http://www.globalresearch.ca/nato-s-eastern-anchor-24-nato-bases-in-turkey/23205, retrieved July 12, 2013.
3. The same was true of international public opinion: In a survey of forty-seven nations conducted in June of 2007 by the Pew Research Center, only Israel and Kenya were in favor of NATO forces remaining in Afghanistan.
4. http://www.eurasiareview.com/10032013-what-is-office-of-high-commissioner-of-human-rights-ohchr-doing-about-usnato-atrocities-oped/, retrieved July 14, 2013; http://www.alternet.org/story/153042/the_us_has_been_bombing_iraq_since_1991_without_stopping--until_now, retrieved August 10, 2013; The actual death toll over the past 22 years in Iraq is extremely difficult to calculate, and the numbers are probably much higher than the aforementioned statistics: in part because there are now over one million refugees there and it is difficult to determine how many people have been dying each day from malnutrition, disease, a lack of medical care and clean water, unexploded ordinance, continued militant aggression, and street violence. There were also countless wounded during this period—some of whom were exposed to chemicals and depleted uranium, and these unfortunate people have been relegated to a long, slow, and miserable death. While difficult to tally with precision, *it is estimated that over one million Iraqis have died since the occupation began.*
5. This explosive devise is so brutal and notorious for not exploding until some unsuspecting civilian detonates it, that an international treaty, the Convention of Cluster Munitions, was ratified on August 1, 2010, but of course the U.S. and Israel—the last country to use cluster bombs in Lebanon in 2006—refused to sign.
6. http://www.dodccrp.org/files/Ullman_Shock.pdf, retrieved July 19, 2013, p.23.
7. Not because of his human rights abuses as BP has plenty of its own, with a long list of major environmental disasters, exploitation of labor, as well as a willingness to do business with anyone, including South Africa during the international oil embargo on the Apartheid government, and in what was then Rhodesia (now Zimbabwe) violating the UN embargo on its white-supremacist government. See: "BP: A Legacy of Apartheid, Pollution and Exploitation": http://www.multinationalmonitor.org/hyper/issues/1992/11/mm1192_11.html, retrieved August 1, 2013. Keep in mind that while BP was still state owned, Margaret Thatcher was a supporter of Apartheid in South Africa. So was President Ronald Reagan—Thatcher and Reagan were two pees in a pod. See: http://mg.co.za/article/2013-04-19-00-margaret-thatchers-shameful-support-for-apartheid, retrieved August 3, 2013; http://www.presstv.com/detail/2013/07/03/312093/s-african-apartheid-backed-by-thatcher/; http://www.cnn.com/2013/04/08/politics/thatcher-reagan, retrieved August 3, 2013; http://www.realclearpolitics.com/articles/2013/04/09/margaret_thatcher_reagans_most_resolute_ally__117862.html, retrieved August 3, 2013; http://www.nytimes.com/2013/04/09/opinion/thatcher-reagan-and-their-special-relationship.html, retrieved August 4, 2013; http://www.salon.com/2011/02/05/ronald_reagan_apartheid_south_africa/, retrieved August 4, 2013; http://www.democracynow.org/2004/6/11/allied_with_apartheid_reagan_supported_racist, retrieved August 4, 2013.
8. Bear in mind that all of this has happened long after George W. Bush, on May 1, 2003, declared that "Major combat operations have ended," during his "Mission Accomplished" speech from the flight deck of the U.S.S. Abraham Lincoln in San Diego. The aircraft carrier came in handy, not only for the symbolic significance of its name, but also for this propaganda stunt

as the vessel had just returned from combat operations in the Persian Gulf where bombers and fighter jets used its deck for the massive air campaign. The president arrived in the co-pilot seat of a Navy S-3B Viking, which made a tail-hook landing that was widely televised domestically and internationally. There he was, Commander and Chief George W. Bush—a man who was essentially a deserter from the U.S. Air Force back in the day, dressed in a fully equipped flight suit for what was surely the shortest flight in military history. With a helmet secured under his arm, and a big grin on his face, he took advantage of this staged photo opportunity to shake hands with the pilots onboard and the ship's crew just under the massive banner that said "Mission Accomplished." Amidst this grotesque pomp and circumstance, the mainstream corporate media took its orchestrated place in the celebration and relished the moment without doing their job of asking any hard questions about the reality of the situation on the ground in Iraq. This absurd event infuriated many people here in the States. Just imagine how Muslim communities around the world felt. At the time of Bush's glorious declaration, the Iraqi insurgency had really just begun. As the violence intensified, so did the number of civilian and military casualties. On January 10, 2007, President Bush, in a televised address to the U.S. public, announced that he was deploying an additional 21,500 troops to Iraq and extending the tour of most of the service personnel already there, in what was being referred to as the "surge," or more officially as "the New Way Forward."

9. See: http://us.mg6.mail.yahoo.com/neo/launch?.rand=1021641614&cleolblock=1#mail , retrieved July 14, 2013
10. Jeremy Scahill, (2013). *Dirty Wars: The World is a Battlefield*. New York: Perseus.
11. See: http://www.cbsnews.com/8301-201_162-57585776/attorney-general-holder-drones-killed-4-americans-since-2009/, retrieved July 21, 2013; http://www.cbsnews.com/8301-202_162-57585798/who-were-the-4-u.s-citizens-killed-in-drone-strikes/ retrieved July 22, 2013.
12. Thom Shanker, (2012). "U.S. Arms Sales Make Up Most of Global Market." *New York Times* (August 26): http://www.nytimes.com/2012/08/27/world/middleeast/us-foreign-arms-sales-reach-66-3-billion-in-2011.html retrieved August 27, 2013
13. See: http://www.dw.de/china-supplies-fewer-arms-to-dictatorships-than-us/a-6388021 retrieved July 19, 2013; http://sciencenordic.com/united-states-arms-most-dictatorships retrieved July 19, 2013; http://andrewgavinmarshall.com/2013/03/26/in-the-arms-of-dictators-america-the-great-global-arms-dealer/ retrieved July 10, 2013.
14. The United States has supported dictators throughout Asia, including in Vietnam, Indonesia, Singapore, Thailand, China, Taiwan, the Philippines, South Korea, Brunei, Cambodia, and Fiji.
15. It's important to note that current job losses in the U.S. are not merely lay-offs caused by hard economic times. With capital flight and global outsourcing, both blue-collar and white-collar jobs have been exported by U.S. corporations to nations, even Communist countries like Vietnam and China, that pay below a living wage and that ensure that workers have little to no protection under labor unions and human rights laws that regulate corporate interests and power. By cheap labor, we're often talking between 13.5 and 36 cents an hour; we're also talking about a total disregard for child-labor laws and environmental protections. The Chinese were invited to be members of all the major global financial governing bodies including the World Bank, the G-20, the WTO, and the IMF; I guess allowing Kentucky Fried Chicken, the fastest growing franchise in a country of over a billion people, to be just across the street from the Forbidden City and Tiananmen Square makes it all fine and dandy—the next best investment in China will be Beano and Pepto-Bismol.
16. See: http://comptroller.defense.gov/defbudget/fy2013/Fy2013_Budget_Request_Overview_Book.pdf, retrieved August 12, 2013.

17. ABC News Exclusive (January 15, 2008). "President Bush in Saudi Arabia." http://abcnews.go.com/Nightline/Politics/story?id=4136209&page=2, retrieved August 1, 2013.
18. See: http://www.cnn.com/2006/POLITICS/02/23/port.security/, retrieved July 23, 2013; http://www.nbcnews.com/id/11474440/ns/us_news-security/t/bush-backs-transfer-us-ports-dubai-firm/#.UgkR5lN1FXY, retrieved July 24, 2013.
19. We sell weapons to Israel and many of their enemies, including Saudi Arabia—there's no real solidarity in any of this, just business. Even Israel is wary of such deals, see: http://www.haaretz.com/print-edition/news/israel-wary-of-u-s-arab-arms-deals-1.265576, retrieved July 29, 2013. But Israel will sell weapons to any one with cash as well.
20. See: http://www.gwu.edu/~nsarchiv/NSAEBB/NSAEBB82/, retrieved July 13, 2013.
21. John Pilger, (2003). "What Good Friends Left Behind." The Guardian. http://www.theguardian.com/world/2003/sep/20/afghanistan.weekend7Piljer, retrieved August 12, 2013. Cooley, John (2002). *Unholy Wars: Afghanistan, America, and International Terrorism*. London: Pluto.
22. See: http://www.larouchepub.com/other/1995/2241_mujahideen_control.html, retrieved July 21, 2013.
23. See: http://www.globalresearch.ca/articles/BRZ110A.html, retrieved July 17, 2013.
24. See: http://presscore.ca/2012/yesterday-theyre-idolized-by-the-u-s-as-freedom-fighters-today-they-are-hunted-as-terrorists.html, retrieved July 14, 2013; http://www.youtube.com/watch?v=Zo17biJzRtc, retrieved July 14, 2013; http://www.project.nsearch.com/video/ronald-reagan-dedicates-space-shuttle-columbia-to-the-taliban, retrieved July 14, 2013.
25. Patrice McSherry, (2005). *Predatory States: Operation Condor and Covert War in Latin America*. Boulder, CO: Rowman & Littlefield.
26. It's important to remember that there is a long history of U.S. violence and support for totalitarian regimes in Central America, the Caribbean and South America, including Omar Herrera-Torijos and Manuel Noriega in Panama; Hernandez Martinez in El Salvador; Francois Duvalier and Jean-Claude Duvalier in Haiti; Rafael Trujillo in the Dominican Republic; Gerado Machado Morales, Carlos Prio Socarras, and Fulgenseo Batista in Cuba; Marcos Perez Jimenez in Venezuela; Gustavo Rojas Pinilla in Columbia; Alfredo Stroessner Matiauda in Paraguay; Forbes Burnham in Guyana; General Jorge Rafael Videla, Admiral Emilio Eduardo Massera, and Brigadier-General Orlando Ramón Agosti in Argentina; Juan Maria Bordaberry, Alberto Demicheli, Aparicio Mendez, and Gregorio Alvarez in Uruguay; Alberto Fujimori in Peru, etc.
27. See: http://www.thirdworldtraveler.com/Middle_East/Israel_Nicaragua_Contras.html retrieved August 1, 2013, this also involved a sophisticated CIA cocaine smuggling operation that helped to fund the insurgency, much as it did in Afghanistan where the U.S. turned a blind eye to the heroin operations used to fund the Mujahideen.
28. http://www.theguardian.com/theguardian/1999/mar/24/guardianweekly.guardianweekly1 retrieved August 3, 2013; Pope Francis is thought to have supported the violence of the "Dirty War" during the junta from 1976–1984 when over 30,000 people were murdered; see: http://www.globalnewsdesk.co.uk/rest-of-the-world/pope-francis-argentina-dirty-war-allegations/03668/, retrieved August 7, 2013.
29. http://www.thirdworldtraveler.com/Israel/Israel_LAmer_TrailTerror.html, retrieved July 18, 2013; http://www.thirdworldtraveler.com/Israel/Israel_LAmer_ILAMC.html, retrieved July 25, 2013.
30. http://www.huffingtonpost.com/2013/01/10/israel-arms-sales-2012_n_2447861.html, retrieved August 15, 2013.
31. http://www.haaretz.com/news/diplomacy-defense/.premium-1.528993, retrieved July 18, 2013; http://www.imemc.org/article/65649, retrieved August 2, 2013.

32. http://electronicintifada.net/content/israel-and-mexico-swap-notes-abusing-rights/12475, retrieved July 28, 2013; http://my.firedoglake.com/wendydavis/2013/06/05/revealed-israelis-are-helping-to-crush-the-zapatista-movement/, retrieved July 29, 2013.
33. http://www.pbs.org/newshour/indepth_coverage/middle_east/conflict/map_westbank.html, retrieved July 23, 2013; http://www.vtjp.org/background/Separation_Wall_Report.htm, retrieved July 23, 2013; http://www.alhaq.org/10yrs/openions-expert-org/international-organisations/604-israel-west-bank-barrier-violates-human-rights, retrieved July 24, 2013; http://www.un.org/apps/news/storyAr.asp?NewsID=6947&Cr=palestin&Cr1, retrieved July 24, 2013. On July 20, 2004 the UN General Assembly accepted Resolution ES-10/15 condemning the separation barrier.150 countries, including all 25 members of the European Union, supported the resolution. Of course Israel and the U.S. stood defiantly opposed, and Israel has systematically disregarded the mandate ever since its ratification, and ignored the International Court of Justice's earlier judgment that compensations be paid for damages caused by the occupation.
34. http://www.jadaliyya.com/pages/index/12040/alone_palestinian-children-in-the-israeli-military-, retrieved August 5, 2013; http://resourcecentre.savethechildren.se/start/countries/occupied-palestinian-territory/crc-reporting, retrieved August 5, 2013.
35. http://www2.ohchr.org/english/bodies/crc/docs/co/CRC-C-ISR-CO-2-4.pdf, retrieved August 19, 2013.
36. http://www.cjr.org/behind_the_news/speech_in_israel_is_not_free.php?page=all, retrieved July 23, 2013.
37. http://thebilzerianreport.com/how-much-does-israel-cost-the-average-american/, retrieved August 12, 2013.
38. Only $500 million in humanitarian assistance will be allocated to the Palestinian Authority. Compared to the $528 that goes to each Israeli citizen annually from the U.S., only $3 per capita goes to the Palestinians.
39. http://www.nclej.org/poverty-in-the-us.php, retrieved July 26, 2013.
40. http://stateofworkingamerica.org/great-recession/unemployment-and-underemployment/, retrieved July 12, 2013.
41. http://www.washingtonpost.com/blogs/the-fix/wp/2013/07/11/the-fight-over-food-stamps-explained/, retrieved August 17, 2013.
42. See: http://www.michaelparenti.org/Honduras.html, retrieved July 15, 2013; http://www.breitbart.com/Big-Peace/2013/07/05/A-Tale-of-Two-Coups-Egypt-vs-Honduras, retrieved July 13, 2013; http://www.theguardian.com/commentisfree/cifamerica/2012/mar/22/democrats-press-obama-us-complicity-honduras retrieved July 24, 2013; http://www.hrw.org/reports/1995/WR95/AMERICAS-08.htm, retrieved July 24, 2013.

    For information on the Obama administration's involvement in the coup that recently ousted Mohammad Morsi, see: http://www.alternet.org/world/america-supports-honduras-and-egypt-coups?akid=10795.240686.nWDm_g&rd=1&src=newsletter881734&t=15 retrieved July 24, 2013; Leo Valladares Lanza and Susan Peacock, (1998). *In search of Hidden Truths: An Interim Report on Declassification by the National Commissioner for Human Rights in Honduras*. Patuca: Comisionado Nac'l de la Derechos Humanos.
43. http://www.michaelparenti.org/Honduras.html, retrieved July 12, 2013; http://www.breitbart.com/Big-Peace/2013/07/05/A-Tale-of-Two-Coups-Egypt-vs-Honduras, retrieved July 26, 2013; http://www.theguardian.com/commentisfree/cifamerica/2012/mar/22/democrats-press-obama-us-complicity-honduras, retrieved August 3, 2013; http://www.hrw.org/reports/1995/WR95/AMERICAS-08.htm, retrieved August 17, 2013.

    It is also the case that the Obama administration has been involved in the coup that recently ousted Mohammad Morsi. See: http://www.alternet.org/world/america-supports-

honduras-and-egypt-coups?akid=10795.240686.nWDm_g&rd=1&src=newsletter881734&t=15, retrieved July 5, 2013; Lanza, Valladares, Leo & Peacock, Susan (1998). *In Search of Hidden Truths: An Interim Report on Declassification by the National Commissioner for Human Rights in Honduras*. Patuca: Comisionado Nac'l de la Derechos Humanos.
44. Phil Gasper, (2001). "Afghanistan, CIA, Bin Laden, and the Taliban." *International Socialist Review*. http://www.thirdworldtraveler.com/Afghanistan/Afghanistan_CIA_Taliban.html. I owe a debt of deep gratitude to Phil Gasper as I used his research considerably in this section on the links between the U.S. and Osama Bin Laden; while there is plenty of credible investigative reporting on this issue, I think that Gasper did an excellent and comprehensive job with this.
45. Associated Press (1998). *"U.S. Next Superpower Foe for Terrorist Leader."* (August 23).
46. Evan Thomas, (October, 1, 2001). "The Road to September 11th." *Newsweek* (p.12). http://www.thedailybeast.com/newsweek/2001/09/30/the-road-to-september-11.html, retrieved July 18, 2013.
47. As cited in Phil Gasper, (2001). "Afghanistan, CIA, Bin Laden, and the Taliban." *International Socialist Review*. http://www.thirdworldtraveler.com/Afghanistan/Afghanistan_CIA_Taliban.html, retrieved August 1, 2013.
48. Obama is continuing to provide military aid in Somalia, see: http://www.reuters.com/article/2013/04/08/us-somalia-usa-idUSBRE93711G20130408, retrieved July 29, 2013.
49. Edward Said, (1998). "In Search of Palestine." Available at http://www.youtube.com/watch?v=ksTgAL-e9yo, retrieved July 24, 2013.
50. Noam Chomsky & Howard Zinn (Eds.) (1972). *The Pentagon Papers: Critical Essays, Volume Five: The Senator Gravel Edition*. Boston: Beacon Press.
51. http://www.imdb.com/name/nm0957016/bio, retrieved August 7, 2013.
52. http://www.revcom.us/a/v20/980-89/987/zinn.htm, retrieved August 17, 2013.
53. Al Haram (2010). "Noam Chomsky: Speaking of Truth and Power." http://weekly.ahram.org.eg/2010/1001/intrvw.htm, retrieved July 4, 2013.
54. Noam Chomsky, Pepi Leistyna, & Steve Sherblom, (1995). "A Dialogue with Noam Chomsky." *The Harvard Educational Review* 65(2, Summer)—Violence Special Issue (127–144).
55. Travel Warning: U.S. Department of State, Bureau on Consular Affairs, Israel, the West Bank and Gaza, June 19, 2013. http://travel.state.gov/travel/cis_pa_tw/tw/tw_6010.html, retrieved August 1, 2013.
56. See: http://www.globalresearch.ca/source-cia-was-smuggling-weapons-to-syrian-rebels-during-benghazi-embassy-attack/5345037, retrieved August 13, 2013.
57. See: http://www.cnn.com/2013/08/22/world/meast/syria-civil-war, retrieved July 23, 2013.
58. Emily Dische-Becker, (2013). "Why Isn't Beirut Bombing Called 'Terrorist'? What's Behind It?" Institute for Public Accuracy. http://us.mg6.mail.yahoo.com/neo/launch?.rand=572372048&cleolblock=1#mail, retrieved July 14, 2013.
59. Noam Chomsky, Pepi Leistyna, & Steve Sherblom, (1995). "A Dialogue with Noam Chomsky." *The Harvard Educational Review* 65(2, Summer)—Violence Special Issue (127–144).
60. Pepi Leistyna, (1999). "Veritas: The Fortunes of My Miseducation at Harvard." In: Leistyna, P. *Presence of Mind: Education and the Politics of Deception*. Boulder, CO: Westview (pp. 127–164).
61. http://www.youtube.com/watch?v=-SOw55BU7yg, retrieved August 18, 2013
62. I came out of Harvard swamped with student debt because Catherine Snow had my Title Seven Grants from D.C. cut because of my political views. It would have paid for my entire doctoral degree. In fact, my application to *The Harvard Educational Review* was initially rejected because Snow's research assistant during the review process for new board members dissed me because of my politics. I was brought on boar only after two people resigned.

63. Cornelius Castoriadis, (1987). *The Imaginary Institution of Society.* Cambridge, MA: MIT (p. 3).
64. See: http://www.youtube.com/watch?v=DykgMyTjWU4, retrieved August 17, 2013.
65. Noam Chomsky, Pepi Leistyna, & Steve Sherblom, (1995). "A Dialogue with Noam Chomsky." *The Harvard Educational Review 65*(2, Summer)—Violence Special Issue (127–144).
66. Paulo Freire, & Pepi Leistyna, (2004). "Presence of Mind in the Process of Learning and Knowing: A Dialogue with Paulo Freire." *Teacher Education Quarterly*, Winter Special Issue: *Critical Pedagogy: Revitalizing and Democratizing Teacher Education, 31*(1), 3–6 (Caddo Gap Press).

INDEX

Afghanistan, 24, 36, 127, 130, 132–134, 136–138, 143, 165, 167
Albertson, D., 154, 164
Alper, L., 56, 62
Alvarez, L., 56, 63
American English, 49, 59
Anzaldúa, G., 57, 60, 61, 161
Apple, M., 4, 6
Aronowitz, S., 56, 61
Assange, J., 144
Au, W., 4, 6, 55, 62

Baird, F., 54, 62
Banking, 54, 62
Barsamian, 24, 40
Barsky, D., 23–27, 29, 36, 40
Bazin, M., 100
Behaviorism, 7–9, 26, 37–39
Behaviorist theory, 8, 26, 37, 38
Bernays, E., 78
Bhutto, Benazir, 137
Black Africa, 98
Bloom, A. 34
Bloomfield, L., 26
Bosch, T., xix, xx, xxii
Boston Globe, 18, 84, 95, 101
Bourdieu, P., 8, 22, 60, 62
Brand Obama, 48
Brazil, 15, 54, 66, 70, 90, 108
British English, 49, 59
Bush, G. W., 17, 44, 47, 48, 70, 71, 88, 99, 127, 130, 132, 133, 136, 143, 155, 161, 165, 166
Bush, G. H. W., 99, 133, 137, 145

Cairo, 71, 140
Cambodia, 24, 164, 166
Capitalism, xiii, xv–xviii, 87, 131, 161
Capitelli, S., 56, 63
Caribbean, xvi, xx, 23, 44, 74, 75, 79, 88, 100, 114, 117, 134, 167
Carothers, T., 44, 80, 82, 83, 94
Carr, P., 4, 6, 54, 59, 62
Carter, S., 134
Castoriadis, C., 160, 164, 170
Chavez, H., 14, 15, 136, 161
Chechnya, 152, 153
China, 68, 72, 73, 131, 136, 151, 166
Chomsky Effect, The, 36, 40
Churchill, W., 56, 62
CIA, 84, 99, 130, 133, 134, 136, 137, 141, 142, 144, 145, 152, 167
Clinton, B., 16, 17, 19, 68, 70, 71, 86–88, 91, 92, 96, 99–101, 105, 161
Clinton Doctrine, 78, 87
Cockburn, A., 24
Colonization, xiii, 3, 37, 66, 97, 98, 114, 115, 120, 123, 161
Columbia, 159
Congress, 85, 99, 102, 130, 134, 137
Contras, 30, 36, 134
Crawford, J., 56, 57, 62
Crocker, C., 91
Cuba, 74, 92, 167
Culture of Terrorism, The, 10, 94
Cummins, J., 56, 57, 62
Czech Republic, 152, 153

Darder, A., 60, 62, 118
Davidson, B., 98

Democracy, viii, xi, xiii, xxi, 4, 5, 15, 16, 34, 43–49, 53–59, 61, 72, 77–85, 87–90, 94, 105, 108, 128, 129, 132, 133, 136, 137, 145, 154
Democracy and Education, 54, 62
Democratic schooling, 2, 3
Demystifying Democracy: A Dialogue with Noam Chomsky, 156
Denzin, N. K., 4, 6, 54, 62
Depoliticized society, 46, 48
Dewey, J., 54, 62, 141
Dische-Becker, E., 153, 169
Dominant language, 43, 49, 59
Duvalier, J. C., 134, 161, 167

Ecological democracy, 53
Economic democracy, 53
Education Under Occupation, 14, 16
Egypt, 71, 107, 130, 132, 135, 151
El Salvador, 30, 31, 167
Ellis, N., 27, 41
Ellsberg, D., 27, 143, 144
Emergentism, 27
Ethnic cleansing, 146
European Union, 165, 168

False consciousness, xx
Farmer, P., 18, 95, 105
FBI, 27, 141, 142, 145
Fetishism, xv
Foreign Intelligence Surveillance Act of 1978, 144
Foucault, M., 51, 60, 62, 140
France, 10, 17, 27, 37, 59, 61, 69, 70, 73, 74, 88, 114, 115, 117, 121, 151, 155
Free market economy, 91
Free trade, 80, 90, 91
Freire, P., 3, 6, 21, 34, 38, 54, 55, 62, 118, 119, 121, 122, 124, 156–159, 161, 163, 164, 170

Gardner, H., 156–159
Gasper, P., 169
GDP, 72
Gee, J.P., 8, 22
Generative grammar, 26
Geneva Conventions, 135, 143
Getting Haiti Right This Time, 18

Giroux, H., ix, xvii, xxii, 4, 6, 21, 54–56, 62, 118
Global meliorism, 78, 89, 92
Globalization, 3, 92, 97, 101, 102, 107, 108, 147
Golan Heights, 135, 147–150, 152
Goodman, A., 18, 19, 25
Gramsci, A., 60–62, 113, 118, 119, 124, 142
Grande, S., 56, 62
Great Britain, 39, 59, 115, 159
Greene, M., 54, 62
Guantanamo Bay, 143, 144
Guevara, C., 119, 163

Haitian Revolution, 10, 98
Harris, Z., 25
Harvard Educational Review, 154, 156, 169
Harvard University, 25, 29, 105, 106, 140, 142, 154, 157, 159, 161
Hebrew, the Story of a Living Language, 25
Hebrew: The Eternal Language, 25
Hedges v. Obama, 143
Hegemony or Survival, 35, 109
HGSE, 154, 156–159
Hirsh, E.D., 34
Hong Kong, 69
hooks, bell, 21, 118, 161
Hopes and Prospects, 25, 66
Horowitz, D., 29, 36
How Europe Underdeveloped Africa, 57, 115

I Walked with a Zombie, xvi, xvii
iconoclastic activist, xii
IMF, 69, 89, 166
Imperialism, xi, 15, 24, 27, 31, 34, 35, 38, 47, 48, 71, 97, 99, 101, 103, 104, 107–109, 113, 116, 119, 120, 122, 136, 154, 161
Inacio Lula de Silva, L., 15
India, 65–67, 70, 72, 73, 97–99, 103, 104, 108, 120, 138, 151, 158
Iran, 45, 66, 71, 72, 127, 128, 130, 131, 133, 134, 149, 151

Jordan, 130, 143, 148–151

Kaufmann, K., 54, 62
Kennan, G., 92, 96, 101, 102
Kincheloe, J., 162, 164
Klein, N., 56, 62
Kyoto Prize, 25

Lakoff, S., 80, 82, 85, 94
Latin America, xx, 14, 23, 30, 31, 66, 70, 74, 75, 79, 80, 82, 87, 90, 94, 101, 109
Lebanon, 84, 126, 127, 132, 140, 141, 145, 147–149, 152–154, 165
Leistyna, P., ix, 8, 10, 56, 62, 113, 123–125, 156, 169, 170
Lewis, A., 83, 85
Libya, 152
Lincoln, A., 81, 99, 105
Linguicism, 9, 113, 115
Linn, R.L., 55, 62
Lipman, P., 55, 62
L'Ouverture, T., 27

Macedo, D., 3, 4, 6, 8, 31, 54, 56, 57, 63
MacWhinney, B., 27, 41
Madison, J., 78, 81
Magic Island, xiii, xxii
Magic-cap of modernity, xxi
Magical Marxism, xx, xxi, xxii
Making the Future: Occupations, Interventions, Empire and Resistance, 25
Manning, B., 144
Manufacturing Consent, xi, xxii, 94
Marable, M., 33
Market revolution, 78
Marx, K., xiv, xv, xvi, xviii, xx, xxi, 28, 29, 61, 63, 117, 124, 155
Marxist Zombies, xviii
McCain, J., 45, 48
McNally, D., xvi–xviii, xxi, xxii
McSherry, P., 25
Merrifield, A., xx–xxii
Mexico, 36, 60, 85–87, 90, 95, 101, 110, 135
Middle East, 23, 45, 66, 125, 126, 130, 131, 141
Moll, L., 61, 63
Monk, T., xvi
Monsters of the Market: Zombies, Vampires, and Global Capitalism, xiv, xxii
Myrdal, G., 56, 63

NAFTA, 80, 85–87, 90, 95, 96, 101, 102, 135
Nativist theory, 7, 8, 10, 24, 26, 27, 37, 40
Neocolonization, 98, 114
Neoliberalism, vii, 2, 3, 16, 20, 65–69, 72, 75, 113, 119, 135, 136, 154
New Mexico State University, 16, 33, 161

New Republic, 83, 94, 95
New World of Indigenous Resistance, 25, 40
New York Times, The, 45, 47, 67, 78, 83, 93–95, 143
Newitz, A., xvi, xxii
Newsweek, 87, 145
Nicaragua, 30, 31, 82–84, 94, 97, 99, 134, 167
Night of the Living Dead, xvii, xxii
Nixon, R., 142
No Child Left Behind, 45, 53, 55, 155

Obama, B., 4, 16, 17, 45, 48, 51, 66, 67, 70, 71, 110, 127, 128, 130–132, 135, 136, 138, 143, 144, 161, 168, 169
OECD, 91, 96
Office of Technology Assessment (OTA), 85, 102
O'Grady, W., 27, 41
Olsen, R., 57, 63
O'Reilly, B., 153
Oslo Accords, 140
OXFAM, 101

Palestine, 19, 45, 135, 141, 163, 165
Participatory democracy, 4, 5, 43, 54, 59
Partners in Health, 18
Patriot Act, 143
Peck, J. 23, 41, 94
Pedagogy of the Oppressed, 54, 62, 156, 157
Pentagon Papers, 143
Phillipson, R., 8–10, 21, 22, 38, 41, 60, 63, 118, 120
Pilger, J., 167
Plato, 53, 54, 163
Porfilio, B., 6, 56, 62, 63
Power Systems: Conversations on Global Democratic Uprisings and the New Challenges to the U.S. Empire, 25, 40
President Evo Morales, 4, 15
President Jean Bertrand Aristide, 11, 15, 38, 68, 69, 87, 88, 100, 101, 105, 106
production of value, xiv
production of wealth, xiv
Prospect, 146
Protestantism, xv
Putin, V., 151

Quneitra Crossing, 150, 151

Ramesh, P., xi, xii, xxii
Ray, A., 36
Reagan, R., 44, 79, 80, 86, 89, 91, 133, 134, 137, 165
Republic, 54, 63
Rodney, W., 57, 63, 114, 115, 118, 119, 124
Romero, G.A., xvii, xxii
Russell, B. 15, 28
Russia, 25, 73, 127, 131, 133, 137, 145, 148, 149, 150, 151, 153

Sachs, J., 105
Sanders, B., xi, xii, xxii
Saudi Arabia, 45, 128–133, 137, 138, 151
Scahill, J., 166
Schatz, C., 25
Science Citation Index, 23
Science of Language: Interviews with James McGilvray, The, 25, 40
Seabrook, W., xiii, xxii
Second World War, 100, 109, 154
Shanker, T., 166
Sherblom, S., 154, 156, 169, 170
Shinawatra, T., 164
Silber, J., 29–31
Six Day War, 148
Skinner, B.F., 8, 22, 26
Skutnabb-Kangas, T., 8, 9, 21, 22, 38, 41, 60, 63, 118
Sleeter, C.E., 4, 6, 55, 63
Smiley, T., 4, 6
Smith, A., 91, 114
Smith, N., 23–25, 28, 29, 35, 39, 41
Snowden, E., 144, 145
South America, 44, 46, 70, 80, 114, 131, 134, 136, 167
South Korea, 69, 72, 166
Spivak, G., 21, 60, 63
Spring, J., 56, 63
Steinberg, S., ix, 56, 62, 63, 162
subjugated language, 3, 9, 43, 59, 60
syntactic structure, 25
syntax, 26
Syria, 126–128, 131, 133, 148–152

"Taiwan of the Caribbean," 88, 100
Taliban 137, 138, 169
Tas, F., 146
Texaco Oil Company, 88, 99

Thiong'o, N.W., 118, 119, 124, 161
Third World, vii, 5, 11, 38, 39, 44, 65–69, 73, 78, 92, 97, 98,103–105, 107, 109, 114, 118–123, 152
de Tocqueville, A., 56, 63
Tolstoy, 73
Tourneur, J., xvi, xxii
Turkey, 71, 107, 111, 112, 126, 127, 129, 146, 151, 152

UN Industrial Development Organization, 92
UNICEF, 77, 92, 93, 96
United Nations, 35, 38, 135, 151
United Nations Disengagement Observer Force, 150
Universal Grammar, 27, 50
University of Massachusetts, 2, 8, 10, 13, 154, 159
USAID, 88, 89, 100, 136
U.S. imperialism, 24, 27, 31, 34, 35, 47, 71, 107–109, 113, 136
U.S. International Trade Commission, 85

Valdés, G., 56, 63
Value theory of labor, xiv
Vejjajiva, A., 164
Verbal Behavior, 22, 26, 40
Vidal, G., 161, 164
Vietnam, 10, 24, 110, 131, 142, 164, 166
Vodou, xiii

Walking Dead, The, xix, xx
Wall Street Journal, The, 85, 95
Washington, D.C., 88, 129, 136
Weber, M., xviii
Weberian Zombies, xviii
West, C., 4, 6, 55, 56, 63
Western imperialism, 15, 38, 48, 97, 101, 108, 109, 122
Western neocolonialism, 103
Williams, E., 57, 58, 63
Williams, R., 160, 164
Wilson, W., 78, 79, 88, 100
World Bank, 69, 80, 88, 95, 166
World Social Forum, 102, 108, 109

Zombies, xiii–xxii
Zombie Apocalypse, xix, xx
Zombiehood, xx
Zombified, xiv, xviii

Studies in the Postmodern Theory of Education

General Editor
Shirley R. Steinberg

Counterpoints publishes the most compelling and imaginative books being written in education today. Grounded on the theoretical advances in criticalism, feminism, and postmodernism in the last two decades of the twentieth century, Counterpoints engages the meaning of these innovations in various forms of educational expression. Committed to the proposition that theoretical literature should be accessible to a variety of audiences, the series insists that its authors avoid esoteric and jargonistic languages that transform educational scholarship into an elite discourse for the initiated. Scholarly work matters only to the degree it affects consciousness and practice at multiple sites. Counterpoints' editorial policy is based on these principles and the ability of scholars to break new ground, to open new conversations, to go where educators have never gone before.

For additional information about this series or for the submission of manuscripts, please contact:

> Shirley R. Steinberg
> c/o Peter Lang Publishing, Inc.
> 29 Broadway, 18th floor
> New York, New York 10006

To order other books in this series, please contact our Customer Service Department:
> (800) 770-LANG (within the U.S.)
> (212) 647-7706 (outside the U.S.)
> (212) 647-7707 FAX

Or browse online by series:
> www.peterlang.com

www.ingramcontent.com/pod-product-compliance
Ingram Content Group UK Ltd.
Pitfield, Milton Keynes, MK11 3LW, UK
UKHW022239230426
12048UKWH00018BA/1353